EARLY MODERN WOMEN AND THE PROBLEM OF EVIL

Early Modern Women and the Problem of Evil examines the concept of theodicy—the attempt to reconcile divine perfection with the existence of evil—through the lens of early modern female scholars. This timely volume knits together the perennial problem of defining evil with current scholarly interest in women's roles in the evolution of religious philosophy. Accessible for those without a background in philosophy or theology, Jill Graper Hernandez's text will be of interest to upper-level undergraduates as well as graduate students and researchers.

Jill Graper Hernandez is Associate Professor of Philosophy at the University of Texas at San Antonio.

EARLY MODERN WOMEN AND THE PROBLEM OF EVIL

Atrocity & Theodicy

Jill Graper Hernandez

Routledge
Taylor & Francis Group

NEW YORK AND LONDON

First published 2016
by Routledge
711 Third Avenue, New York, NY 10017

and by Routledge
2 Park Square, Milton Park, Abingdon, Oxon OX14 4RN

Routledge is an imprint of the Taylor & Francis Group, an informa business

© 2016 Taylor & Francis

British Library Cataloguing in Publication Data
A catalogue record for this book is available from the British Library

Library of Congress Cataloging in Publication Data
Names: Graper Hernandez, Jill, author.
Title: Early modern women and the problem of evil : atrocity & theodicy / Jill Graper Hernandez.
Description: New York : Routledge-Taylor & Francis, 2016. | Includes bibliographical references and index.
Identifiers: LCCN 2015039099
Subjects: LCSH: Theodicy. | Good and evil. | Women.
Classification: LCC BL216 .G73 2016 | DDC 214.082--dc23
LC record available at http://lccn.loc.gov/2015039099

ISBN: 978-1-138-12233-8 (hbk)
ISBN: 978-1-138-12234-5 (pbk)
ISBN: 978-1-315-65054-8 (ebk)

Typeset in Bembo
by Taylor & Francis Books

Printed and bound in the United States of America by Publishers Graphics, LLC on sustainably sourced paper.

For Gustavo, Allie, & Sofie:

"Someday, the light will shine like a sun through my skin

& they will say,

What have you done with your life?

& though there are many moments I think I will remember,

in the end, I will be proud to say,

I was one of us."

(Brian Andreas, StoryPeople)

CONTENTS

ACKNOWLEDGMENTS

The ideas in this book have been germinating for a long time, and as everyone who goes through the process knows, the production of a book is never a solo endeavor. Thanks go out to a number of groups and individuals, for their philosophical, academic, or personal contributions to the project and to helping me turn it into what it finally is. (All the flaws are only my own, in spite of your best efforts.) Although Claudia Card passed during the publication of this book, I hope it honors her memory and that she would have viewed it as excellent fodder for conversation. This book was significantly improved by a generous eight-month Faculty Award from the National Endowment for the Humanities. My gratitude goes to John Cox, Ana Wandless, Amy Ossola-Philipps, Dan Gelo, Sherrie McDonald, and Terri Gerondale for their assistance throughout the award process. As a result of the NEH support, the book was informed by rare holdings in Special Collections at the University of North Carolina-Greensboro (Women's Collection) and Rice University (Woodson Research Center). (Citations for these holdings will include references to the Special Collections in which they were found.) Librarians there provided invaluable support and assistance, especially Jennifer Motszko and Carolyn Shankle at UNCG and Rebecca Russell and Lee Pecht at the Fondren Library's WRC. Thank you!

Participants in a number of conferences provided invaluable insight and were willing to listen to new ideas, sometimes in their infancy. Special thanks to Chris Lauer and Brian Treanor at PACT (and for allowing me the privilege of presenting at the inimitable Getty Museum); Fr. Bryan Kromholtz and Aaron Harburg at Berkeley's Dominican School of Philosophy & Theology; the Iowa Philosophical Society's David Alexander, Evan Fales, Amber Griffioen, and Annemarie Butler, and my own Elizabeth McCoy, who was the best *ever* sounding-board; Clark Butler and James Sterba at the Human Rights Institute at IUPUI; the participants at SWIP, especially Nancy Snow, Allison Merrick, and Rochelle Green; and the Notre Dame Center for Philosophy of Religion's Mike Rea and Sam Newlands, both of whom have asked me important substantive and methodological questions. Thanks also to Larry Jorgensen, Lacey Hudspeth, Joy Ann McDougall, Jim Spiegel, Larry Helyer, Stanley Hauerwas, William Fitzpatrick, Marcy Lascano, Kristen Irwin, Joshua Thurow, Eleanore Stump, Fr. John O'Connor, Jason Fisette, Lewis Powell, Samuel Levey, and Linda Radzik for their insights.

The book prospectus, in various stages, received invaluable input from Steve Daniel, Marilyn McCord Adams, William Abraham, Margaret Atherton, Mike Almeida, Linda Zagzebski, Robin May Schott, Claire Katz, and Dan Whatley. Routledge has been phenomenal to work with, and I am grateful to Eve Mayer for her questions, encouragement, and enthusiasm for the project. The referees Routledge utilized in the vetting and revision process were also very helpful. Thanks very much indeed!

I am delighted to thank Brian Andreas, Annette Laitinen, and StoryPeople for their permission to use "One of Us" for my dedication page. If nothing else, at least I know one thing about the book is exactly right.

Genealogically, this project was birthed when I was asked to keynote the "Art against Violence" event at the University of Texas-Pan American several years ago, and I am indebted to Cynthia Jones, and the Pan American Center for Ethics (PACE) faculty and students for providing liftoff to a long and fulfilling project. UTSA students have engaged with me at various stages of the project, and I especially want to thank Sheila Williams, Alicia White Hernandez, Brian Marks, Meredith Mobley, Brie Charette, Matthew Trevino, Vincent Martinez, and Argon Gruber. Along the way, family and friends have both humored me and challenged me about various things I was thinking about—my folks, siblings, the amazing Christian Thinkers Class at First Pres, Lynn Helmke, Al Philippi, Kristie Dotson, Cynthia McSwain, Deb Dumaresq, Mark Philippi, Tamara Haywood, Deborah Tollefsen, Randy and Doris Johnson, Louise and Loren Peters, Doug and Judith McNeel, Bill Hensley, Irena and Porter Taylor, Eva Cox, Mimi Hart, Helen Miles, David and Emily Peeples, Ruth and Tom Thomson, Nancy and Harold Black, Anne Collins Smith, Jerry Smith, Owen Smith, Kelly Salsbery, Eve Browning, Win Corduan, John Stemen, Becca Anderson, and Erin Carter. And, of course, our Sue B.

INTRODUCTION

The moral issues raised from Claudia Card's atrocity paradigm pose a unique threat to theism: institutions of evil which perpetuate atrocious harms demonstrate the need to rescue 'evil' away from theism, so that the human moral liability for such harms can be assessed. The atrocity paradigm holds theism accountable for transferring blame away from the people who perpetuate suffering in the world by relying on a divine moral sense of justice. Treating evil as an abstract, logical category removes human agency away from the horrors produced by evil. Agency is required not only to be able to hold someone responsible but also to fully understand the impact of suffering on the world. Bat-Ami Bar On writes, "One stops witnessing when one abstracts so much and gets away from the phenomenological experience of the suffering of real people. Abstractness undermines the work on … [which] a spectator depends in order to connect to embodied people in pain" (Bar On 2007, 196). An enduring legacy of the atrocity paradigm surely will be its demand that humans are culpable for inexcusable harms which threaten the ability to live a tolerable and decent life. Whether the atrocity paradigm can succeed in its moral project—to rethink evil and refocus its role in the human institutions which facilitate suffering—depends at least upon two aspects of an atrocity: its systematicity and its transmutativity. Atrocious harms result from systems or structures of oppression that suppress human flourishing in a way that irretrievably and negatively alters the sufferer.

To date, theists have not specifically responded to the atrocity paradigm, although some philosophers of religion have started to think about whether theodicy should account for concrete harms. This book is unique, then, in that it offers the first thoroughgoing theistic reply to the challenges suggested by the atrocity paradigm. But it is also unique in the source of inspiration for its theistic reply. Just as scholarship on the atrocity paradigm has been spearheaded by a woman, so too, the responses provided in this book are derived from those given by women, specifically within the early modern period of philosophy. There is a current (and necessary) resurgence of interest in the work of early modern female scholars in philosophy. This book marries the theistic need to respond to the atrocity paradigm's rejection of theodicy with philosophy's need to reclaim important work done by women in the early modern period.

I argue that theodicy would be better served against the atrocity paradigm critique if it could appropriate the atrocity paradigm's view of evil, which requires theodicy to be able to discuss concrete harms. I argue that early modern women share the atrocity paradigm atheist's conception of evil, yet argue for divine perfection in spite of evil in the world. The best demonstrations are found in the writings of female contemporaries of G.W. Leibniz, especially Mary Hays, Catharine Macaulay, and Mary Astell and including Margaret Cavendish and Mary Wollstonecraft.[1] These scholars should be considered early modern philosophers of religion, who were committed to a concept of 'evil' that was situated in civil rights abuses and oppression but who also defend divine perfection in distinctive ways. Hays (1798), for example, argues that certain pernicious harms are perpetuated especially within the moral agency of a patriarchal political structure. On Macaulay's (1790) view, political atrocities stem from human institutions which propagate systemic injustices, and were never divinely intended to "enslave female nature". Astell (1697) wrote that suffering resulted primarily from preventable harms, such as civil rights abuses and keeping women and the poor from being educated. Although Cavendish (1666b) was skeptical about what could be predicated of God's nature, she also provides a foundational account of transformative moral encounters which aids in an understanding of early modern female theodicy. And, Wollstonecraft (1798b)—though more skeptical of theodicy's ability to redeem the particular suffering of women—still argued that virtue and moral improvement help women overcome evil and to better identify with the divine. Read together, the theodical arguments provided by these scholars can be considered as a political statement centered on the human agency of moral evil—tied to, though independent of—the theoretical notion of suffering.

The book is structured to acquaint readers with the main claims of the atrocity paradigm that are relevant to traditional theodicy, especially from Leibniz's perspective, to set up the importance of looking at the problem of evil from the perspective of women who also conceive of evil concretely. Chapter 1, then, introduces the atrocity paradigm, concrete harms, and the contention that theodicy fails because it cannot speak *to* those who truly suffer from atrocious harms, nor *from* the perspective of those who suffer, since historically, the authors of theodicy were largely writing from positions of social and epistemic privilege. Rather than evaluating the merits of this view, this chapter argues that the atheist worry over whether theodicy must connect with sufferers is persuasive: for theodicy to effectively persuade those who truly suffer, it must speak directly to their plight. So, are theists and atrocity paradigm atheists at a standoff over concrete evil?[2] Chapter 2 moves the atrocity paradigm to the early modern period, to demonstrate that the scholarship of female women scholars who have been excluded from the philosophical canon emphasizes harms that are defined by atrocity paradigm scholars as those which threaten the great good of someone's life. 'Moral evil' as these women thought of it was inseparable from concrete suffering in society and in the home, and so, Chapter 2 focuses on systemically generated concrete harms such as oppressive patriarchy, rape, abusive political power, and the suppression of rights and access to education. The discourse on theodicy ought to include a notion of evil with which those who suffer can readily identify, if the purpose of theodicy is to salvage divine perfection (including God's relational qualities, like omnibenevolence) in the face of evil. Chapter 3 picks up on the concept of the 'situated knower' as weighing in on the tension between the atrocity paradigm and theodicy. Contemporary narrative theodicy attempts to bridge this gap, by arguing that narratives can better serve the function of theodicy because stories can more effectively convey theological knowledge to situated knowers. Chapter 3 uses narratives by early modern women scholars to demonstrate that a second-person standpoint cannot sufficiently account for situated expressions of suffering, nor for the loving relationship theists want to express through theodical narratives. Whereas Chapter 3 bridges contemporary analytic philosophy of religion with the theodical narrative work of women in the early modern period, Chapter 4 shows that early modern women provide at least three genres of theodical arguments that are distinct in various ways from traditional theodicy: *Natural Balance Accounts* (theodicy that centers on our personal efficacy in eradicating evil); *Virtue Accounts* (moral arguments that focus on con-tinually improving the moral landscape for the oppressed); and *Transmuted Goods Accounts* (defenses of God that are grounded in viewing the system of human morality itself as a divinely-inspired response to atrocity). Although none of these women explicitly set out to do theodicy, each defends God against blame for pernicious evil as they attempt to fight political and moral injustices against women. These scholars provide distinctive contributions to the philosophy of religion, then, while relying upon a situated notion of suffering. Finally, Chapter 5 anticipates criticisms of the arguments presented within the book—from atheists, theists, early modern scholars, and ethicists; from those who worry that I am arguing for sufferers to take one on the chin for God, to those who worry about the scope of atrocities and transmuted goods; from concerns about objective knowledge and standpoint theory, to those who wonder if the book is an attempt to 'gender' evil (quick hint: *it's not*). Chapter 5 also summarizes ways in which I think the book, and early modern female theodicies, can succeed. First, it is a philosophical discovery of import on its own if these women actually make contributions to theodicy. Further, these arguments are successful *at least to the extent* that they answer the contemporary atheist's contention that theodicy is divorced from concrete, atrocious harms. If they make contact with the atrocity paradigm, they enable a conversation with contemporary atheism—a conversation that is precluded by most versions of theodicy today. My hope is that the many issues that motivate the writing of this work will also go on to provide a point of departure for many to enter into the debate about them.

Notes

1 A pure reclamation project on the philosophy of religion of early modern women would surely include the interesting scholarship of more scholars than I could hope to cover here. The focus of my inquiry is on those who contribute to a unified, concrete notion of evil and who share some aspect of their theistic commitments. Scholarship on early modern women is enjoying new attention, however, and much more could be added to my humble offering. Marcy Lascano has a forthcoming article that touches on Lady Anne Conway's theodicy in her co-edited (with Eileen O'Neill) volume *Feminist History of Philosophy: The Recovery and Evaluation of Women's Philosophical Thought*, but there are numerous other subjects who could serve as fodder for continued work, including Marie le Jars de Gournay, Laura Cereta, Gabrielle Suchon, Demaris Masham, Mary Ann Radcliffe, Emilie Du Châtele, Charlotte Turner Smith, Maria Edgeworth, Margaret Killam, Sarah Chevers, Lady Eleanor Davies, etc.

2 Interestingly, contemporary theologians have expressed a growing disenchantment with theodicy that is removed from concrete evil. See Mark Stephen Murray Scott, "Theodicy at the Margins: New Trajectories for the Problem of Evil," *Theology Today* 68:2, (2011) 149–152, John Swinton, *Raging with Compassion: Pastoral Responses to the Problem of Evil* (Grand Rapids, MI: Eerdmans, 2007); Sarah Katherine Pinnock, *Beyond Theodicy: Jewish and Christian Continental Thinkers Respond to the Holocaust* (New York, NY: State University of New York Press, 2002); Kenneth Surin, *Theology and the Problem of Evil* (Eugene, OR: Wipf & Stock, 1986); Terrence W. Tilley, *The Evils of Theodicy* (Eugene, OR: Wipf & Stock, 2000).

1

THE ATROCITY PARADIGM AND CONTEMPORARY THEODICY

The traditional problem of evil says that the existence of an all-knowing, all-powerful, and all-good God is inconsistent with the presence of evil in the world. A perfect creative being would know how (and would have the abilities) to prevent systematic and pernicious harms. Just over three hundred years ago, G.W. Leibniz's *Theodicy* became the most significant philosophical monograph devoted to the problem of evil. Since that time, theodicy—a demonstration of whether divine perfection is consistent with evil in the world—has faced significant obstacles. Contemporary atheists forcefully argue that theodicy is a doomed project because it justifies God's role in undeserved suffering by relying on a concept of 'evil' which is too abstract and removed from human agency and brings about atrocious, foreseeable harm.[1] Even recent theists have agreed that traditional theodicy may not be sufficient to account for egregious, historically situated evils.[2] Fueling this worry from atrocity paradigm scholars is that since the *Theodicy*, men almost exclusively have been taken seriously as leading contributors to the philosophical project of theodicy, despite the fact that several female contemporaries of Leibniz made noteworthy strides in philosophy of religion, often writing in the guise of political treatises or novels which emphasized civil rights. This book answers the call for philosophers of religion to address whether theodicy can adequately account for concrete moral evils and the suffering of the powerless, meets a need for a comprehensive analysis of the contributions made by female scholars in the early modern period as serious philosophers of religion, and argues these women support the goal of traditional theodicy although they each offer examples of suffering that today would be ultimately rooted in the atrocity paradigm of contemporary atheists.

Can Traditional Theodicy Account for Atrocious Harm?

Theist Marilyn McCord Adams calls these "horrendous evils", atheist Claudia Card calls them "atrocious harms", but both agree at least that the category refers to evils as a genre that are culpable, preventable, create intolerable harm, and threaten the great good of someone's life.[3] Such evils must be distinguished from merely concrete instances of evil. The atrocity paradigm scholar does not worry that theodicy does not tell me why I suffer uniquely, nor is she concerned with my problem of feeling separate from God. Instead, the worry is over a certain genre or class of evil.[4] Atrocious evils are "reasonably foreseeable intolerable harms produced (maintained, supported, tolerated, and so on) by culpable wrongdoing" (Card 2002, 3). Atrocious evils are distinguishable by the pernicious harm caused by the atrocious act, rather than any evil motive of the agent, since the atrocity paradigm focuses on disclosing the vitriol of the evil act rather than blaming persons. Atrocious evils are also avoidable and inexcusable (though they need not be extraordinary). It is not necessary for murder (as an example) to be an atrocious evil, but genocide always is because it results from a system of evil which perpetuates lasting, denigrating harm.[5]

The atrocity paradigm, then, zeroes in on a class of evil. For the atrocity paradigm, what distinguishes evils from lesser wrongs is *harm*, so the focus of the model is to eradicate systemic evil practices and institutions (Card 2010, 5). That class includes things like racial cleansing, rape, genocide, bombings of children, and hate crimes. What makes a class of harms 'systemic' or 'institutional' is that the rules that define the power structure foreseeably result in intolerable harms when normally or correctly applied (Card 2009, 214). What makes a systemic harm 'intolerable' is that they deprive a person from what is basically and ordinarily necessary to make "a life tolerable and decent (or to make a death decent)" (Card 2002, 16). They are "intolerable" not in the sense that individuals cannot in fact tolerate them but rather that a good life cannot include them so that a victim of an intolerable harm is deprived of something typically needed to make an experience "decent". The atrocity paradigm atheist's problem with theodicy is that as a class, these atrocities present a particular difficulty for any defense of a perfect God, since as a system they could and should be eradicated—mere humans are morally culpable when we have the ability to eradicate them and do not. Theodicies suffer for their insufficient accounting for God's omniqualities against pernicious harms as a class, since an all-good God would want to prevent atrocious evils, an all-knowing God would be able to see when and where they might occur, and an all-powerful God would be able to thwart those actions he sees and wants to prevent.

The atrocity paradigm specifically calls out theodicy as a failed project because it cannot speak *to* those who truly suffer from (especially) atrocious harms, nor *from* the perspective of those who suffer, since historically, the authors of theodicy were largely writing from positions of social and epistemic privilege. "[Our] concern is more basic than the classic theological conundrum of how a world that contains evils could have been created by a benevolent Supreme Being. Our concern is with certain logically more fundamental questions of philosophical ethics: What distinguishes evils from lesser wrongs? What kinds of evils are there and how are they related to each other? What responses to evils are honorable?" (Card 2010, 4).

Though the atrocity paradigm moves past the theological worry of whether this is the best of all possible worlds (since it dispenses with the notion of God altogether), theodicy has been firmly situated as a debate between theist apologists and atheist detractors at least since the time at which Leibniz posited that this is the best of all possible worlds. Recently, however, some theists have agreed with atrocity paradigm atheists that traditional theodicy (i.e., whether evil in the world is logically consistent with a perfect God) may not be sufficient to account for systemic, historically situated evils. One theistic response to this difficulty is to distinguish between abstract and concrete senses of evil, and then to provide corresponding theodical arguments for each.[6]

Leibniz's theodicy seems particularly susceptible to the atrocious harm worry, given that many atheists historically have rejected Leibnizian theodicy particularly for its perceived inability to respond to concrete evil.[7] It is not a secret, for example, that Voltaire's *Candide* was written in part to ridicule the suspected insensitivity of Leibniz's *Theodicy* in light of the 1755 Lisbon earthquake. To date, however, Leibniz scholars have not addressed the specific worry about how it is that concrete evil could be accounted for by a Leibnizian theodicy—although some point out that Leibniz's work is not entirely disconnected from actual pain and suffering in the world since he uses examples such as famine, disease, and death while defending God's goodness in the world.[8] If Leibniz's theodical ambitions (and those of traditional theodicy that take Leibniz's lead) fail to extend to concrete cases, when particular evils call out for justification, the Leibnizian rejoinders could be either that we cannot know that God does not already limit evil[9] (he writes, "Therefore it is sufficient to have confidence that God does everything for the best and that nothing can harm those who love him. But to know in detail the reason that could have moved him to choose this order of the universe—to allow sins, to dispense his saving grace in a certain way—surpasses the power of a finite mind, especially when it has not yet attained the enjoyment of the vision of God"[10]), or that, any individual harms are outweighed by a collective good within the best of all possible worlds.[11] (Leibniz notes at T169 f/189, "It is not strictly true (though it appears plausible) that the benefits God imparts to the creatures who are capable of felicity tend solely to their happiness .... The felicity of all rational creatures is one of the aims he has in view; but it is not his whole aim, nor even his final aim. Therefore it happens that the unhappiness of some of these creatures may come about *by concomitance*, and as a result of other greater goods.") But, each response has a difficulty: either the necessary connections between good and evil stay on an abstract plane and theodicy appears to lack contact with real evils, or theodicy hedges closer to detailing likely explanations of individual evils, in which case, some say, it descends into farce.[12]

It may be possible, however, to retain Leibniz's commitment to the best of all possible worlds and to integrate concerns about concrete evil without having to capitulate to the "farce" of explaining every individual instance of suffering. Theodicy could disregard concrete, particular evil—so, worries about my insecurities, disappointments, and inconveniences—and focus on concrete, atrocious evil.[13] Particular harms are "evils in the amounts and of the kinds and with the distributions of the sort found in the actual world".[14] Atrocious harms are distinguishable from particular harms on the basis of whether the systemic denigration and intolerable harm stems from a human institution that is perpetuated and maintained culpably (Card 2002, 102). Differentiating between concrete, particular and concrete, atrocious evils is subtle, but important. The former rejects theodicy because God does not prevent suffering for any one person, and the latter represents the atheist's worry that theodicy cannot explain an entire genre of harms against humanity. Traditional theodicy—whose strongest early expression is Leibniz's *Theodicy*—so far has largely focused on justifying each instance of evil with an instance of good. But, this focus limits theodicy's ability to engage in dialogue with atrocity paradigm atheists, since the atrocity paradigm already asserts that atrocious harms are preventable and gratuitous (so, outside of the ability to be trumped by some later good). Theodicy could treat atrocious harms as the atheist does—as a class—and then could provide reasons for how and why that class of evil is accounted for within a creation of an omnibenevolent, omnipotent, omniscient God who would want to prevent atrocious evils, would be able to see when they might occur, and would be able to thwart those actions.

Rather than assess the merits of the contemporary distinction between abstract and concrete evil, we can use it to revisit Leibnizian theodicy to answer, first, whether there is textual support in *Theodicy* for the distinction, and second, if traditional theodicy like Leibniz's can justify divine perfection in the face of atrocious harms. It will be difficult to justify the category of 'atrocious harms' directly from Leibniz's text, but I will argue that there is just enough space created by it that others (such as Astell, Macaulay, and Hays) can fully address atrocious harms while also producing theodical arguments. Delineating between concrete, particular and concrete, atrocious harms has several benefits for theodicy. It creates the possibility for theodicy to rigorously (rather than incidentally) engage with concrete evil—and so proponents of theodicy can duck the atheist's contention that their arguments fail to engage with the lived experience of suffering. My distinction also removes the burden from traditional theodicy to demonstrate that, for each person who suffers, evil contributes to the good whole of the individual's life, since the concrete evils that are explainable by theodicy are a genre, rather than an instance.[15] Finally, it preserves the uniformly theistic view that the goodness of God extends to the particular, relative to the whole—a result which continues to prove the relevance of theodicy to contemporary philosophy. I will conclude this chapter with a reimagined picture of the actual world—a world in which a system of transmuted goods is created by God for humans to alter the consequences of the atrocious harm they perpetuate. I will then later show that such a picture is supported by scholarship of women in the early modern period, and that transmuted goods can properly address the system of atrocity provided by contemporary atheists.

What to Do with the Concrete?

Atrocity paradigm scholars fault theodicy's effort to justify God's role in undeserved suffering because the problem of evil does not, as a metaphysical exercise, require the concept of 'evil', since the very notion of God creating an imperfect world suffices to "cast major aspersions on the character of the supreme being" (Card 2002, 13). Theists who remove the power of evil from the concrete in order to salvage the idea of evil as a logically possible concept want both to remove God from culpable wrongdoing and also to contend that God foresees suffering and does not want suffering to occur. Maria Pia Lara writes:

> Attempts to justify the existence of both evil and God were not seen as addressing theoretical or moral problems, but rather as a religious burden to explain why suffering is possible if God exists. Thus, philosophies of religion and their theodicies were failed attempts to anthropomorphize nature and God, without really confronting why evil seems to be a definite part of human nature, and why it is necessary for us to take this reflexive step if we are to find a way of accepting human weakness, our dark side, or as Martha Nussbaum would say, our own 'fragility'.
>
> *(Lara 2001, 1–2)*

Theodicy which evaluates only the logical compatibility of divine existence with an abstract evil misses just what it means to suffer, and what it means for an individual to feel as though God has abandoned her in her suffering. Some theists would agree. Marilyn Adams (1999, 3) notes, "[Christian theism's] propensity for generic solutions—our search for a single explanation that would cover all evils at once—has permitted us to ignore the worst evils in particular and so to avoid confronting the problems they pose." Adams's worry hints at the fact that theodicy faces the practical difficulty of effectively communicating that a perfect God exists in spite of the significance and felt impact of evil, but it also suggests a stronger philosophical difficulty. In the very least, a theodicy which takes heinous evils to be merely possible ignores that pernicious harms seem to be preventable.[16] (Mere humans, after all, use their considerable abilities to prevent more grotesque harms from occurring every day.)

Card does not regard the enduring interest in theodicy as stemming from a true theological difficulty that must be solved, but from a human moral fault that seeks to place blame elsewhere, and this fault results in "truly gross defects that produce intolerable harms" (Card 2002, 13). A purely abstract conception of evil fails to capture that evil is "a higher order moral concept ... [that] presupposes culpable wrongdoing in a moral agent as the source of the harm it does or risks" (2002, 12). Tying 'evil' to God removes it from human agency and culpability and leads to a rhetoric in which the oppressed are told to value suffering. Theists, particularly, must shoulder blame for (on one hand) arguing that God is neither complicit with nor culpable for atrocities in the world, and (on the other) encouraging those who are oppressed to turn the other cheek.[17] Those who suffer are told that through one's personal 'struggle' with evil, an individual can "prove one's moral mettle and worth".[18] But if evil is instead tied to concrete, systemic expressions of moral evil—those thick instances of evil, 'institutions of evil'— atrocity paradigm scholars argue the philosopher's focus can be on preventing atrocities and holding human agents responsible for them. On their view, placing the blame for evil on a non-existent God undermines our human ability within communities to eradicate atrocities.

If theodicy can meet the challenges of the atrocity paradigm, its first obligation is to admit that some evils are atrocious and produce harms that are both fore-seeable and intolerable. Since human agents who commit or allow atrocious evils could choose to do otherwise, and should choose to do otherwise, they are morally culpable for the harm brought about by them. Subsequently, God is at least initially implicated by the existence of atrocious evil in the world, despite the atheist's purpose to move beyond that implication to a discussion of how humanity can limit atrocious harm in the world. Theodicy's focus on evil as a possibility alone obfuscates how to thematize evil, the critics argue, and so the project of theodicy should be rejected in favor of a treatment of human suffering that uses a secular notion of evil that is inextricably tied to the experiences of the victim.

The Argument from Atrocious Harms

An atrocity paradigm argument against the existence of God on the basis of atrocity can be logically represented as follows:[19]

1. If one world, W1, contains less pain than another, W2 (and there is no respect in which W2 is better than W1), then W1 is better than W2.
2. There is a possible world, Wx, such that Wx contains individual concrete harms but not atrocious concrete harms.
3. The actual world, Wy, contains atrocious concrete harms and there is no respect in which Wy is better than Wx.
4. If God exists, then no world is better than the actual world, Wy.
5. Wx is a better world than Wy.
6. Therefore, God does not exist.

The success of this argument hinges on two questions: (a) Does Wx contain less pain than Wy in virtue of the fact that it does not contain atrocious harms?;

and, (b) Does the systematic nature of atrocious harms lead to a *qualitative reason* against the existence of God? If the atrocity paradigm atheist would engage in dialogue with the theists about her reasons to reject the idea that God exists, she would argue 'yes' to both. We already know that (b) is affirmed by the atrocity paradigm, since proponents of it already believe that we can improve upon the systems of injustice and pernicious harm that we (ourselves, as humans) are morally responsible for eradicating. As to (a), atrocity paradigm atheists could contend that a world in which there are individual harms (but not atrocious ones) is overall better than a world in which there are atrocious harms (so, a system which ensures atrocious harm will be suffered). This contention is consistent with the atrocity paradigm, since it argues that it is our moral responsibility to fight atrocious harms even if they persist because humans continue to fund, maintain, and participate in them. Lara (2001, 2) explains, "The challenge is to create a meaningful account of evil that allows us to comprehend why we are capable of exercising cruelty upon our fellow human beings. Absolutely central to considering the problem of evil is its relation to human agency. Evil belongs to the domains of action where agency is related to moral and political responsibility."

If theists take seriously the worries produced by the atrocity paradigm and believe that there are proper responses available, they ought to work within the parameters set by it, and then ascertain whether salvageable responses are plausible. The first step for the theist is to distinguish atrocious harms from merely concrete instances of evil. The atrocity paradigm scholar does not worry that theodicy does not speak to why any given individual suffers uniquely, nor is she concerned with any person's individual feeling of being disappointed with or separate from God. She focuses on systems of evil, rather than motives of agents, and she focuses on disclosing the debilitating consequences of the evil acts rather than on finding out who specifically to blame. Since atrocious evils are avoidable and inexcusable, philosophers ought to work to discover where they reside and use their considerable intellect to defeat the system.

The systemic evil practices and institutions (Card 2010, 5) that are atrocious are caused and encouraged by—or are the likely practical consequences of—political, religious, legal, or social systems. Harms of this nature fundamentally alter (whether physically, psychologically, financially, or otherwise) the ability of a person to emerge out of the harm tolerably and decently (see Card 2002, 16). The atheist's problem with theodicy is that as a class, these atrocities present a particular difficulty for any defense of a perfect God, since as a class they could and should be eradicated—still more, the world is worse off with atrocities in the world, and we are worse off morally when we do nothing to prevent and eradicate atrocious harm. Theodicies, thus, insufficiently account for God's omniqualities against pernicious harms as a class, since an all-good God would want a world without atrocious evils, an all-knowing God would be able to see when and where they might occur, and an all-powerful God would be able to thwart those actions he sees and wants to prevent.

At first blush, the atrocity paradigm seems to blame theodicy on the same grounds as other formulations of the problem of evil, and structurally that is true. But the systemicity condition on evil makes atrocious harm as a class specifically different than other evils tackled by the problem of evil. Most human moral evil does not lead to atrocious harm, although our evil actions can harm people and cause suffering. The atrocity paradigm carves out atrocious harms as its own set among harms. Perhaps it could be the case, the atheist might go so far as to say, that a free will defense or Leibniz's best of all possible worlds argument could succeed if the truly troubling bits of evil in the world are the individual sorts that each of us (individually) would like to be eradicated: murder, adultery, theft, jealousy. In those cases, perhaps if there was a God, a better world would be one in which the possibility of evil is necessary for the exercise of free will. It might yet be the case that if we were able to quantify the individual harms suffered by immorality and the goods incurred by moral action, at the end of the day, an all-things-considered good would win out. But, this stipulation does not take into consideration a system of evil that is culpable, preventable, and creates atrocious harms. If there *are* atrocious harms *and* an all-knowing, all-powerful, all-good creative and existing God, then by their nature, that system of harm could only be trumped by a system which produces overriding good. (It is insufficient, from the atrocity paradigm, to assert that there are gratuitous evils—that argument only needs to stipulate that there is at least one evil that is not morally justified in relation to some other good, and the existence of atrocious harms necessarily includes gratuitous evils, since atrocious evils definitionally are those that could never be justified by some other good.[20] Instead, the atrocity paradigm picks out a genre of evil, whose consequence is harmful, denigrating harms.)

The theist ought to concede this point to the atrocity paradigm atheist. We cannot even *conceive* of a system in which overriding good is produced *as a result* of atrocity—any goods that could emerge after an atrocity would come *in spite of* the atrocity. (We frequently speak this way in everyday life, "She went through x, but look at how caring a person she is!") We can (and do) conceive of a world in which some people emerge out of their suffering to become beacons of moral virtue, and it seems almost perverse to suggest that the reason why there is atrocity is so that people can emerge victorious on the other side of it. If such were true, we would have to say that specific horrendous evils are *justified* because some people became virtuous after having undergone the effects of the atrocious acts. It seems as though the atrocity paradigm atheists have the upper hand here when they reply that nothing could justify horrendous evils. Of course, if there is no system in which overriding good is produced as a result of atrocity—and there are atrocities—then, they conclude, God does not exist. (As it goes, the atrocity paradigm atheist doesn't just deny the existence of God—she argues that 'evil' itself ought to be 'rescued' from the theist.[21] Rescuing evil allows her to focus on human agency for evil, and on the culpability we share in allowing atrocious harms. Ada Jaarsma (2003, 59) observes, "The problematic of evil ... explicates and enacts this ongoing critical process. If we take up the word 'evil' in this context, then, we are referring to this imperative to reread and transform the tradition. Rereading theological words such as 'sin' opens up the possibility of rethinking salvation as well.")

Leibniz's *Theodicy* and Atrocity

One of the most potent responses in the early modern period of philosophy to the problem of evil came from G. W. Leibniz, whose *Theodicy* argued that a perfect Creator would make the best of all possible worlds, and a world containing human free will with the possibility of moral evil is a better world than one without free will and the possibility of moral evil. He writes, "Although God is the ground of sins, nevertheless He is not the author of sins. The ultimate physical cause of sins, as of all created things, is in God, but the moral cause is in the sinner. I suppose this is what is meant by those who have said that the substance of the act is from God, but nevertheless not the evil aspect."[22] Theodicies like Leibniz's treat moral evil as a mere theoretical possibility since it is necessary that humans have the free will to choose to commit atrocious acts, but it is contingent that those acts be performed. The challenge is to discover whether more could be found within the text to relate Leibniz's *Theodicy* to atrocity.

Prior to assessing the text of *Theodicy* for clues about the conundrum over concrete, atrocious harms, Andrea Poma's (2012, 149) pronouncement is helpful, so that "we should not forget that the basic assumption on which the discourse is founded is that the eminent goodness of this world is not a thesis to be demonstrated but an axiomatic starting point. The arguments put forward, then, are not aimed at demonstrating that which, being a mystery, is incomprehensible, but only at partially explaining it." Of course, this assumption is not left groundless in *Theodicy*. Leibniz writes,

> it appears that Bayle asks a little too much: he wishes for a detailed exposition of how evil is connected with the best possible scheme for the universe. That would be a complete explanation of the phenomena: but I do not undertake to give it; nor am I bound to do so, for there is no obligation to do that which is impossible for us in our existing state. It is sufficient for me to point out that there is nothing to prevent the connection of a certain individual evil with what is the best on the whole. This incomplete explanation, leaving something to be discovered in the life to come, is sufficient for answering the objections, though not for a comprehension of the matter.
>
> (T *196/214*)[23]

So, Leibniz confirms his belief that individual evils are trumped by an eschatological, all-things-considered good. But, our focus is on concrete, atrocious harms. Could Leibniz's discussion of individual evils transfer to adequately address the atrocity paradigm—or could it be that there is textual support to engage *Theodicy* directly (and successfully) with atrocious harms?

The easy answer (and so, the one that I'll engage with first) is 'no'. Most of *Theodicy*'s energy is directed towards the logical rather than evidential claims that contemporary scholars like to discuss, often when Leibniz discusses (what could be characterized as) concrete evil, he seems to play into the hands of atrocity-scholar atheists who deny that *Theodicy* can account for concrete evil at all. There are a number of passages that could be drawn from, but the leading contenders follow below:

> 122.VII All these objections depend almost on the same sophism; they change and mutilate the fact, they only half record things: God has care for men, he loves the human race, he wishes it well, nothing so true. Yet he allows men to fall, he often allows them to perish, he gives them goods that tend towards their destruction; and when he makes someone happy, it is after many sufferings: where is his affection, where is his goodness or again where is his power? Vain objections, which suppress the main point, which ignore the fact that it is of God one speaks. It is as though one were speaking of a mother, a guardian, a tutor, whose well-nigh only care is concerned with the upbringing, the preservation, the happiness of the person in question, and who neglect their duty. God takes care of the universe, he neglects nothing, he chooses what is best on the whole.

In this section, Leibniz indeed mentions the particularity of moral evil, and the physical evil (i.e., for Leibniz, the pain and suffering that ensues from moral evil) that can cause us to question the goodness of God. He admits that God allows suffering and death. In this admission, Leibniz could be read to be admitting that individual instances of suffering occur for concrete reasons. But, he clearly is not giving a defense of God's permission of suffering, since he also chastises the person who questions the goodness of God in light of evil in the world, "Vain objections … which ignore the fact that it is of God one speaks". The end result of blaming God for suffering, Leibniz thinks in this passage, is a false comparison with (it should be pointed out) lesser authorities in the world (such as mothers and mere care-takers). Instead, God is the ultimate authority, and since the information from which God chooses is faultless ("he neglects nothing") so too God can only choose what is best.

This section, therefore, cannot on its own be read to contribute to a dialogue with the atrocity paradigm. It is open to the idea that there are particular instances of suffering; however, it derides anyone who would question God's role in allowing evil to persist in the world. Other passages hold a bit more promise:

> 238–9 [quoting Theodore de Bèze:] "… if his mercy and his justice are not declared; for this cause simply by his grace he decreed for some men life

eternal, and for others by a just judgment eternal damnation. Mercy pre-supposes misery, justice presupposes guilt". (He might have added that misery also supposes guilt.) …. 239. This system is not of the best conceived: it is not well fitted to show forth the wisdom, the goodness and the justice of God; and happily it is almost abandoned today. If there were not other more profound reasons capable of inducing God to permit guilt, the source of misery, there would be neither guilt nor misery in the world, for the reasons alleged here do not suffice. He would declare his mercy better in preventing misery, and he would declare his justice better in preventing guilt, in advancing virtue, in recompensing it.

Here Leibniz takes up Bèze's conception of mercy and misery, and agrees with and amplifies Bèze's contention that misery and guilt are entwined. (Where he diverges with Bèze is on Bèze's thesis that the fall of man was "by the providence of God; in such a way notwithstanding, that God was not involved in the fault, inasmuch as man was not constrained to sin.") The passage assures us that if God had overriding reasons to prevent suffering (and interestingly, moral evil—which contributes to feelings of guilt) he would have done so. This text links into Leibniz's belief that God, as a perfect being, can only act from the best reasons, and absent better reasons, God was compelled to permit the evil in this world in order that the overall best possible goods would be a part of the actual world.

But, the link between misery and guilt and its relationship to the problem of evil is problematic, for a number of reasons that an atrocity paradigm scholar would find interesting. First, in this selection Leibniz is explicit that suffering comes as a result of wrongdoing. (The atheist would deny that atrocious harms could ever be instances in which the guilty party gets what is coming to them, since by their nature atrocities strip away the ability to emerge out of harm decently. In fact, since the atrocity paradigm atheist denies that there could be goods that could overcome systemic evils, this instance of Leibniz in which misery is linked to guilt simply would be irrelevant in discussing atrocities.) Leibniz could at least reply that *for the wrongdoer*, suffering is a result of moral evil. In a later section of *Theodicy* (270), Leibniz hints at this,

> They [the miserable] will love their state, unhappy as it will be, even as angry people, lovers, the ambitious, the envious take pleasure in the very things that only augment their misery. Furthermore, the ungodly will have so accustomed their mind to wrong judgments that they will henceforth never make any other kind, and will perpetually pass from one error into another.

But, the atheist could argue that Leibniz's inference from guilty party to suffering soul ignores exactly what is the atheist's contention: in a world created by a perfect being, guilt is not the source of misery (and suffering), but *God*. Recapitulating that God would have reasons to permit guilt (especially given that God does *not* declare that his mercy prevents misery, nor that his justice prevents guilt) does not account (in this passage) for the problem of the origin of atrocious harms if God does exist.

This is not the only section of *Theodicy* that links suffering to sin—of course, the category of 'physical evil' for Leibniz is an entire category of evil that comes because of sin. At 246, he argues, "Bayle will say that there is a difference between a privation of good and a disorder; between a disorder in inanimate things, which is purely metaphysical, and a disorder in rational creatures, which is composed of crime and sufferings. He is right in making a distinction between them, and I am right in combining them." The experience of suffering (a physical evil) as a result of moral evil inextricably ties guilt (*Malum Culpae*, for Leibniz) with (especially) a "penalty" (*Malum Poena*), which for Leibniz serves as sufficient evidence of divine justice,[24] but such a stance does not differentiate between the guilt of the evildoer and the suffering of the godly. Poma takes Leibniz to task for lumping the two together,

> It is certainly true that this notion of suffering as a penalty for sin is unsatisfactory, since it is undemonstrated and, indeed, in the case of the suffering of the just, it is plainly disproved. In truth, it would seem that on this point Leibniz, rather than basing his approach on rational arguments, rather adheres to scripture and its traditional interpretation, with particular reference to the doctrine of suffering as representing a consequence of original sin.[25]

As for whether Leibniz wonders whether the righteous suffer disproportionately to their acts, Leibniz writes, "In this sense [as guilt (*Malum Culpae*)] physical suffering usually derives from moral evil, even though it does not always fall on the same subjects. This latter fact, which may appear an aberration, is, however, compensated for by such a great reward that those very innocents themselves would not wish *not* to have suffered" (*GP VI* 443). The righteous may indeed suffer (and their suffering is only an *appearance* of injustice), though for Leibniz they also can take hope that their suffering will pay off in eternal well-being. Such a response does not adequately account for the worries of the atrocity paradigm, and relies upon the epistemic inaccessibility claim mentioned earlier, but it does show at least that it is false for Leibniz that individual instances of suffering are merely phenomenal appearances and so non-substantive.

> III. 241 Now at last I have disposed of the cause of moral evil; *physical evil*, that is, sorrows, sufferings, miseries, will be less troublesome to explain, since these are results of moral evil. .... But one must believe that even sufferings and monstrosities are part of order; and it is well to bear in mind that only it was better to admit these defects and these monstrosities than to violate general laws, as Malebranche sometimes argues, but also that these very

monstrosities are in the rules, and are in conformity with general acts of will, though we be not capable of discerning this conformity. It is just as sometimes there are appearances of irregularity in mathematics which issue finally in a great order when one has finally got to the bottom of them, *which is why I have already in this work observed that according to my principles all individual events, without exception, are consequences of general acts of will.* [italics mine]

A key difference between the third text and the two before it is the use of the term "monstrosities" that is apparently distinguished from "less troublesome" sufferings (in contemporary terms we would call these 'mild pains') as greater sufferings that are built into the order of things. Could it be possible that the monstrous could shed light on whether Leibnizian theodicy can speak to atrocious harm? (We remember, here, that the term 'monstrous' went through a thoroughgoing evolution in the early modern period, from Bacon's emphasis on the fetal monster to a term that encapsulated everything from hermaphrodites to a person who is unable to achieve a 'certainty of truth'. For Leibniz, monstrosity refers to a possibility of generative mistakes or errors—such as Ariew (1998) points out, the horns of unicorns—but the actuality of monstrosities is impossible since it throws doubt, albeit very tentatively, on the jurisdiction of a divine will.[26]) In this specific section, Leibniz is clear that the 'monstrosities' he thinks of are not the results of moral evil, but are aberrations of the appearance of the physical system of laws. In contrast, the concrete moral evil he refers to is of the particular variety—those 'individual events that are the consequences of the will', and without exception, any *appearance* of a system of moral evil (and consequent suffering) is an aberration, an appearance of a deformity in the system of harmony in which this work operates.

In several technical, textual senses, then, this passage could not use the monstrous as a way to enter into dialogue with atrocious harms. Atrocious harms, after all, are not merely appearances, and are not reducible to individual events (since they indicate a system or genre of evil). But, III.241 does create a possibility to begin to formulate a response. First, Leibniz is committed to concrete harm. Some instances of concrete harm are easy to discuss in relationship to God's existence, and others, he admits, are more difficult. If there are harms that are more difficult to explain, what *makes* them more difficult is not, as many contemporary arguments suggest, their *quantity* or (here, I am adding) their gratuitous nature, but that they do not at least *seem to fall within the system of rules* established for creation. Now, we know that for Leibniz, that 'seeming' is simply that—there are harms that are *apparently* against the system but (like a troublesome premise within a proof), they eventually will be worked out. Reading Leibniz to incorporate concrete harm in *Theodicy* is consistent with the rare texts outside of *Theodicy* which suggest that there are concrete pains, such as in *Discourse on Metaphysics*. There, he argues that the feeling of pain (similar to the apparent injustice above) is a positive evil, and not merely ephemeral,

It seems to me that we cannot say that pain is the privation of pleasure any more than we can say that pleasure is the privation of pain. Instead, both pleasure and pain are positive. Moreover, the relationship of pain to pleasure is very different from that of darkness to light. Indeed, shadows cannot spread and melt away where light is excluded, and where light is absent there are not greater and lesser degrees of shadow. Pain, instead, does not exist solely where pleasure is eliminated and one pain may be stronger than another.

(GP I 214)

The 'pain' experienced by the agent is a true suffering, and so not merely an appearance or absence. What I would like to suggest is that the 'seeming' in the III.241 passage could also be read so as not to exclude the possibility that there are atrocities in the world. Rather, there are atrocities, and when they are present, atrocities are more than mere appearances of disorder in the system. They are part of a system whose consequences are inconsistent with the system of moral goods that reflect humanity's best purpose. They are a system of atrocious harms and need to be responded to by the theists. In this chapter's last section, I will provide a possible response to the atrocious harm argument—one that is not textually identical to the *Theodicy*, but consistent enough with it. In subsequent chapters, I will demonstrate how this response is grounded in the scholarship of early modern women and provides several clear paths for the theist to enter into dialogue with contemporary atrocity paradigm atheists.

A Response to the Systemicity Condition of the Atrocity Paradigm

Let's grant the atrocity paradigm scholar that there are atrocious harms. There are gratuitous evils that are not trumped by some greater good, and there is a system of harms which perpetuates injustice, indignity, and lifelong suffering and which threatens our ability to think of a good, loving, and powerful God. Let's also grant that this system and its evils are culpable and preventable. By granting the existence and nature of atrocious harms, we agree with the main premise of the atrocity paradigm: that if there *are* atrocious harms *and* an all-knowing, all-powerful, all-good creative and existing God, then by their nature, they could only be trumped by a system which produces overriding good. This puts pressure on the theist to prove what the atheist denies—that there is a system which produces overriding good.

Before I carefully approach proving this, I want to anticipate a powerful criticism that also hails from the atrocity paradigm: that redemptive accounts of suffering have been used to oppress those who already suffer. The Church itself has, passively or actively, perpetuated the suffering of women (and other minorities). Christianity has been a primary—in many women's lives *the* primary—force in shaping the acceptance of abuse. The central image of Christ on the cross as the savior of the world communicates the message that suffering is redemptive. Women can sacrifice themselves for the good of their loved ones because God was willing to sacrifice himself through the incarnate Christ, and calls us to emulate his example. Believers promulgate this image when they juxtapose caring for oneself (especially when those needs compete with those of their families) with being a faithful follower of Jesus.[27] My own belief is that this is a matter of empirical fact and rather than be threatened by it, the theist needs to recognize it prior to formulating a response to the atrocity paradigm, and recognize it for what it is: a truth and an injustice. Attempts to articulate a system which can produce overriding good should avoid the pitfalls of Leibniz (namely, minimizing concrete evils, tying suffering exclusively to sin, and suggesting systemic evil is an appearance) *as well as* the pitfalls of an extremely conservative theism that—in addition to Leibniz's pitfalls—would encourage those who are in an oppressed situation to suffer more.

Now we are able to explore the possibility of a system which produces overriding good. If such a system was possible, *it would not be that goods take place* because *of evils*. For theodicy to be more than an exercise in monologue, the theist position should not be that evil is the condition for the possibility of good.[28] If there is a system in which overriding goods take place in spite of evils, then this system already avoids the foundation of the atrocity paradigm critique mentioned above: people do not need to suffer in order that good can be produced. Neither do they need to suffer *in order to experience* redemption—whether redemption occurs is in fact ancillary to my view. Since atrocities transmute a person's well-being into a life without dignity by removing her ability to experience a 'great good',[29] they can never be justified by some later good. The divinely-inspired moral system must likewise be maintained by human action and produce overriding goods—goods that do not justify the atrocity, but which are difficult to explain on the basis of the atrocity paradigm. Whereas atrocious harms cause life-altering ruin for the people who suffer from them, 'transmuted goods' could replace that result with something qualitatively different—whether the ability to have a future, to create possibilities for oneself, or to live a moral life. Transmutation alters the individual who has experienced a real harm, and brings about consequences other than what the atrocity should have generated (those that are essentially debilitating and degrading). Transmuted goods share the characteristics of an atrocious harm: they could have been otherwise (since they are the products of human choice); humans are accountable for bringing them about; and they are ultimately praiseworthy (rather than blameworthy) since they non-negligibly benefit the person who experiences them (just as an atrocious harm non-negligibly alters the person who suffers it). That the transmutation occurs is itself a net positive (since it transmutes the harm's negative impact on an agent), and the resulting transmuted goods can yield a life in which meaning (and more, flourishing) can occur despite suffering.

Theists can thus assent to a human moral system that threatens the belief in a perfect God—we'll call this 'atrocity'. But there is an equally forceful moral system, perpetuated by human action, which can work against the impact of atrocious harm. We'll call this system 'transmutation'. (In physics, 'transmutation' is the changing of one element into another by radioactive decay, nuclear bombardment, or a similar process.) The system of atrocity produces life-altering demise in the people who suffer from horrendous evils, but if there is a system of transmutation, it is possible that the demise wrought by the atrocity can be replaced by something qualitatively different, something good. A key similarity between the systemic evils of the atrocity paradigm and the systemic goods of transmutation is that humanity is at the center of its moral praise and blame. Atrocious harms result from human interference with the world, and humans are to blame when they come about. Similarly, transmuted goods require human action to be produced, and we ought to laud humans when they come about.

How might a theory of transmuted goods alter the landscape for the theist in responding to the atrocity paradigm's treatment of the problem of evil? For starters, the transmuted goods account is distinct from traditional theodicy's commitment that good and evil are binaries which, when weighed against each other, are inevitably found in good's favor. Rather, transmuted goods free the theist who wants to talk about whether God cares about concrete evil from having to justify every instance of evil. The moral math moves from attempting to account for every evil with some (perhaps a yet-unknown) good, to a one system-to-one system correspondence: God created morality, within which humans choose to participate, whether within a system of goods or a system of evils. Some of those goods are transformative, as are some of those evils. But, ultimately, we are held accountable for our participation in either, and are called to eradicate atrocities. The emphasis on human participation in bringing about transmuted goods to alter the trajectory of a harm presents a real difficulty to the atrocity paradigm—the existence of such goods is evidence against the paradigm's contention that atrocious harms deprive a person from what is required to live a tolerable life, and so also undermines the paradigm's rejection of the theist response to the problem of evil.

Some further qualifications are necessary to flesh out transmuted goods. It is false, in my view, that all suffering is transformative and that all suffering can be redeemed. In fact, the system of transmuted goods I posit is distinct from a 'redemptive' account of suffering. Under a redemptive account, individual evil acts are justified by some consequent good as long as the evil act is redeemed by the good, and the harms that come about from the evil acts are wholly eliminated by some other good. Neither need be true on my account—indeed, the position I am proposing is skeptical of redemptive goods.[30] Atrocious harms are culpable, preventable, and blameworthy, whether there are transmuted goods. Their presence in the world does not become permissible as long as there are transmuted goods. Not only is their presence impermissible, it is also gratuitous, since within a *system* of evils, there is not a moral math that could happen to weigh individual pains and pleasures against the whole. The system ensures that there is gratuitous suffering. But it is also true that the system of transmutation ensures that there are gratuitous, transmuted goods. There are culpable, preventable, praiseworthy goods that come as a result of human interference, and come despite the evil suffered by the individual. There is virtue where there ought not to be, there is undeserved kindness, there is unexplainable generosity, and there is inexplicable forgiveness towards those who have perpetrated atrocities. Lives alter—against reason and evidence—after atrocities have been suffered. It is true that there are some people who suffer who will not experience transmuted goods—but the system is not to blame for this (people are) just as people are to blame for the atrocity paradigm. It is also true, of course, that there are concrete instances of evil that are not transmuted, and these seem readily explainable as predictable results of the harm suffered. But the atrocious harms brought about by the system of atrocity are transmutable. Transmuted goods do not justify atrocity—nothing can justify atrocity. But, correlatively, atrocities cannot justify transmuted goods. Nothing within the nature of atrocious harms admits of good as an allowable result from atrocity, given that horrendous evils diminish the good of someone's life. And yet, there are transmuted goods that alter the lives of individuals who have suffered atrocious harm, and derive from a system of human action that works to mitigate the harmful impact of atrocity.

Perhaps the strongest criticism of a system of transmuted goods would be that the theist would have the inside track towards transmuted goods, as long as their theism included a concept of redemption. Even if this is evidentially true (and it is not obvious that it is), I'd like to urge against it. I have suggested that (as far as such a theistic position that believes this actual world is the created order of God) the system of transmutation is divinely willed to allow humans to defeat the system of atrocity which they perpetuate. So, to the extent that God has created the system, the critic could be right. But the success of the system of transmuted goods depends upon human action and participation. We participate in our own transmutation if we are receptive to the great suffering around us—in fact, we participate in our own transmutation if we take the atrocity paradigm atheist seriously and work to silence systemic injustice and institutional harms. The hard work of service throws us into the system of goods, whether we are theists or atheists. We work to fight against the causes of atrocious harm, and we replace it with systems of sustainable health, fulfillment, and existential flourishing.[31]

Transmuted Goods and Theodicy

If a system of transmutation could successfully be posited, would it suffice as a theistic response to the atrocious harm? Logically, I think so, for two reasons. First, the system I've imagined in this chapter produces the consequent that was required by the atrocity paradigm's argument: a system of overriding goods. (I take transmuted goods to be overriding at least in the sense that atrocious harms are overriding: they transform the life of the person experiencing them. If atrocious harms are overridingly negative because they suppress the ability to live meaningfully, transmuted goods are overridingly positive because they enable meaningful life in a person who had lost the ability to have one.) Although the atrocity paradigm's condition that atrocious harms could only be overcome by a system of overriding goods might seem daunting to theodicy, it actually frees theodicy a bit from the requirement that most theodicies are burdened with: that of justifying each individual harm with an overriding good. To answer the (quite difficult) challenge of the atrocity paradigm, theists need to address whether there is a system of overriding goods, but such a system need not address whether each instance of harm is answered by a particular good. But, a further logical reason to think that transmutation can defeat the theodical problem of atrocious harms is that I have explained at least one respect in which the actual world is better than possible worlds that do not contain atrocious harms. Even possible worlds that include individual evils but not atrocious harm are comparatively less valuable than a world in which a system is in place to transmute and battle a system of atrocious harms. The value of the actual world in part comes from its system of gratuitous goods, maintained and preserved by human action, and such a world is better than any in which there is no system of good—including worlds that do not contain atrocious harms.

More needs to be said of the system of transmutation, and throughout the rest of the book, I will more thoroughly articulate the contours of transmuted goods, seen through the purview of theodical scholarship of women in the early modern period. But prior to that, one further critique should be evaluated. Some might wonder as to whether a system of transmutation really is consistent with Leibniz's theodicy, as was suggested earlier. Leibniz does not, after all, argue that there are transmuted goods that are the by-product of a system, and certainly, Leibniz would deny that there are gratuitous evils, since he instead argues that all evils will be justified within the best of all possible worlds, in a manner consistent with divine justice. Leibniz stops short of *demonstrating* that all evil is consistent with being part of a divinely-willed creative order, as noted by Burgelin (1959, 5), "How can moral evil, which we introduce into creation, agree with the overall harmony of the whole? This must remain a mystery for us, which we will be unable to penetrate until everything is fully revealed to us—i.e. until we fully transcend the egocentric point of view of our present condition. The role of faith is not hereby cancelled out, since it is highly reasonable to believe." The most literal reading of Leibniz's denial that evil is overridable excludes as possible an authentic dialogue with atrocity paradigm atheists.

But that does not mean that a system of transmutation is not entirely inconsistent with Leibniz's larger theodical project. Leibniz thinks, after all, that the actual world is part of a creation that was created in a system of pre-established harmony. It is not inconceivable to say that a system of transmutation is part of the created natural order, so that just as the worst evils *apparently* violate (but do not actually violate) natural law (as is evidenced in *Theodicy* III.241), transmuted goods are those that are not readily explainable by physical laws. (Upon further inspection, we might find that a system of transmuted goods resides within the balance of physical laws which is enough explanation for their possibility in the world. To explain how they become actual, when typical consequences of horrendous evil are atrocious, philosophers would need to do good work at least in moral philosophy.) Such a result might make transmuted goods an aspect of theodicy that sounds much more Kantian than Leibnizian, since a main goal of Kantian theodicy is to emphasize the ways in which free human action can defeat an interest in vice. In fact, transmutation's emphasis on the human participation in producing transmuted goods might resemble closely the *atrocity paradigm's* emphasis on the need for humanity to eradicate systems of injustice. But, this should be read as a strength of transmutation rather than a weakness. (Later, I will argue that theists like Astell actually provide a *better account* for transmuted goods than could be provided on the basis of the atrocity paradigm.)

So, are transmuted goods part of Leibniz's theodicy? A close literal read would have to conclude 'no'. But, traditional theodicy *like* Leibniz's can include concepts like 'atrocities' and 'transmuted goods', and when they do, the possibility opens for them to enter into dialogue with atrocity paradigm atheists. Such a possibility has, to date, been incredibly limited. Contemporary theists would agree that it is relevant to discuss human responsibility for moral evil, still they would disagree that doing so requires a concept of systemic harm like 'atrocity'. The theist's emphasis on affirming the coexistence of God and an evil world, and underscoring the purposes God might have for allowing evil in this created order, is tone-deaf to the worries of atrocity paradigm atheists. In the very least, it seems that the atheist worry that theodicy must connect with sufferers is persuasive: if theodicy can effectively persuade those who truly suffer, it must speak directly to their plight. Creating the possibility of discourse between atheists and theists on the topic of atrocious harms allows the two sides to reevaluate the soundness of theodical arguments in direct relationship to those who suffer. In the next chapter, I will demonstrate that the atrocity paradigm's claims were presaged by important scholarship of *theist* women in the early modern period of philosophy, especially Mary Hays, Catharine Macaulay, Margaret Cavendish, Mary Astell, and even Mary Wollstonecraft. These thinkers were conceptualizing harms in a similar way to today's atrocity paradigm—concrete evils stem from systems of injustice, and so are preventable, culpable, create intolerable harm, and threaten the great good of someone's life. Not only is evil concrete and systematic, these women also recognized that evil could threaten our ability to rationally believe in God's existence. But this limitation was never assumed to be a logical problem about evil that could be isolated from the lived experience of suffering. Their work does, then, what Leibniz's text is constrained to do: it collectively confirms the problem of concrete atrocious evil (that is, the problem of evil need not refer to the logical problem of evil, but to whether atrocious harms are pernicious to a perfectly existing moral being), which can later be juxtaposed against their competing claims that a perfect creative God cares about those who suffer.

Notes

1 A representative sample includes Claudia Card (2002, 2010), *The Atrocity Paradigm* and *Confronting Evils: Terrorism, Torture, Genocide* ; Bat-Ami Bar On (2007), "Terrorism, Evil, and Everyday Depravity"; and Jennifer L. Geddes (2007), "Banal Evil and Useless Knowledge: Hannah Arendt and Charlotte Delbo on Evil after the Holocaust."

2 See, for example, Marilyn McCord Adams (1999, 2006), *Horrendous Evils and the Goodness of God* and *Christ and Horrors*; Andrew Chignell (2001), "Infant Suffering Revisited"; and Morny Joy (2010), "Rethinking the 'Problem of Evil' with Hannah Arendt and Grace Jantzen. Interestingly, while theistic philosophers have been slow to address concrete harms, contemporary theologians have expressed a growing disenchantment with theodicy that is removed from concrete evil.

3 See Adams (1999), 26–29 and (2006), 32–34; Card (2002), 9, 12–13, and (2010), 5–7. Card has recently focused on the *inexcusability* of atrocities and less on their *culpability* because we can be culpable for something minor, whereas inexcusability indicates that there is no excuse that could justify the atrocity (Card 2009, 216).

4 I thank Larry Jorgensen for helping me see the importance of drawing this point out. Leibniz, of course, gives examples of particular instances of suffering, such as the extreme distress he underwent when he was almost tossed overboard – Jonah style – by the Italian crew members of a boat, who all thought the violent storm they were in had been caused by some sin Leibniz must have committed.

5 Card (2010), 8. Card explains there may be murders that are morally excusable, 6.

6 The best arguments for this are found in Adams (1999).

7 Card, Bar On, and Geddes all do. Interestingly, theists raise a similar worry; see, Adams (1999), 3, and Joshua Seachris and Linda Zagzebski (2007, esp. 85), who note that theodicy should account for those who undergo a maximal quality of suffering.

8 Larry Jorgensen and Samuel Newlands (2014, 3) make this observation in their introduction to *New Essays on Leibniz's Theodicy.*

9 Against evidential worries, we must assume that God does *in fact* prevent and limit evil in the world, "God always acts according to wisdom, goodness, and justice, never in an arbitrary manner, even if we are unable to understand all the reasons of his Providence. Generally speaking, we can affirm that God does not permit any evil to occur in the world unless he knows that a greater good will occur because of it – so that the evil is only admitted as a condition *sine qua non* or as a means to the best. But this does not necessarily mean we are able to identify this greater good in particular" (Rateau 2014, 94–5).

10 Leibniz 1989, "Discourse on Metaphysics", GP IV 430.

11 All references to *Theodicy* are from Leibniz, *Theodicy*, ed. A. Farrer and trans. E. M. Huggard (Chicago: Open Court), 1998, print and Kindle editions, unless otherwise noted. *T* 241, G VI, 261. Maria Rosa Antognazza (2014) writes "The reason for God's permission of congenital deformities and malfunctions, and, in general, natural defects or irregularities, is to be found in the natures of things which are compossible in a given world. As the notorious Leibnizian refrain goes, these defects and irregularities are justified by the fact that the world containing them and selected by God is the best of all possible worlds. Such a world contains the maximum of compossible perfection and goodness" (123–4).

12 J. Franklin (2002, 50) is helpful here.

13 See Adams (1999), 26–29 and (2006), 32–34; Card (2002), 9, 12–13 and (2010), 5–7. Horrendous, or atrocious harms, then, are a genre or class of evil (which include racial cleansing, rape, genocide, bombings of children, and hate crimes) that present a particular difficulty for any defense of divine perfection, since as a class they could and should be eradicated – even humans are morally culpable as a group when we have the ability to eradicate them and do not. See also my (2014), 28.

14 These non-horrendous concrete evils are described by Adams (1999, 14).

15 Marilyn McCord Adams (1999) places this constraint on theodicy, "Appeals to global goods or to the overall preponderance of good over evil are not enough. An individual who participates, as victim or even as victimizer, in horrendous evil must be shown to have a life that constitutes a great good for the person in question. God must be shown to be not only good in general but *good to the individual suffering person* by enabling her life to be a good whole in a way apparent and relevant to the individual herself .... Further, the evil suffered must be *organically related* to the good whole of the individual's life. It isn't enough for the evil to be covered over or drowned out by countervailing good" (26–8).

16 Jennifer Geddes (2007, 110–120) argues that because evil makes people victims, we ought to consider "the relational aspect of evil".

17 Joanne Carlson Browne and Rebecca Parker (1989, 1) write, "Christianity has been a primary – in many women's lives the primary – force in shaping our acceptance of abuse. The central image of Christ on the cross as the savior of the world communicates the message that suffering is redemptive. If the best person who ever lived gave his life for others, then, to be of value we should likewise sacrifice ourselves. Any sense that we have a right to care for our own needs is in conflict with being a faithful follower of Jesus. Our suffering for others will save the world."

18 Bar On (2007), 196. This isn't to say that all atheists want to rescue the concept 'evil' – some want to move away from using the term to identify particular evils, simply because of its religious connotations. Alison Jaggar (2007, 219) for example, in an article specifically about terrorism, notes "I do not attempt to justify terrorism, but I suggest that the language of evil, because of its theological and absolutist associations, is distinctly unhelpful for understanding and figuring out how to respond to the complex and contested phenomenon of contemporary terrorism."

19 So far, the focus of scholarship concerning Leibniz on individual pains has centered on an underachieving God and slight pains. See, for example, Morgan Luck (2014), from which I borrow to provide this modified argument.

20 See, for example, Bryan Frances, 2013, 21.

21 See, for example, M.P. Lara (2004), 186; and Card (2002), 9.

22 G. W. Leibniz, 2006, 121.

23 Cf. 108/129, 177/197, 178/197 f., 248/264, 250/265 f., 253/268, 264/279.

24 See Poma (2012), 171ff.

25 Poma (2012), 171ff, relies upon Leibniz, T104/125, 275/290, 410 f./415.

26 Andrew Curran and Patrick Graille (1997), 4.

27 This leads to further suffering, especially in cases in which women stay in abusive marriages out of a duty of fidelity. Browne and Parker (1989), 1–30.

28 This is *not* to say that there could not be some particular goods that require certain wrongs. Plantinga has argued, for example, that the goods of Christ's atonement and redemption *necessarily* require that there is evil in the actual world. (See Plantinga 2004, 12.) My position here is that a system of evil is not required in order that good is produced. There is a system of evil, and there is a system of good. Both are human systems, both are evidenced in the world by the harms and goods produced by them, and both are products of a world in which the predicate 'moral' applies to human action. Such a view is consistent with a further view that there are certain instances of good that are brought about in order for God to minimize particular instances of suffering.

29 The "coercive effects" of an atrocity "trample individual autonomy ... erase self-determination," and "the associated harm can be expressed as the harm of dehumanization," see Sarah Clark Miller (2009), 57.

30 The notion of redemptive goods seems to be something reserved for work that a divine being could do, in which case the reasons for which we would believe God would redeem would reside in something similar to Leibniz's eschatology. I've already

demonstrated why this theistic response is disconnected from the atrocity paradigm. What I am suggesting in this section is not the only theistic account that has rejected the necessity of redeemed goods. Michael Almeida (2012, 228), argues that, though there is reason to suspect that this is not the best possible world, even if this is a bad world, God does not intend that anyone brings about evil, and his "redemptive response to evil and suffering is *not* part of a theodical account of evil and suffering. It is not the purpose for which God allows evil and suffering .... the redemption of bad worlds is the very hard work of divine and non-divine atonement". Although Almeida's work goes far to expand a theistic response to gratuitous evil (in part rejecting that this is the best of possible worlds), I will argue that gratuitous evil need not be inconsistent with this being the best possible world.

31 On this point, Almeida's work (2012, chapter 8) is consistent with the system of transmutation.

2

CONCRETE EVIL AND
ATROCIOUS HARMS

To properly understand what is at stake with the atrocity paradigm's repudiation of theodicy, and the upside for theism to address it, the systematicity and transmutativity conditions of the paradigm should be located in actual examples of evil in the world. Suffering results from social, political, economic, and religious power structures, it is developed and maintained by humans, and the harms generated by them erode the dignity of humanity. The existence of a perfect, creative God is undermined by the lived misery of this created humanity. Chapter 2 will move the atrocity paradigm to the early modern period, where scholarship of long-overlooked women on evil shares important characteristics with the atrocity paradigm's use of evil, including that concrete harms are structurally supported, preventable, culpable, and intolerable. This view of evil stands in contrast to that used by Leibniz, although I will argue at the end of the chapter, each of the women presented here are theists and believe that the existence of God can coincide with human moral evil.

Prior to engaging the scholarship of early modern women with the atrocity paradigm, there are two potential criticisms that should be anticipated (although they will be expounded upon in Chapter 5). The first is whether these women add something new to the atrocity paradigm. If the atrocity paradigm succeeds on its own as an ethical framework, and the work of early modern women does not inform the atrocity in new ways, is it really essential to engage in a focused inquiry into early modern women's notion of evil? For the aims of this book to be met, it is not necessary to show that their views add to the atrocity paradigm, since it is philosophically significant enough to highlight that their work presages the paradigm, despite their theist point of departure. But in actuality an investigation into the scholarship of early modern women on evil does obviate a critical feature of the atrocity paradigm that otherwise might be overlooked. In Chapter 1,

I argued that what sets the atrocity paradigm up uniquely among atheist perspectives is its focus on the systematicity of evil and harm. And, though this is true—Card, Lara, Bar-On and others all emphasize the systemic oppression and harm that comes about through institutionalized atrocity—it is not altogether an obvious point. I will try to show in this chapter, however, that the women of the early modern period did focus their efforts on preventing systemic harms. I will draw upon their oft-used examples (patriarchy, political systems, rape, education, and rights suppression) to demonstrate that they believed it was significant not only to *name* (or call out, identify) injustice at a systemic level but to eradicate it.

The second worry is a bit broader, but threatens the effectiveness of my endeavor. Could it be that the project is purely interpretive so that, although these thinkers were concerned about injustice, they were in such disparate circumstances (and a century apart), that their theories about, and examples of, institutional inequities are just too different?[1] For starters, it must be denied that contextual differences for these women create impassible philosophical barriers. We read Macaulay, Hays, Astell, Wollstonecraft, and even Cavendish similarly as early feminists—that is not a new project, certainly, since they share a vision to expand the rights and the living conditions of women, though separated by decades, class, political parties, and in some instances, geography. Analogously, each of the male writers in the early modern period of philosophy made distinctive contributions to the doctrine of 'substance', but we would reject as a live criticism that the differences in the authors' times and locations result in 'substance' not being a legitimate philosophical topic within the period. So, that there are variations in the contextual scenarios of these women is not enough to reject out of hand an attempt to assess their perspectives on God and evil. Of course, it is true that I will end up making an interpretive case. As I noted in Chapter 1, the purpose of the scholarship of these women was not *theodicy*, and the intended result of their scholarship was different than Leibniz, for example, whose purpose was theodical. But, the interpretive move will be at the level of theodicy (in Chapter 4), and not truly at the level of concrete atrocities. It is significant philosophically that we read these contributions not only for what they were intended to be—attempts to increase women's access to civil rights and social resources—but also for what they *are*—identifications of systems of injustice that perpetuate atrocious harm. Once that identification has been highlighted, then the interpretive work to address the contemporary atheist worries over theodicy can be performed.

Systems of Evil

Although they would not deny altogether Leibniz's best of all possible worlds argument in *Theodicy*, early modern women would find traditional theodicy to be insufficient for a number of reasons. First, traditional theodicy like Leibniz's is grounded on an abstract conception of evil in which the possibility of evil must be necessary for God to instantiate a best of all possible worlds. (Leibniz writes,

"[God] has permitted evil because it is involved in the best plan existing in the region of possibles, a plan which supreme wisdom could not fail to choose. This notion satisfies at once the wisdom, the power and the goodness of God, and yet leaves a way open for the entrance of evil. God gives perfection to creatures in so far as it is possible in the universe. One gives a turn to the cylinder, but any roughness in its shape restricts the swiftness of its motion," (*Theodicy* III.327). But Macaulay, Hays, and Astell would agree with atrocity paradigm atheists that this use of 'evil' is too removed from harms in the world for the task of theodicy to truly speak to the problem of divine concurrence of moral evil.[2] 'Moral evil' as these women thought of it was inseparable from concrete suffering in society and in the home, and so, correlates importantly with today's atrocity paradigm, though atrocity paradigm theorists do not share their theist conclusions. Given that the work of these early modern women on evil is rooted in the concrete, it proves more readily identifiable with those who suffer. If the theist wants there to be discourse on theodicy, and wants to include a sense of evil with which those who suffer can readily identify, then it is imperative to look at their conception of concretely-situated evil.

One more qualification should be made. It is true that the work of early modern female scholars collectively confirms the problem of concrete evil (the problem of evil is more of a problem because suffering is lived, rather than whether evil must be logically possible for God to create the best possible world) and so atrocious harms are pernicious to the existence of a perfect being. But it is also true that these women were not writing as a collective. So, not all of them will have written extensively, for example, on rape as a systemic evil (although many of them do). Instead, when each writer has something important to say about systemic injustice, I have noted it. Rather than being an exhaustive representation of each scholar's view of systemic injustice (which would be wildly unwieldy) I mean to provide here evidence first, that these women believed that evil and harm were systemically grounded and, anachronistically but properly, atrocities; and secondly, that the early modern concrete examples provided here of systemic harm are also examples of institutional injustice today. This will allow me to suggest, in Chapters 4 and 5, that these women can offer a unique theodicy grounded in the saving power of God's own suffering and experiences of creation, and the restorative power of secular and Christian service. Those arguments will prove all the more compelling for having been written in response to egregious civil rights abuses and rampant domestic violence of their day. If insight can be gained into the transformative power of transmuted goods, then rather than speculating about the metaphysical nature of the divine, we might understand divine perfection in light of evil in the world.

Tying oppression into a systemic (changeable, human) framework is similar to today's atrocity paradigm. Hacking at the roots of suffering is to dare, Mary Hays might say, "to trace, to their springs, errors the most hoary, and prejudices the most venerated, emancipate the human mind from the trammels of superstition, and teach it, that its true dignity and virtue, consist in being free" (Hays 1796, 219). For atrocity paradigm theorists, criticizing the institutions that perpetuate harms allows us to transform the beliefs and values that keep the institutions in power.[3] For early modern women, suffering is not a logical, necessary consequence of a created order, nor is it brought about by God or bad luck. Rather, in a way that resounds with the atrocity paradigm, they take the source of suffering to be human action, "I allow we are not impelled from a blind fatality without us; for the sources of our actions originate in the frame of our nature, and in the force of motives" (Hays 1793, 168). Any theory of evil that is divorced from human agency is too abstract, and so is distanced from the experiences of the exploited. Suffering comes from evil, evil comes from base intentions to enslave others, which most perniciously evidences itself in political power. Concrete individual harms often result from political systems which create anguish.

Catharine Macaulay identifies the harm suffered by women specifically as *systemic abuses* of a natural order that was designed for good by the Creator but perverted (especially) by men's desire for power:

> I do not intend to give a history of women, but to trace the sources of their peculiar foibles and vices; and these I firmly believe to originate in situation and education only, for so little did a wise and just Providence intend to make the condition of slavery an unalterable law of female nature, that in the same proportion as the male sex have consulted the interest of their own happiness, they have relaxed in their tyranny over women, and such is their use in the system of mundane creation, and such their natural influence over the male mind, that were these advantages properly exerted, they might carry every point of any importance to their honor and happiness.
>
> *(Macaulay 1790, 207)*

The systematicity required by the atrocity paradigm resounds in Macaulay's emphasis on men's unnatural tyranny, the improper exertion of male advantage, the slavery of women at the hands of the mundane systems men use—and these violations are in sharp contrast to any untoward act of women, which are relegated as mere 'foibles'.

The systemic harm Macaulay identifies as abuses of advantages men are given is evidenced in Hays's work as well, but Hays more strongly argues against the view that evil is not natural. For her, moral evil is an aberration whose origin is in the human will (which at times acts on bad information or improper reasoning), so that any horrendous harm that comes out of an evil system is contingent on a human person's will and so is not a necessary part of the moral order. (This point is important. The moral order is part of the created system, but exercises of will depend upon each person.) Whereas atrocity paradigm theorists emphasize that fighting against some evils requires the disaggregation of systemic harms (Lara 2004, 189), Hays analogously suggests that the purpose for humanity is an equal responsibility under equal law, and can be protected only when people overturn the institutions that suppress individual rights. God's purpose is that we use our free choices to overcome oppression:

> I must therefore repeat, that is a most extraordinary circumstance, and not to be accounted for upon any of the common principles of reasoning; that a wise, a just, a beneficent Creator, should frame laws and enact punishments for a race of beings, all equally dependent upon him, and equally responsible for disobedience; yet allow some to deviate from his will with impunity, and others not. Indeed it has always appeared to me so shocking to imagine, if either of the maledictions had been intended by the Creator to have been handed down to posterity, that they should not have literally taken place; that if I may be permitted to give my explanation of the passages, I think the plain and obvious meaning of them must have been, a punishment for the first pair, and for them only.
>
> *(Hays 1798, 5–6)*

Falling with the "first pair" (those who "deviate from his will with impunity") are those who hold to "the antediluvian claim of divine authority, to domineer over women…—Where peace to its manes! And oblivion to its memory!" (7). Those who are in power must instead strive "to restore to woman that freedom, which the God of nature seems manifestly to have intended, for every living creature!" (105).

Although Mary Astell is less direct about arguing for particular civil rights for women, she does not shy away from aligning harm with systems of injustice, which negatively impact those on the margins of power. "As the World became more Populous, and Men's Necessities whetted their Inventions, so it increased their Jealousies," she observes, "and sharpened their Tyranny over us, till by degrees, it came to the height of Severity, I may say, Cruelty, it is now at in all the Eastern parts of the world, where the Women, like our Negroes in our Western Plantations, are born slaves, and live Prisoners all their lives" (Astell 1697, 21–2). The reader gets a sense of her tongue-in-cheek reply to those who want to differentiate the genders on the basis of a natural inferiority of women. The differentiation is instead one that is taught and enforced by social structures, "Only let me beg to be inform'ed, to whom we poor Fatherless Maids, and Widows who have lost their Masters, owe Subjection? It can't be to all Men in general, unless all Men were agreed to give the same Commands; do we then fall as Strays to the first who finds us?" (Astell 1706, 174).

Examples of what Astell, Hays, and Macaulay, and others were thinking of by 'evil' can show that they mean institutional harms, rather than individual concrete harms. Although there are different examples that could be used, there are four that are common among most of these intellectuals: patriarchy (specifically, domestic abuse of men over women), political power, rape, and the suppression of education. As fascinating as each case study is historically (and, to be sure, each one could potentially serve as its own chapter), I will highlight the most important philosophical aspects contained about them within the scholarship of early modern women. These examples are especially significant because they are also used by contemporary atrocity paradigm atheists as representations of systems that effectuate atrocious harm.

Patriarchy as Systemic Evil

If the atrocity paradigm calls out systems of evil as those that violate the great good of one's life, it could include systems that would not ordinarily be thought of as creating atrocious harm. Indeed, Card's work infamously faults marriage and motherhood as systems which can perpetuate atrocious harm. She writes, "the social institutions of marriage and motherhood are controversial among gay men, bisexuals and transgender people" (Card 2005, 139) and that this skepticism is justified—even though there are many examples of both that do not produce atrocious harm—because "these hallowed institutions encourage, shelter, and facilitate terrorism in the home". (Of course, Card is not the first to condemn traditional relational social structures for perpetrating oppression on women, either among philosophers or theologians. Mary Daly, one of the most notable contemporary feminist thinkers, argued against the "religion" of patriarchy, whose message is essentially "necrophilia" because it legitimizes oppression as "infrastructures … erected as parts of the male's shelter against anomie" wherein "women are the objects of male terror" (Daly 1978, 83).[4] Card is the first, however, to articulate the contours of the genre of evil produced by the structural injustices women and others suffer under as part of these social structures). Not all atrocity paradigm scholars agree with the extension of her theory to what many non-scholars think of in positive, comforting, terms—Maria Pia Lara, for example (Lara 2007 and 2009), argues that the atrocity paradigm theorist should start theorizing with particular concrete instances of evil and move out to making judgments about the systems that might perpetuate them. "Rather than formulating an abstract definition of what makes an action or institution evil" she posits, "a primary task for a theory of evil is to examine the concreteness of examples and explore possibilities for thematizing some of them within a larger framework of atrocities" (Lara 2009, 201).

So, whether atrocities are committed within a particular system or whether a system perpetuates evil really are two different things. Particular atrocities can be committed within *any* system, but there are systems whose primary function is to produce atrocious harm. Patriarchy, for example, is an institution that has certain benefits,[5] not only for those who can exercise their power as a result of it, but for those who experience some level of protection because of it. But, upon investigation, the institution of patriarchy persists as a system that typically and predictably produces atrocious harm—even if those who suffer as a result of it sometimes need to learn that their suffering is not natural and is in fact the result of an immoral act. Lynne Tirrell reports that women often, "still need to be taught that sexual harassment is a basic harm, that incest is not a personal failure, that rape is a macroscopic problem, not an individual lapse in self-protection, that we need to learn these things is evidence of the thoroughgoing hegemony of a patriarchal world in which women's status as a person has not yet fully caught hold, even amongst women" (Tirrell 2009, 45). Patriarchy is a system marked by the subjugation of others and the suppression of the rights of the weak, and it also fosters other systems that produce atrocious harm, such as rape (an action marked by an expression of power over another) and the stifling of rights by preventing (for example) the education of women.

This is true today,[6] but worries with contemporary patriarchy also founded many of the 'appeals' of women in the early modern period, who saw patriarchy as a leading institution of suffering, both in and outside of the home. For her part, Hays argues against the position that the evil of patriarchy is a natural occurrence— or, conversely, that it is unavoidable because men are born evil (for example, with original sin). She writes that it would be "a most extraordinary circumstance" if "a wise, a just, a beneficent Creator, should frame laws and enact punishments for a race of beings, all equally dependent upon him, and equally responsible for disobedience; yet allow some to deviate from his will with impunity, and others not" (Hays 1798, 506). If social atrocities come about as a result of being created sinful, the only way to explain their impact in the world is to blame the creator. But, this view is inconsistent with divine justice, goodness, and mercy (Hays 1798, 10–11). The better explanation is that neither men nor women are perfect physical or intellectual creatures, and their inability to have perfect knowledge causes many people to act immorally.[7]

The impact of imperfect reason is more significant for women who live in a subordinate state to men, because they are also likely to believe that men are intellectually better equipped than women. Women see themselves already at a physical disadvantage compared to men, though Hays points out that human nature is actually the same for men and women. Mind, she writes, is of no sex (Hays 1798, 121). If the will is tied to the mind, and minds are equal, we should see a fairly proportionate scope of action between men and women, but we do not. Men, rather, use their political and familial power to commit evil through tyrannical ways that women would never do—even if women were given the same power as men. In God's divine providence, the different sexes were created equal in rank, but men use their power to attempt to persuade women that they are naturally inferior and subordinate to men.[8] Over time, females become convinced that laws framed by men supersede the laws of nature, and so they come to believe that any harms they suffer are the natural result of created gender differences in intellect and physical prowess.[9]

Hays views the male propensity to abuse power as intentional rather than accidental, in the same way as it is not accidental that the system of political power creates suffering for women. Patriarchy thrives when millions of reasonable beings remain ignorant of their rights and incapable of learning new skills that might take them outside the home. Men fear that if women are educated and understand that they are given full rights through the natural order then they would not submit to being governed. Hays, an Englishwoman, compares all women—when they lack opportunities to exercise basic rights and when they are unable to expand their nondomestic talents—to an underestimated political powerhouse. She posits (Hays 1793, 44), "I cannot perhaps explain myself better, than by saying that it appears to me, that women, with respect to mental abilities, compared with men, are like the French nation compared to every other nation upon earth; who under the appearance of lightness and frivolity, possess a capability of everything useful and agreeable, or great and good." Men fear the advancement of women, however, because they believe that a system in which women do not submit to patriarchal authority would "produce the most fatal consequences in society"[10] and so men intentionally continue to perpetuate political and civil injustices against women.[11] So despite the fact that human nature is the same, men ensure women will suffer exquisitely more than men by enforcing a system of laws—written by men for men—that dooms women to having and exercising fewer rights than their male counterparts.

Although women suffer as a result of a suffocation of their abilities, education, and rights, patriarchy in the political realm is not the only manifestation of atrocious evil on Hays's account. Moral evil represents itself in political patriarchy, but is not exclusive to it. Rather, the suffering that women undergo daily at home is more insidious, largely because in Hays's day, once a woman married, she had a single opportunity for happiness or justice, "and this one chance is, that of her husband happening to be a sensible, a reasonable, a humane man, in a more than ordinary degree" (Hays 1798, 282). (Mary Wollstonecraft, however, went farther, and cast aspersions on the idea that the humane treatment of women by their husbands could ever be properly motivated, "A fondness for the sex often gives an appearance of humanity to the behavior of men, who have small pretensions to the reality, and they seem to love others, when they only are pursuing their own gratification" (Wollstonecraft 1798b, 138–139).) Anecdotally, Hays believes that most women will not be privy to this 'single opportunity' for domestic equality, since Hays only ever saw one instance of a man who could perform his husbandly duty to be moral and just—her own betrothed (Luria 1977, 25). If all men behaved as John Eccles did before his untimely death, perhaps women would not suffer as they do. Instead, women experience "too frequently" a power whose engine is too dangerous as well as marriages that leave women utterly subjugated, and at the mercy of their spouse for a safe and meaningful existence. "And to call much less than absolute and unlimited power, that which men may, and often do, exercise over their wives; is only deceiving ourselves, and prevents us perhaps from searching to the bottom an evil, which can never be remedied, till that is faithfully done" (Hays 1798, 263–64).

Women are told by society that there are two primary reasons for their domestic suffering: first, the social and familial structure demands that women be subordinate, since the home and social relationships depend upon the superiority of men; and second, the natural order dictates the subordination of women, since nature ordains the treatment of any person based on their intellectual and physical abilities. In the first case, men propagate the worry that the family will be the sacrificial lamb of giving women equal rights as men. If women are not duped into submission, men might risk their places at the head of the family, after all. To ensure their powerful positions, men must have the goal to "stamp a marked inferiority on the whole sex when they insinuate that women are made of baser materials" (Hays 1798, 203). The irony is that the continued, intentional subjugation of women by men is actually the biggest threat to social advances. Hays writes, "It is time, perhaps, to endeavor at least to stop the progress of folly which has already taken too deep root among mankind; much to the injury of the best interests of society, and which in the end is equally pernicious to those who inflict injury, as to those upon whom it is inflicted" (Hays 1798, 204).[12] Of course, if women buy into the "natural order" reasoning that results in the idea that women are naturally inferior to men, a more pernicious spiritual reason for the continued, intentional mistreatment of women in the home is revealed: women deserve inferior treatment because they are created by God with inferior intellect and physical abilities. The social argument for subjugating women twists the intended purpose of the social order, and so too, this natural argument takes what should be positive (i.e., a physical difference between man and woman) and uses it to justify moral evil. As for most things in nature, Hays contends, physical differences between men and women indicate complementary natural functions.

The female body is designed to create life, whereas the male body is designed to protect that life. Men use female "frailty," however, as justification for abuse in the home and for ensuring that women cannot exercise their basic human rights. Early modern women as a whole reject the idea that nature prescribes these abuses, because although there are created differences in nature, there are no naturally ordered injustices, nor anything in nature that is irrational. And, there are no created differences which evidence themselves as differences in intelligence. Mary Astell allows that any difference that could be a foundation for inequality would have to be a *created* (and so, divinely intended) inequality, but she finds no evidence for such a difference:

> To proceed therefore if [women] be naturally defective, the Defect must be either in Soul or Body. In the Soul it can't be, if what I have heard some learned Men maintain, be true, that all Souls are equal, and alike, and that consequently there is no distinction as Male and Female Souls; that there are no innate Ideas, but that all the Notions we have are derived from our External Senses, either immediately, or by reflection.[13] ... Neither can it be in the Body, for there is no difference in the Organization of those Parts, which have any relation to, or influence over the Minds.
>
> *(Astell 1721, 10)*

God created men and women with the same genderless, intellectual soul, that is a reflection of divine rationality—and so both are morally obligated to facilitate the development of their minds through self-discipline and rational contemplation (Ruether 1998, 135). The subjugation of women by men undermines our collective purpose. Astell writes, "This is our Case; for Men being Sensible as well of the Abilities of Mind in our Sex, as of the strength of Body in their own, began to grow Jealous that we, who in the Infancy of the World were their Equals and Partners in Dominion, might in the Process of Time, by Subtlety and Stratagem become their Superiors; and therefore in good time to make use of Force (the origin of Power) to compel us to a Subjection, Nature never meant" (Astell 1696, 21). As for those who would argue that women provide tacit consent to being subjugated to men by signing a marriage contract, Astell's response links to the difficulty of systemic political injustices within the home. Those who claim that authority is derived from the consent of the governed are hypocrites because men who are oppressed would be able to seek an audience to vent their concerns, "If the Matrimonial Yoke be grievous, neither Law nor Custom afford her [the wife] that Redress which a Man obtains. … but Patience and Submission are the Only Comforts that are left to a poor People, who groan under Tyranny, unless they are Strong enough to break the Yoke, to Depose and Abdicate, which I doubt wou'd not be allow'd of here" (Astell 1706, 20).

Rather, the rationality with which men rule over women is the same rationality given to women. In fact, men and women were created so alike that God ordained that all intellectual pursuits—even those in the sciences and those that improve humanity—be explored by both sexes (Hays 1798, 176–77). The fear women have at home is thus rooted in the "willful prejudices of men" rather than nature and this fear persists through inconstancy and absurdity. The result is that the evils perpetrated by husbands on wives are without natural or social justification. (Christianity for Hays, too, could never justify these harms, since Christianity mirrors the laws of nature and reason.) Instead, domestic tyranny (as Hays calls it) is "only established by men, and it is totally incompatible with natural justice, not always even consistent with humanity; and consequently ill calculated to promote the happiness of either party" (Hays 1798, 274). The only way that the matrimonial imbalance of justice can be sustained is when the subjected party believes either that she deserves her treatment or that her husband really treats her as well as he can. And to these women, Hays writes, "Of the first, women never were, nor I fear never will be convinced. And the last, the daily and sad experience of many, will not permit them to believe" (Hays 1798, 275).

Similarly, Catharine Macaulay's objections to gender inequalities also frequently target the role of women at home. Upon entering a marriage contract during Macaulay's time, a woman consented to wed and vowed to submit to her husband, and at such a time, the woman's civil existence was voided: since man and wife were one in the law, the woman vanished into the man as her husband became her sovereign.[14] But, then and now, a man would never rationally enter into a contract that invalidates his civil rights or his status in the political community, nor should anyone under the natural order created by God. Macaulay contends, as Hays did, that the paternalistic injustices of politics are the result of human volition. She writes, "The power Adam had over his children is not mentioned as of the monarchical kind. We find him no where exercising this power or claiming it as his due; and yet there could not have been a more equitable occasion for exercising it, than the perfidious murder of Abel presented" (Macaulay 1769, 10). The intentional, systemic patriarchy Macaulay sees within the marriage contract is a worry that Astell also shares, who thinks of the marriage relationship analogously to the political systems which oppress a citizenry. "Astell deploys the Whig critique of arbitrary power (the framers held that James II had broken the 'original contract' between king and people, and had 'abdicated the government') in order to expose the reality of male power and tyranny to which women voluntarily subject themselves when they enter into the marriage contract" (O'Brien 2009, 12–13).

Abusive political power as systemic evil

The location of evil in the political is socially expedient but is also necessary to obviate the concrete significance of atrocious harm. A situated sense of moral evil makes all claims against God equal, because whether it is disease, or suffering that parents bring upon their children, or mental illness (or other factors that impinge on the ability to act rationally), or pains from physical labor, or daily circumstances that test one's integrity, identifying evil with these injustices makes the problem of evil relevant to all people (not just philosophers, lords, and priests). There are differences, certainly, among the viewpoints of female scholars as to what extent political power, especially, is an evil, and to what degree it creates systemic harm, although at a minimum, all agree that social and political structures can facilitate systemic injustice. Mary Astell, for her part, focused on advancing women's access to education, and rarely engaged in arguing directly for political rights for women. She was hopeful that a legitimate monarch could provide enlightened leadership, and thought that some of the inequities among race and class were inextricably tied to the proper functioning of society. In spite of this, "she deeply resented the domination of ignorant and morally inferior men over women of quality such as herself, especially when such men were presumed to have power over women simply because they were males, while women were denied the possibility of self-improvement because they were women" (Ruether 1998, 134). Mary Wollstonecraft's *Vindication of the Rights of Women* is largely considered to be the first significant feminist tome, and yet, it is but one of her works in which she argues against various structures of oppression. "Men are strange machines," she writes, "and their whole system of morality is in general held together by one grand principle, which loses its force the moment they allow themselves to break with impunity over the bounds which secured their self-respect. A man ceases to love humanity, then individuals, as he advances in the chase after wealth; as one chases his interest."[15] Women are more susceptible to suffer under the political power structures, "Born as a woman—and born to suffer—in endeavoring to repress my own emotions, I feel more acutely the various ills my sex are fated to bear—I feel the evils they are subject to endure, degrade them so far below their oppressors, as almost to justify their tyranny, leading at the same time superficial reasoners to term that weakness the cause, which is only the consequence of short-sighted despotism" (Wollstonecraft 1798b, vol. 2, 108–9). The political 'tyranny' Wollstonecraft believes imprints itself onto moral reasoning establishes a cycle in which women are mentally and physically subordinated. She explains, "A false morality is established which makes all the virtue of women consist in chastity, submission, and forgiveness of injuries" (Wollstonecraft 1798b, vol. 2, 150).

Even Margaret Cavendish, who was a staunch advocate for "rank" (as a monarchist who believed that the right rule for a society was in a strong monarch), argued against oppressive political systems—especially when those institutions worked against the education of women.

Certainly, Catharine Macaulay's reputation as an intellectual to be reckoned with comes in part from her arguments for the rights of women, and she shared Cavendish's belief that suffering often derives from human institutions which propagate systemic injustices. Macaulay argued that these systems were never divinely intended to enslave female nature (Macaulay 1790, 207), and provided concrete political examples to try to persuade the men of Great Britain not to rely on 'barbarism' when interacting with women. Although "it wouldn't be her purpose to relate" the details of the problem in Europe, she contends (205), "certain it is, that some degree of inferiority, in point of corporal strength, seems always to have existed between the two sexes, and this advantage in the barbarous ages of mankind, was abused to such a degree, as to destroy all natural rights of the female species, and reduce them to a state of abject slavery." The physical strength of men over women (coupled with the ability of men to own property) affords them a great power. Power tends to corrupt, however, and in civil society a pattern emerges, in which those who are in power invoke natural law within God's perceived created order to deceive women into believing they are intrinsically inferior to men, and that oppression is thereby naturally justified.

Any inferiority of women is not natural, Macaulay insists, but comes about as an accident of living within a society that perverts justice. She writes:

> They give to their own color only, the quality of external beauty, and they persuade themselves that the swarthy inhabitants of India and Africa are a degree below ... but if we reflect on the rise and fall of nations, we shall find, that accident alone, without the assistance of internal excellence, has produced this superiority, and that it has appeared and disappeared in the same society, as accident was favorable or unfavorable to its existence.
>
> *(Macaulay 1790, 249–50)*

Macaulay argues that human nature exerts its selfish bent through political power, but that this selfishness can be evident at any stage of a person's life (12). The natural tendency towards power could be beneficial, since if people are essentially good (and only accidentally evil), those in power will generally use their positions to benefit the powerless. If this is true, political power is a virtue to be sought, especially for those who would place the corporate good before their own individual happiness. Tabling the paternalistic undertone of this position, Macaulay agrees that it is pragmatically possible that the thirst for power could be used altruistically and towards the benefit of society (12). It is especially true that most people do not understand how intricately connected they are to others, so they might miss how interwoven their individual happiness is to the interests of society.

Unfortunately, despots often win positions of power and they use their power to convince the masses that violations of individual liberty are imperative to keep the public peace, although what the despot wants is personal happiness. For Macaulay, power driven by self-absorption corrupts the mind, which thus contributes to a warped disposition toward self-gratification. Becoming enamored with the self makes one's own self the object of one's desire. But if individual happiness is the rule by which life is governed, the "rule" becomes as variable as each person's subjective 'dispositions'. She explains, "The gross selfish man would have a rule for himself, in which we may be sure that benevolence, temperance, and moderation, would have no part ... and if a man is only to be directed by his notion of happiness in the conduct of life, then making a wrong choice can never be esteemed vice, nor can any harder term be given to it than an error in judgment" (413–15). In an ideal world—a world in which political power is guided by the ethical application of the virtues—those in power would benefit those who suffer, but such a world is actually disconnected from what happens when people obtain the political power they seek.

The political systems which foster what we would now call 'atrocities' spread the disease of harm to other social institutions, including the Church. "Is it any wonder?", Macaulay asked (Macaulay 1783, 158), "that justice should be so little considered by those who agree that a perfect God created two species of creatures with equal intelligence and similar feelings[16] and yet consigned one as a kind of property—deprived of any qualities that could prove sufficient to prevent the enormous abuse of such power?" The subordination of justice to power observed in politics was also displayed by theists in Macaulay's day, especially by religious leaders who would reason that any human suffering is eventually offset and outweighed by a later, greater good:

However, the teachers of Christianity [are] condemned for admitting so gross a solecism in religious sentiment, as to preach Christ crucified for the universal good of the human race; because it is not congruous to any just idea of divine perfection, to permit the sufferings of an innocent being for the advantage of transgressors; although according to the fundamental principle of this condemned doctrine, the highest reward that omnipotent power can bestow is annexed to this act of obedience and benevolence in the person of the Messiah.

(Macaulay 1783, 85–6)

Macaulay presages here contemporary atheism's worry that theism's message of eschatological justice (which seems to be predicated upon the suffering of the oppressed at the hands of those who benefit) is irreconcilable with the God of scripture. Although they end up making different conclusions, both would agree that if God is perfect and loving, God's created order would not require the suffering of the most needy and innocent.

Whereas male philosophers in the early modern period articulate a version of moral evil in which human immorality is inconsistent with divine perfection,[17] their version also manifests a tension between contingent, free human actions (so, those that people can be held morally accounted for) and necessary events set in motion by God (so, those for which God might be morally praise-or-blameworthy).[18] Although Macaulay agrees that moral evil leads to human suffering, she places much more emphasis than Leibniz (for example) on the role human volition plays in making morally flawed choices, and she argues that human depravity is created and sustained by the concrete social and political structures ruled by the world's elite. The point of departure for Macaulay's view on moral evil, then, is a systemic ground of political evil which perpetuates unjust gender inequalities. A depraved human need for power is at root for atrocities that evidence themselves politically and socially.

Margaret Cavendish, considered by many to be a bit of an eccentric (though impactful) scholar, differs a bit from Macaulay, Astell, and Hays in that, although she agrees that misery is a moral evil that frequently results from human action, she also thinks that the question of whether God is responsible for evil is ultimately unknowable. The religious is tied to the political, so that political injustice is implicit in whatever has a religious function in society.[19] But, with a particular focus on issues of women's liberty, Cavendish does position evil firmly in the realm of the concrete—in injustices that limit, especially, the ability of women to think for themselves. These injustices occur in the lack of education of women, from political abuses, and as a result of domineering patriarchal domestic and civil rule. A goal of her writings is to "delineate the traits of a fanciful and witty dimension parallel to the masculine dominion of objectivity, where she manifested and realized the inalienable right of a woman to think within the intimacy of her mind and her house."[20] And, while her work focuses on the specific areas in which women are excluded from the scope of considerability, she also was responding to concrete horrors of civil war. Cavendish rejects the (in some ways, still fashionable) idea that God could endorse the horrendous suffering that comes with war, "Rationally one would think that God should not take delight in shaven heads, or bare and dirty feet, or cold backs, or hungry stomachs" (Cavendish 1655, 29–30).

Rape as Systemic Evil

But, for the positive impact the atrocity paradigm has had on focusing attention on foreseeable and preventable harms, the history of philosophy indicates that female scholars in the early modern period presaged focal elements of the atrocity paradigm, with different conclusions. Indeed, many of these intellectuals understood that 'evil' connotes suffering that is situated concretely in political and civil structures. Mary Wollstonecraft's scholarship, easily identifiable among the women this book highlights, was an outspoken advocate for women's civil and domestic rights. Her posthumously published *Maria, or the Wrongs of Women* [21] has been viewed as an early (though excoriating) accusation against the sexual, physical, and mental abuse women suffer in society. One of the characters, Jemima, laments after her rape, "But youth and a strong constitution prevailing, I once more crawled out, to ask myself the cruel question, 'Wither [sic] I should go?'" (98). The question is not simply a physical lament, but a *moral* one, since it indicates that Jemima's assault left her completely bereft of everything, including the ability to choose to be moral. Wollstonecraft goes so far as to suggest that immorality is a privilege reserved for those who actually have the resources to be tempted when she pens Jemima's statement, "I had not even the pleasure of being enticed into vice," (99) which suggests that choosing vice is itself a privileged position—because those who are able to choose to act immorally are free, a luxury not afforded to many who suffer.

Those who exert power through rape facilitate an individual's suffering and squelch freedom, but the impact is corporate, and not merely individual. Wollstonecraft's characters indict the system that eradicates ways out of suffering, as well as individuals who do not act to prevent the suffering of others. "How writers, professing to be friends to freedom, can assert that poverty is no evil, I cannot imagine" Wollstonecraft writes (112), because poverty as an institution creates other avenues for a person to suffer[22]—physically (the poor are more likely to become imprisoned, sexually and otherwise[23]) and mentally, "The mind is necessarily imprisoned in its own little tenement; and, fully occupied by keeping it in repair, has not time to rove about for improvement" (113). Knott and Taylor observe that Wollstonecraft's arguments against systemic evil are meant to positively impact all women, "not just women of a particular class. She articulated the stories of women facing poverty and sexual abuse. While Wollstonecraft concentrated on women's private woes, she knew that they needed the public status of citizens to enforce their private rights" (Taylor and Knott 2005, 577).

Wollstonecraft was not alone in developing literary works that speak directly against the ill-treatment of women at the hands of the powerful, and of using stark sexual imagery to facilitate systemic change. Mary Hays (who, like Wollstonecraft, was famous for her work in literature), also provides philosophical justification for conceiving evil in concrete ways. For Mary Hays, certain pernicious harms are enacted especially within the moral agency of a patriarchal political structure. Her focus (Hays 1796 and 1994) on the systemic, legal (and human) injustice that allows for rape and domestic violence sparked widespread controversy. Much to the chagrin of certain critics, Hays specifically calls out the political, legal framework as a main culprit for the myriad political and social injustices suffered by her female characters (Ward 2009, 131), and as a denunciation of the real systemic injustices of the oppressed. Within her works, there is a striking example of a most vicious concrete evil in the world: rape. Moral evil has its concrete rigging in social and familial injustice, and rape is the visceral physical representation of the depravity of human systems, especially since Hays views rape and sexual assault as a stark and excoriating analogy to the private violence and public subjugation of women (Ward 2009, 132).

Hays's *A Victim of Prejudice* (1799, Hays 1994) tells the story of Mary Raymond, who was born to a prostitute but later became educated. After Mary's mother dies tragically, Mary is raped. After the rape, her attacker tells her not to take the rape too seriously, especially since he was a little drunk. Hays provides unsparing details of Mary's feelings of horror and self-loathing, her sense of impotence and abandonment, and her realization that she is utterly powerless against society and the law (Ward 2009, 137). The inexorable and brutal subjugation of Raymond indicates Mary Hays's, "consuming need to engage the real horrors suffered by real women in late-eighteenth-century England. Eighteenth-century literature was, of course, suffused with Mary Raymonds, some raped, most deceived, all fated by the pretences of morality and the harder demands of the 'system of property', as Hays put it, to suffer the inevitable consequences" (Ward 2009, 139). Another Haysian heroine, Emma Courtney (the namesake of *Memoirs*), laments that the self is, "modified by circumstances: the customs of society, then, have enslaved, enervated, and degraded women" (Hays 1796, 71) and that, "we may trace most of the faults and miseries of mankind to the injustices and errors of political institutions, their permanency having been their radical defect" (91). Courtney tries to uncover the intrinsic cultural roots of evil against women, which she believes includes legal chicanery and the hypocrisy of the established Church—both of which are likely to "check the freedom, and contaminate the purity of the mind, and, entangling it in an explicable maze of error, poison virtue at its source" (193). The Haysian heroines are philosophically compelling since they suggest that the grossest incarnations of moral evil are perpetuated systemically, originate in human despotism, and result in the suppression of female liberty.

A critic might argue that rape, as a worst-case example of concrete moral evil, is not really a proper example of structural evil that produces atrocious harm. Rape might be egregious and a violent immoral act, but most injustice (and so, most evil in the world) is not brutal, as the acts Wollstonecraft and Hays depict. But, for these women, rape is the perfect instance of concrete evil because it demonstrates the powerlessness of women in any system where women are treated as property, rather than as equal partners in the created order. Wollstonecraft's language supports this, "But a wife, being as much a man's property as his horse, or his ass, she has nothing she can call her own" (Wollstonecraft 1798b, vol. 2,

45–6). Real women in late eighteenth-century England suffered real horrors, and the subjugation of rape victims—as vicious as these scholars illustrate it—is symbolic not only of rape, but of the deprecation of all women—women who were fated by law and morality to suffer under harsher demands than men as items of property (Ward 2009, 139).

Another potential critique is that early modern women did not view rape in the *same* negative light that atrocity paradigm scholars do. Some have made this claim. Roy Porter (1986), for example, argues that although early modern women spoke out against sexual blights such as child prostitution and sexual abuse, they did not view rape as an atrocious harm. Others instead argue that women in the eighteenth and nineteenth centuries always viewed rape as a harm, but the discourse over rape was differently impacted by the perception of rape in early modern England.[24] There, and at that time, "women would have been more aggrieved by the damage of a rape assault to their social standing or respectability" (Smith, 2010, 29). In spite of the fact that women in the period were more heavily impacted by a social stigma against rape victims, Smith points out that most scholars would repudiate the idea that rape was not viewed in that era as an atrocity. First Wave feminists, following Wollstonecraft's lead, did campaign against sexual violence, including marital rape and the sexual abuse of children, and more scholars (including Wolfthal 1999 and Smith 2010) argue that women were as fearful of the rape act then as they are now, and were not merely concerned about becoming a social or domestic blight. Coupled with the stringent evidential demands placed on women who publicly declared that they had been raped,[25] the fact that early modern female novelists like Hays and Wollstonecraft were willing to write in such open terms about rape is a sign of bravery, rather than capriciousness, to socially condemn the power structures that were in place to further victimize victims. Their bravery is high-lighted even more when we remember that there was a lack of access for women to write philosophical treatises against assault, and if they found an avenue in which to write, any arguments they wrote were required to be rigorously systematic and objective, which can be difficult when talking about a topic as personally damaging as rape.

The Suppression of Rights and Access to Education as Systemic Evil

For as long as there have been opportunities to be educated, women have had a more difficult time gaining an education than men. Even today across the globe, examples abound for those who think the status quo is sustainable only if women are not afforded the opportunity to better themselves intellectually, and those who prey on the intellectual suppression of women and girls. The subjugation of women politically, socially, and domestically is maintained by denying access to education. Early modern women are famous for arguing against the institutional injustice of preventing women from gaining an education, and they identified it as the form of slavery and oppression that those in power intended it to be. It has already been noted that they agree that men and women begin life with more or less equal intellectual endowments, but Hays (1798, 69) directly linked oppression to the lack of intellectual access. Any group of people, "can be held in a state of subjection and dependence from generation to generation, by another party, who, by a variety of circumstances, none of them dependent on actual, original superiority of mind, may have established an authority over them" (Hays 1798, 69). And when anyone is subjugated to oppression, Hays argues, both the body and the mind degenerate (69). Women who are kept in ignorance are easier to manipulate and, so will more willingly buy into the idea that they ought to be treated as objects worthy of degradation. When the weak and ignorant are at a greater disadvantage, this leads to further disenfranchisement of women, who will be prevented from an education—which is required to pursue health and moral well-being.

Gender inequality has already been identified as a chief contributor to atrocious harm for the women that we are looking at. For Macaulay, any true differences that exist among the genders come from education and situation only, and were never intended by God to serve as the foundation of what Macaulay deems as slavery of the female nature (Macaulay 1790, 206–7). The continued physical subordination and mental slavery of the oppressed become ingrained within a political system, such that those who suffer under it believe both that the injustice is ordained by God and that they deserve whatever they receive from the system. Mary Astell would agree, and she argues in *A Serious Proposal to the Ladies* that women are imprisoned and confined to a life of petty concerns whenever they are not educated—especially in philosophy and religion (two disciplines that help us understand the higher purposes of life[26]). She speaks off the page directly to her women readers, "How can you be content to be in the world like Tulips in a Garden, to make a fine *show* and be good for nothing?" For Astell, women's incapacity, if it is present at all, is hardly natural. Instead, it comes from generations of forced inactivity—long hard years during which women are kept from serious education, turned away from productive intellectual work, and kept from using their minds in ways that had advanced a culture. "Women are from their very Infancy debar'd those Advantages, with the want of which they are afterwards reproached", they are "nursed up in those Vices which will hereafter be upbraided to them. So partial are Men as to expect Brick where they afford no Straw" (Astell 1696, 24). Astell was not simply in favor of extending the opportunity for formal learning to more people, but instead she thought the capacities of the female mind and spirit had to be completely reassessed as a result of their subjugation (Taylor and Knott, 2005, 360).

Astell was skeptical of natural law arguments for the subordination of women, and she also sarcastically contrasted men who are afforded by their social systems liberties that are not afforded to women—with men who, for reasons of financial exigency, have to forego public education and be intellectually satisfied with private contemplations.[27] Just as poor men think it is a grave injustice to be compelled to give up their education, so, too a woman's lack of access to education is, according to Astell, at the core of institutional abuses of power. In *Proposal*, Astell argues, "The Cause therefore of the defects we labour under is, if not wholly, yet at least in the first place, to be ascribed to the mistakes of our Education, which like an Error in the first Concoction, spreads its ill Influence through all our Lives" (Astell 1697, I.16). Of course it's true that preventing females' education has a deleterious impact on society, but for Astell, the moral impact of not educating girls and women was more than just social—it was at the root of all individual immoral acts. The system is pernicious because it creates the possibility for women to act immorally (and so, to spread harm and to model immorality for others), "And seeing it is Ignorance, either habitual or actual, which is the cause of all sin, how are they like to escape *this*, who are bred up in *that*? That therefore Women are unprofitable to most, and a plague and dishonor to some Men is not much to be regretted on account of the *Men*, because 'tis the product of their own folly, in denying them the benefits of an ingenuous and liberal Education, the most effectual means to direct them into, and to secure their progress in the ways of Virtue" (Astell 1697, I.19). The vision Astell has is that the genderless soul, whether embodied male or female, can ascend towards communion with God through godly activities, self-discipline, and rational contemplation. Disallowing women an education ultimately denies them the opportunity to cultivate their minds, achieve new ways to physical health, foster improvement in their families, and to live a complete life as she believed God intended.

The upshot to Astell's repudiation of educational injustice is that she projects a world in which political systems create individual agency to fight immoral, oppressive acts. Education—especially in those disciplines that bring us closer to knowledge of teleology—can overturn the individual and corporate impact of abuse and can erode systems of harm. The power of rational autonomy—a much stronger doctrine in Astell than even in Locke (Harol 2007, 96 argues)—prioritizes moral and intellectual development and places her firmly as an arbiter for civil rights for women. Moral and intellectual growth are always in tandem, since moral understanding is the vehicle through which education successfully mitigates harm. When the human will is shaped by practical and moral education, the passions are directed away from "fully and unreasonably" seeking out material objects of desire (Astell 1697, II.137). Astell explores more fully the relationship between education and molding the will according to morally perfect principles:

Especially since the Will is blind, and cannot choose but by the direction of the Understanding; or to speak more properly, since the Soul always *Wills* according as she *Understands*, so that if she Understands amiss, she Wills amiss. And as Exercise enlarges and exalts any Faculty, so through want of using it becomes cramped and lessened; if therefore we make little or no use of our

Understandings, we shall shortly have none to use; and the more contracted and unemployed the deliberating and directive Power is, the more liable is the elective to unworthy and mischievous choices. What is it but the want of an ingenious Education, that renders the generality of Feminine Conversations so insipid and foolish and their solitude so insupportable? Learning is therefore necessary to render them more agreeable and useful in company, and to furnish them with becoming entertainments when alone, that so they may not be driven to those miserable shifts, which too many make use of to put off their time, that precious Talent that never lies on the hands of a judicious Person.

(Astell 1697, I.48)

Whereas education can successfully guide the will and the passions, a life void of the benefits of education leads to desires that are unmoored. When we are denied an education, our unguided desires become evil by "deluding our expectations" and causing "us to fall into Air and Emptiness" (Letter, 119) through a materialism that evidences itself "in a thousand Extravagancies," and makes us fall prey to "pleasant Dream[s]" (Letter 7, 88, 96) (Astell 1705b).[28]

Astell's views on education are similar to Margaret Cavendish—people err because social customs prevent people (especially women) from thinking for themselves, and human nature and development (in which the will asserts itself before the understanding has a chance to develop) is unduly influenced by a lack of education. For Cavendish, the most atrocious forms of suffering result from intellectual rather than physical abuses of liberty (given that physical abuses are originally sourced in intellectual abuses). "We go wrong," Cavendish observes, "either because we are ignorant of the ends which we ought to pursue or because we know what ends we ought to pursue but we willfully deviate from them" (Cavendish 1997 [1664], 509f). Cavendish disparages men of England for acting like other cultural groups who exclude women arbitrarily, especially when they place constraints on the intellectual pursuits of women, especially within the Church, "I thought you had been either Jews, or Turks, because I never perceived any women in your congregations; but what is the reason you bar them from your religious assemblies?" (Cavendish 1666b, 20). At the time of her writing, of course, only men were citizens and had vast amounts of power beyond that of women, and so Cavendish expressed astonishment that such powerful entities would suppress the ability of women to act, behave, and to think freely. When corresponding directly to men, in "Citizens of the Market Place," Cavendish takes a tack that differs from Hays, Macaulay, Astell, and Wollstonecraft and appeals to natural law (as well as female beauty[29]) to argue against oppressive action, "It is not only uncivil and ignoble, but unnatural, for men to speak against women and their liberties, for women were made by Nature for men, to be loved, accompanied, assisted, and protected; and if men are bound to love them by Nature, should they restrain them by force: Should they make them slaves, which Nature made to be their dearest associates, their beautifulest objects and sweetest delights?" (Cavendish 1666b, 247). But Cavendish uses starker terms about the phenome-nological experience of being 'Inferior Women' when her audience is women (in "Female Orations"), "But alas, men, that are not only our tyrants but our devils, keep us in the hell of subjection, from whence I cannot perceive any redemption or getting out; we may complain, and bewail our condition, but they will not free us; we may murmur and rail against men, yet they regard not what we say" (248). The situation of women against men is without hope, and leads Cavendish to compare the tears women cry from their suffering to unfelt "puffs of wind" and "fruitless showers" (248). Not only do women suffer, when they do, no one takes any notice of their suffering.[30]

Should the critic argue that these injustices are *too* particular—that they fall out of the realm of the atrocious harm category—it should be noted that the intel-lectual injustice Cavendish focuses on is systemic, pernicious, and denigrating, perhaps more significantly because the harms are intellectual. Broad and Green observe that, for Cavendish, "Women are not free because they are, quite simply, coerced, threatened, or forced into obedience. In this way, men keep women in the subordinate position of children and fools—human beings without the full use of their reason" (Broad and Green 2009, 220). The subjugation of women by men occurs in the public sphere, although, Cavendish would here agree with the other early modern female scholars, it is perpetuated within the home:

> A telling passage from *Loves Adventures* sums up the contrast between Cavendish's ideal of a patriarchal marriage and the reality. Lady Ignorance expresses Cavendish's ideal: "if a Husband loves his wife, he will be careful to please her, prudent for her subsistence, industrious for her convenience, valiant to protect her, and conversable to entertain her, and wise to direct and guide her." Her husband corrects her: "To rule and govern her, you mean wife." Husbands may have the natural authority to "direct and guide" women, Cavendish is suggesting, but once they interpret that to mean "ruling and governing," they have overstepped their role, and this results in conflict (or even violence) and further limitations on women's freedom.
>
> *(Boyle 2013, 528)*

By treating women's intellectual pursuits as vacuous, men actively disenfranchise women. The pragmatic consequence of the disenfranchisement is that women are at a disadvantage intellectually, but also in the realms of civics (where they are seen as property, at best), politics (where they have no voice), and religion (where they are subjugated to the wills of their husbands).

As strongly as Macaulay, Hays, Astell, and Cavendish argue for the equalization of access to education, Mary Wollstonecraft's arguments have, out of all those from early modern female scholars, been singularly lauded as philosophically trailblazing and legally significant, and I highlight that point here for two reasons.

First, although so much has been written by[31] and on[32] Wollstonecraft and education, the reasons for which Wollstonecraft wrote to encourage educational access to women reflect concerns similar to today's scholars over atrocious harms that impact women globally. Second, her arguments point towards a need for theists to address the concrete suffering endured by women particularly and not just humanity generally. Amartya Sen (2005, 5–6) observes that Wollstonecraft's initial language defended in general the 'rights of men' (utilizing the common general description 'men' to also refer to women) but "by the time Mary wrote the second of those two books on rights—*A Vindication of the Rights of Women*— she had seen clearly the need to separate out the particular problems of women, in addition to the general problems of disadvantaged human beings—men as well as women."

The philosophy of religion of women like Hays, Astell, Wollstonecraft, Macaulay, and Cavendish takes its starting point, then, in a political statement centered on the human agency of moral evil. The relationship between political injustice and suffering mirrors the description of atrocious harms provided by contemporary atrocity paradigm atheists. A key difference, certainly, is that Hays, Macaulay, and Astell were theists, and Wollstonecraft and Cavendish produced arguments consistent with theism. So, can their concrete expressions of evil and suffering be reconciled with their theistic commitments? A situated sense of moral evil equalizes claims against God for the presence of evil, for whether it is disease, or suffering of children, or mental illness (or other factors that impinge on the ability to act rationally), or pains from physical labor, or daily circumstances that test one's integrity, locating evil within these injustices makes the problem of evil a question that is relevant to those who suffer (and not exclusively philosophers, lords, and priests). In the rest of the chapter, I will argue that the theistic conclusions that emerge from their scholarship are not only accessible to women or the oppressed, but to all those who are marginalized. As Catharine Macaulay observes, "There can be but one rule of moral excellence for beings made of the same materials, organized after the same manner, and subjected to similar laws of nature" (Macaulay 1790, 201–202). Their views are meant to be a description of how things are within systems of oppression, from which we can think about prescriptions for how things should be to overcome the systems that oppress.

Systemic Evil and a Rational Belief in God

Framing evil systemically, as these women and contemporary atrocity atheists do, means that suffering is seen as a product of systemically-imbedded injustice, which is experienced differently. But this is *not* to say that evil is 'gendered'. (Critics who do not understand the atrocity paradigm or standpoint epistemology might make an erroneous inference that including contextual aspects of one's lived experiences—such as suffering as a result of being female—makes evil understandable only in terms of gender. This does not follow, of course.) The result is not that evil must be approached as 'gendered' but that it should be considered as 'situated'.[33] This is an important result for theists. Chapter 1 demonstrated that those who deny that the problem of evil is tied to real, concrete evil in the world are already at a disadvantage when doing theodicy, because the arguments that emerge from their point of departure are already disconnected from the atrocity paradigm atheist, whose entire worry is about the lived experience of suffering in the world. Theists who understand the lived experiences of those who suffer atrocious harms are in a better position to discuss divine benevolence with a critic who is worried about atrocities through which real people suffer.

These early modern women understood the situated component of evil, and so developed approaches to facilitate transformation of the social and legal systems that denied women's rights, enabled horrendous evil, and waged war. Scholars informed by today's atrocity paradigm would recognize the various degrees to which Hays, Astell, Macaulay, Wollstonecraft, and Cavendish grounded evil systemically and rejected a conception of morality that was not tied to the misery of women and others on the periphery of moral considerability. Thus, early modern women and atrocity paradigm atheists share several unified perspectives on moral evil: they agree that injustice is foisted on women (and the weak, the poor, the marginalized) as a result of social and political structures; they agree that concrete, systemic evil ought to be otherwise and so is culpable; they agree that there are no natural or essential advantages given to oppressors that could justify oppression; they agree that these culpable harms are perpetuated by the elite, who benefit from them; they agree that suffering is always a result of a freely chosen action that takes advantage of either a lack of knowledge or an imbalance of power; and, despite their disparate theistic beliefs, they agree that moral evil does not come from God, but is an abuse of what is given (for the theist, by God; for the atheist, by advantage).

Localizing moral evil in systems of harm, however, is not enough for any of these women to make their view of evil consistent with their various theistic commitments. God might, after all, be morally culpable in bringing about—or, in the least, in allowing—the dominant power-brokers of the world to oppress others. Indeed, the scholarship of the women this chapter has focused on is fully consistent with the atheist arguments from atrocity that were provided in Chapter 1: systems of evil exist in the world, are not overrideable, and threaten the great good of our individual and collective projects. Wollstonecraft observes (1798a, note 17, 185–6), "There does not appear to be any evil in the world, but what is necessary. The doctrine of rewards and punishments, not considered as a means of reformation, appears to me infamous libel on divine goodness." If humans in power are to blame for perpetuating harm on those who are unable to prevent it, then it seems an all-powerful, all-knowing, and all-good God would at least have to share some blame for atrocity, if such a being is able (and would be willing) to prevent some of the systems of atrocity described by Hays, Astell, Macaulay, Wollstonecraft, and Cavendish. Further, if patriarchy, rape, political abuse, and the inability for women to gain an education are genuine examples of concrete atrocity, then they also present a rather damning counter to the typical theodicy that defends God's goodness and power in the world. These systems of harm present a challenge to the perfections of a Divine Being, yet, a number of these women would still contend that it is impossible—blasphemous, still—to imagine "that Infinite purity could implant in the creatures of his power a natural propensity to evil" (Hays 1793, 208–9). Macaulay argues against skepticism about God's power and goodness in the face of evil, since skepticism:

> threatens the annihilation of every found principle in morals and religion. The unbeliever triumphs in his newly acquired strength, urges the contest, and boldly challenges the religious world to fight the battle on the ground which themselves have marked out. And whilst he uses the weapons of the adversary with a commanding success, the anxious believer finds his hopes gradually decrease, and the sublime prospect of a happy eternity clouding by degrees, till at length it vanishes into the chaos of doubt and uncertainty
>
> *(Macaulay 1790, 360–361).*

But, if there are horrible, concrete, and systemic moral evils that are propagated against women, and God cannot be blamed as their originator or as their source, what is the cause of moral evil in the world? On one hand, to read early modern female scholarship as engaging with the atrocity paradigm has a huge advantage: it places the theist in conversation with the atheist. These women did not approach evil only as a logical problem that Christian philosophers have to iron out in damp, ill-lit rooms (or large, well-funded conferences). They were committed to identifying the institutions within society and the home that create—or create the conditions for—horrendous suffering. Suffering is concrete, and so the problem of evil is concrete. On the other hand, the concrete depictions of the nature of evil actions and institutions provided by early modern women are quite distinct from impactful male thinkers of their time (such as Leibniz). Evil and suffering ought not to happen, and they at least appear to be gratuitous (as argued in Chapter 1). If early modern women can be read as presaging the conception of evil put forward by the atrocity paradigm, it may also be difficult to imagine how their theistic commitments could mesh with their vision for evil's eradication, especially if theodicy ends up as one of the systems that create harm.

One recent way contemporary theism has tried to connect with atheists who are disenchanted with a too-abstract conception of evil is to introduce narratives (stories) as a theodical tool. Although traditional responses to the problem of evil might (to differing degrees of success) demonstrate that there could be morally sufficient reasons for God to allow evil in the world, stories can communicate in a more relatable way the process through which characters come to accept that God might have reasons to allow their suffering. The use of narrative has more than an emotional point—the narrative's philosophical purpose is to communicate knowledge that differs from the propositional knowledge that logical theodical arguments seek to convey. Daniel Barber (2011, 541) gives an example of the type of knowledge towards which narratives aim:

> Theodor Adorno infamously remarked, "To write poetry after Auschwitz is barbaric".[34] While some may find a lack of precision in this statement, it is no doubt possible to discern in it a non-propositional, affective glimpse of truth …. What I am gesturing at, then, is the possibility of countless narratives of suffering that do not end in the consolation of divine love, or even the possibility of narratives that remain uncommunicated precisely because they are so beset by suffering.

Philosophers have a tendency to "suppose that left-brain skills alone will reveal to us all that is philosophically interesting about the world" (Stump 2010, 24–5). Literary and scriptural narratives are meant as resources to supplement the theist in her attempt to unpack the quagmire of possible reasons for suffering in the world—difficulties which appear to us as logical, evidential, and (even) existential problems.

A limitation for contemporary theists is that appropriating narratives as one of their methods of defense against the problem of evil requires a situated conception of evil. But, relying upon situated evil would require narratives that are relatable from the point of view of the oppressed. In Chapter 3, I will argue that contemporary theodical narratives suffer from similar difficulties as traditional theodicy when it rejects a concrete conception of evil. (I will also argue that of particular concern is the—currently *en vogue*—attempt to use the 'second-person standpoint' as a way to frame narratives that could be especially effective as theodicy.) If theists want to be in dialogue with atheists—and, since the pragmatic point of doing theodicy is to demonstrate that God exists in spite of evil in the world, it seems theists *would* want to be in dialogue with their opponents— theodicy must be relatable enough that an atheist could engage with its content. But, narrative theodicy to date is derived mostly from the position of epistemic privilege (whether told from the perspective of the elite, the wealthy, or those in power).

Theists would be better served if they look at the various narratives of the spectacular female scholars in the early modern period. And it is within these narratives that we can find clues as to how theodical narratives (specifically) might be relatable to those who suffer atrocious harm. Their work can thereby bridge a gap between theism and atrocity by tying atrocity to systemic injustice, in which people willingly abuse the moral systems put into place within the natural order. The challenge for theodicy will be to show that the perfect benevolence of God is not mitigated by a lack of divine ability to prevent or limit evil in the world, since this would lead to an irrational belief in an unprincipled system of morality or a loss of faith in evidence for the justice of God.

Notes

1 And, undeniably, their situations are importantly different. Margaret Cavendish's work is positioned from the royalist perspective, and was less concerned about broad issues of social justice than someone writing from the Whig tradition (such as Catharine Macaulay) or from republicanism (like Mary Hays).

2 See Morny (2010), 17–32, who does not discuss early modern women, but spotlights the problematic fact that analytic theodicy does not take up the topic of violence against women.

3 See, for example, Lara (2004), 190.

4 There are too many important contributions to note, but a good start to the literature would include work by Daly (including 1978, 1993), Rita Nakishima Brock (2002), Marie M. Fortune (especially her work on domestic violence, Fortune et al. 2001), Daphne Hampson (1990), Emily Holmes and Wendy Farley (2011), Joy Morny (2010), Kristine Rankka (1998), Rosemary Radford Ruether (1993, 1998), and Dorothee Soelle (1984).

5 This seems *prima facie* obvious, but has been a source of some consternation. See, for example, Clatterbaugh (2003).

6 We do not have to leave the front pages of our newspapers to see that genocidal rape remains a weapon of choice in various wars, and that, across the globe, women and girls are consistently and persistently denied education—and are even the subject of mass kidnappings when they risk being educated.

7 God created the world in the best possible way, but God did not create humans with either omnipotence or omniscience. The moral law must be tied to what humans are able to do, so no requirements of the moral law depend on people knowing or doing more than they are able. Perhaps a critic could contend that a better alternative to creating metaphysically limited beings is to create nothing at all. Mary Hays would reply (1793, 183), "And these teach us (as I before observed) that a Being of infinite power and boundless benevolence could not have created intelligent creatures, without intending their ultimate benefit; and though on account of their limited capacities in this first stage of their existence, they are liable to much evil and woe, yet these very sufferings may have a reifying tendency, and may be links in a chain of causes and effects, that will eventually terminate in the highest felicity." For Hays, it would not be better for God to not create; rather, a better option is for us to be created with temporal limitations, which eventually will either fade or will no longer matter.

8 Could it be that God could be responsible for creating us with too weak a will? Perhaps if the will were stronger, we would be better suited to avoid temptation. But such a critique misses the balance between reason, will, and desire endemic to human nature, for Hays. God could not have created us with unlimited reason, and because we are animals, we have desires. Will is the sticking point, because when reason indicates a desire is contrary to what is best for us, will is what can remove us from moral danger. If that will is free, God does not intervene in it. That isn't to say that the will cannot be impacted from without. Rather, education can aid natural reason and develop natural capabilities that can strengthen the will. Hays writes, "Nature is so simple, so uniform, and so decided, in her moral as well as physical operations, that she never counteracts herself. Thus if the practice of truth alone, in all its different branches, were faithfully and universally followed out; it would of itself bring about every other reformation" (Hays 1798, 205).

9 Hays (1798, 21). Of course, to buy into the idea that there are disproportionate and natural intellectual and physical differences between the sexes that make a moral difference, women first have to be deceived to believe they are less valuable intellectually and physically. This initial deception is the most morally egregious. Hays writes, "of all bondage, mental bondage is surely the most fatal; the absurd despotism which has hitherto, with more than gothic barbarity, enslaved the female mind" (1793, 19–20).

10 Hays (1798, 98–99). The entire quote is quite fascinating: "But let us consider further, that men not only fear, that if women were permitted to be what they call too wise, and knowing, they would not so easily submit to be governed; but they likewise fear that this want of submission, might produce the most fatal consequences in society. For this truth cannot be denied, in every case as well as the present, either that authority must be vested in one side, and that explicitly for the general good of mankind, for the same important purpose, authority must be so nicely balanced and arranged, alas! So very nicely, that it is almost too much to expect from human integrity, that it shall voluntarily enter upon a task of such trouble and difficulty; or that a party already in possession of so flattering a distinction, no matter how or by what means obtained, shall set about to dilapidate or garble it by participation.—No! No! It is in vain to think, that any man, or set of men, or men in short taken in the gross, shall by frequent appeals to their best feelings seek out for reasons to portion it away. With a bad grace do men entrusted with power, devise it to each other, and still they keep it within as narrow a circle as possible; but when through necessity, and for the common purposes of life, they admit women to certain puny privileges, and delegate to them a scanty portion of power .... With so many useless and mortifying precautions indeed do they trammel their gifts, that they become by passing through such hands, equivalent to prohibitions."

11 Hays discusses the "fatal" moral and pragmatic consequences of suppressing women's education, activity, and rights. For example, she warns against "the fatal effects of wrong, or neglected education" and contrasts these with "the knowledge of them which imports life and safety" and she notes that, "of all bondage, mental bondage is surely the most fatal; the absurd despotism which has hitherto, with more than gothic barbarity, enslaved the female mind" (Hays 1798, 155 and 249), and, "that inactivity of mind and body in which a great part of the subjects of despotic governments must necessarily be plunged, and which is the most fatal and universal enemy to all great and good actions" and, finally, that the "happiness of domestic and social life" have its fatal moment at the exsanguination of "the rules of common justice" (Hays 1798, 134 and 158).

12 Fittingly, Hays's own work received criticism for being "employed in a manner highly dangerous to the peace and welfare of society" The Critical Review, 12, quoted in Kelly (1993).

13 Astell does here pay homage to Locke, "whose Essay on Human Understanding makes large amends for the want of all others in that kind," Astell 1696, 54.

14 Wendy Gunther-Canada (2006) clearly and succinctly draws out this point.

15 Letters Written during a Short Residence, Letter XXIII, 212, in the Woman's Collection at the University of North Carolina at Greensboro, (Wollstonecraft 1796). (Wollstonecraft even warns England and America, who "owe their liberty to commerce," to "beware of the consequence; the tyranny of wealth is still more galling and debasing than that of rank", Letter XIV, 142–3.)

16 Who are consequently capable of an equal degree of suffering.

17 See, for example, Flemming (1986), Hernandez (2010), Kondoleon (1973), and Vabalaite (2010).

18 See, for example, Adams (1994), Groarke (2001), Look (2007), Morris (1984), and Sleigh (1999).

19 Interestingly, according to many of her contemporaries, Cavendish did not correctly tie the political to the religious. Lisa Walters (2014) notes that many considered Cavendish to be an atheist because her version of monarchism did not ground the absolute right of kings on religion (something that even constitutional royalists did), 142–3.

20 Yaakov Mascetti, (2008) 3. Some feminists have worried that Cavendish's reticence to seek to directly abolish systems of patriarchy means that she was less committed to what we would now call a "feminist" project. And, indeed, Cavendish equivocates on issues contemporary feminists would think are important, for example, whether

married women really are free; Cavendish at points argues that they are because their natural beauty gives them power over their husbands. Yet at other points, "Cavendish shows a keen awareness of the fact that many early modern women do suffer from a debilitating loss of negative liberty in the patriarchal marriage state," Jacqueline Broad (2014) 113. Mascetti replies to this criticism by noting that Cavendish's "philosophical feminism was, therefore, carved out of a conscious and supportive acknowledgment of male hegemony, and not turned into a method of gendered opposition and subversion. The dimension of feminine fancy that she created was innocuously and respectfully parallel to that of male wisdom" (Mascetti 2008, 13).

21 References here are to the first edition (Wollstonecraft 1798b), among the holdings at the University of North Carolina at Greensboro's Women's Collection (London: J Johnson, and GG & J Robinson), 1798.

22 Wollstonecraft is not alone when she identifies poverty as a systemic vice that results from the power-grab of men. Mary Astell excoriates those who would allow the powerless to suffer from poverty, and goes so far as to argue that such behavior is not fit for animals, "To introduce poor Children into the World and neglect to fence them against the temptations of it, and so leave them exposed to temporal and eternal Miseries, is a wickedness for which I want a Name; 'tis beneath Brutality; the Beasts are better natured, for they take care of their offspring, till they are capable of caring for themselves" (Astell 1697, I, 17–18).

23 In volume two (1798b), Wollstonecraft examines the plight of women with means compared to men, "The tender mother cannot lawfully snatch from the grip of the gambling spendthrift, or beastly drunkard, unmindful of his offspring, the fortune which falls to her by chance; or (so flagrant is the injustice) what she earns by her own exertions. No, he can rob her with impunity, even to waste publicly on a courtesan, and the laws of her country—if women have a country—afford her no protection or redress from the oppressor, unless she have the plea of bodily fear, yet how many ways are there of goading the soul almost to madness, equally unmanly, though not so mean?" 46–7.

24 Jane Monckton Smith (2010, 29–30) draws helpful historical contrasts about the impact the perceptions of rape have on the punishment we ascribe for it.

25 Which needed to include: providing torn garments, displaying a disheveled appearance and hair, producing witnesses who could testify that the victim cried out, and showing physical bruising (especially around the wrist). See Wolfthal 1993.

26 See Barbara Taylor and Sarah Knott (2005, 359).

27 Robert Aldrich and Garry Voltherspoon (2005, 30) are helpful here.

28 Also in William Kolbrener (2007, 49).

29 It should be noted, however, that some scholars observe the tension with which Cavendish's poems describe the relationship between women (as objects of love) and men (who seek to objectify women through the love act). Jennifer Low (1998, 160) writes, "Cavendish displays both the cruelty and the power relations inherent in the Petrarchan ideal through [her] lyric … By literalizing the trope of lovers' pains, Cavendish brings new life to the convention of the cruel beloved".

30 Cavendish famously defends a monarchy as the proper government to better address civil inequalities. Broad and Green (2009) note, "For Cavendish, as for Hobbes, it is crucial that the sovereign's power be simple and undivided. This is the only way in which human beings might gain some unanimity in their opinions about right and wrong: that is, by subordinating their judgement to the judgement of one individual. Thus in Cavendish's utopia, there is 'but one sovereign, one religion, one law, and one language, so that all the world might be as one united family'", 212.

31 Her earlier work, *Thoughts on the Education of Daughters* (Wollstonecraft 1787) is less of a philosophical treatise than a guidebook for parents on proper raising of children, but it does establish a foundation for later arguments she makes (for example, in 1792).

32 For good examples of this, see Susan Laird (2008), Kirstin Hanley (2013), and Susan Laird and Richard Bailey (2014). There are literally thousands of articles and book chapters on this, but a good introduction to her views is Alan Richardson (2002).
33 Some would argue that evil *is* gendered. One need not commit to that to agree with early modern *and* contemporary women that evil is often tied to systemic horrors.
34 Adorno 1983, 34.

3

THEODICY, NARRATIVES, AND STANDPOINT

Thus far, the need for a dialogue between the atrocity paradigm and contemporary theodicy has been established, as has the inadequacy of Leibnizian theodicy to satisfy the challenges of atrocious harm. If a dialogue between atrocity and theodicy is possible, it can only come through a discussion of a system of (what I am calling) transmuted goods which can battle the consequences of horrendous evils. The scholarship of women in the early modern period is unique because it presages the conception of evil used by contemporary atrocity paradigm atheists, establishes that a system of moral goods can also be at work in the world, and argues that we are responsible morally for both atrocities and transmuted goods. Their arguments are all the more compelling for having been written in response to egregious civil rights abuses and rampant domestic violence of their day. If we can gain insight into the system of goods that we are called to use to transform the world, then rather than speculating about the metaphysical nature of the divine, we can instead understand divine perfection in light of the system of goods and evils within the world. Prior to determining whether these systems in the work of Astell, Hays, Macaulay (and others) can be put to theodical use, it is imperative to consider that the means through which these women often put forward their philosophy of religion was through narratives. But the success of narratives as theodicy depends upon the ability of a narrator to effectively communicate a story to a listener who is epistemically in a position to understand and relate to the story.

Chapter 3 evaluates the 'situated knower' as significantly weighing in on the tension between the atrocity paradigm and theodicy. The type of situated, experiential knowledge which is important for standpoint epistemology, for example, is (interestingly) also important to narrative theodicy: not a *knowing that*, but a knowing-from-the-stance-of-which. Such knowledge is the focus of some contemporary theodicy, especially work by Eleanore Stump and Nicholas

Wolterstorff,[1] who contend that narratives can sometimes better serve the function of theodicy because stories can more effectively communicate theological knowledge that cannot be represented propositionally. The meaning of suffering in a world in which God exists, for example, is best conveyed by a second-personal standpoint, and narratives do this in a more relatable way than traditional, rational arguments.[2] Although Stump thinks narratives can succeed as theodicy if they are told within a second-personal framework, Chapter 3 demonstrates that a second-person standpoint cannot sufficiently account for situated expressions of suffering, nor for the loving relationship theists want to express through theodical narratives. Some critics contend that biblical narratives can never successfully defend against the problem of evil because Scripture fails to speak *to* those who truly suffer from (especially) atrocious harms, nor *from* the perspective of those who suffer, since the biblical authors were largely writing from positions of social and epistemic privilege.[3] Although the project of using narrative as a way to do theodicy should be preserved, this chapter will cast doubt on the ability of second-personal narratives (specifically) to meet the criticisms of the atrocity paradigm. Narrative's theodical use, after all, is meant to relate to those who suffer, so theodical narratives spoken only from the standpoint of the privileged may already be suspect. It is not enough to convince a critic that there are biblical narratives of suffering that are relatable, but the narratives must be relatable *and* effectively communicate a defense of divine perfection in the face of human suffering. It is possible to accept that biblical narratives could be relatable and still reject that they explain second-personally God's goodness and love. Addressing the problem of evil through narratives seems to require that those narratives speak directly to the plight of those who truly suffer, and (to be successful as theodicy) that the narratives allow the powerless, unprivileged, and oppressed to have access to religious knowledge.

Rather, I will argue[4] that the interpersonal, relational goals for narrative theodicy[5] are better achieved if we model the potential standpoint for theodical narratives upon the first-person plural. Turning to the first-person plural creates the framework for a discussion of the possibility of Stump's 'strong sense' of the presence of God in our lives. This presence allows for a reciprocal relationship in which agents answer the calls (moral, practical and spiritual) made upon them. If this is true, the first-person theodical narratives of the early modern women are more effective, because they better facilitate self-identification with the stories of suffering they tell by utilizing the language of identity. For any theodicy to be persuasive and create dialogue, it must communicate to its opponents, and so for narratives to succeed as theodicy, those that use the first-person (with its relatable concepts, situations, and characters) are at an advantage.

Narratives and Theodicy

Philosophers of all stripes have attempted to account for how narratives can instruct, guide, or change behavior. Philosophers of language, such as Donald

Davidson, argue that to understand or interpret any linguistic utterances, a speaker must stand in relation to another speaker and the world.[6] Ethicists, like Martha Nussbaum, have argued that narratives can create receptivity to others which objective philosophical detachment by itself can undermine.[7] Axel Honneth (Honneth and Margalit 2001) and other epistemologists apply narrative to truth and meaning relations, among other epistemic notions. Among philosophers of religion, Nicholas Wolterstorff (2001, 206ff) suggests that textual narratives are able to guide us only as long as there are relatable points of contact between the narrative and individual lives.

Creating that point of contact is the source for narrative's theodical function.[8] Narratives that could function as theodicy, in any event, would have to be relevant to the person who hears the narrative, and the extent to which the person is guided by the narrative is tied to whether the person sees herself as represented in the story. To date, Eleanore Stump provides the best effort of analytic philosophy to produce narratives that have a theodical function.[9] She explains that if the narrative is well done, the character within it is made "available to us in somewhat the same way the character would have been if he had in fact been immediately present to us" so learning from a story comes when we have an experience with the character that "recreates for us an image of one person's relations to others" (Stump 2010, 80). The availability of a character in a story, Stump contends, communicates knowledge that cannot be quantified propositionally. Narratives move beyond "knowledge-that"[10] by their "antiphonal" structure, which allows narratives to be considered in their "disorderly richness" (26). Rather than being relegated to mere analogy, however, narratives produce philosophical knowledge in non-traditionally philosophical ways (27) by creating new experiences and relationships for the hearer.

Stump gives an example to show how a narrative can communicate knowledge beyond a knowledge-that. Imagine that you have visited China frequently over recent years, and grow to love it in such a way that you decide to move there. Your friends in the U.S. do not understand your decision, and though you share with them your love of the culture, traditions, language, and people, they still do not understand how you could trade your American roots for an Eastern home. Your knowledge of China cannot be simply condensed down and communicated to them propositionally. Stump suggests you could purchase a novel for them—a story set in China would better, and differently, communicate your reasons for moving to China by providing them, through the text, with their own experiences of Chinese culture. Stump suggests that some forms of Scripture communicate knowledge beyond a knowledge-that, in a similar fashion as the Chinese novel can to your family. By engaging with theodical narratives, non-believers can have new experiences that can help them see the general reasons God might use to allow suffering in particular cases.[11]

A defense of those reasons can also be provided through the narratives. Stump argues that it is "eminently debatable" that "there is no morally sufficient reason for … God to allow suffering in the world" (4). It is possible, for example, that we could imagine the existence of such a 'morally sufficient reason'. Narratives allow believers to share stories which provide reasons for why God allows some people to suffer; the possible worlds created by narratives provide morally sufficient reasons for God to allow evil in those possible worlds. When those possible worlds relate enough to the actual world, the theodical function of the narrative can succeed (19). The stories offer various examples of how to live through grief and undeserved suffering, and help explain how a rational person could receive suffering as a gift (79). Of course, narratives that depict believers who experience God, "will be received differently by those who have their own religious experiences to draw on" (224) just as, for any story, persuading an audience to share a perspective is "much more likely to be successful with those people who have themselves had some experience of the sort being described in the story" (224).

The primary reason that most run-of-the-mill narratives are effective towards the purpose they intend (whether to illicit fear, tension, anger, pleasure, or joy) is because the hearer or reader can relate to the narrative. Those who use narratives as theodicy, then, accept that for narratives to produce philosophical insight, they must be communicable to those who engage with the story. William Hasker (2011, 436) observes, "The importance of narrative here is that it can impart to us something similar to this even in the absence of direct contact with the person known. Thus, in reading a novel we may 'come to know' the persons portrayed, may come to have a sense of the heroine, say, as a person." For Stump, the significance of narrative's relatability means that knowledge preserved (and conferred) by narratives requires that the story be excellently constructed, and that those who receive the narrative are cognitively able to gain knowledge from the narrative (79–80). Others have suggested that more is required; to actually convey religious knowledge, a narrative would have to be read along with some analysis to give context to the story itself, so that the hearer could return to the biblical account on its own to imagine himself in the stories (Vitale, 2013).

But, narratives come in as many perspectives as there are persons to tell them— and those who believe that narratives have theodical force are looking for a *particular* perspective for their narratives. Stump takes the narrative accounts of suffering explicated in the biblical stories of Job, Samson, Abraham, and Mary of Bethany to supply *second-personal* justification to show that God has morally sufficient reasons for allowing suffering within the narrative. Stump believes that the second-personality of the experiences captured in narrative helps the knower to see that God and evil can be co-present in the world. She writes,

> If everything knowable in a second-person experience could be expressed in terms of knowing *that*, with regard to either oneself or the others with whom one interacts, then no doubt a second-person experience could be captured by first-person and third-person accounts, and there would be no room for anything that could be considered a second-person account. But

the cumulative weight of the evidence and arguments I have given about the knowledge of persons is sufficient to show its distinctive character. Second-person experiences cannot be reduced to first-person or third-person experiences without remainder, and so they cannot be captured by first-person or third-person accounts either. As I have shown, knowledge of persons accessible in second-person experiences is not reducible to knowledge *that*.

(77–8)

Stump thinks that the first- and third-person perspective cannot explain the relational knowledge which comes from experiencing and interacting with others. Only the second-person standpoint (which Stump takes as "a direct and immediate sort of personal interaction" (75–6)) can properly frame the type of narrative that could do some theodical work. Generally, when a story is told, she explains, we take "a real or imagined set of second-person experiences of one sort or another and make it available to a wider audience to share" (78). What makes these experiences second-personal is that, through the story, the hearer experiences "some of what she would have experienced if she had been an onlooker in the second-person experience represented in the story" (78).

Thus, on Stump's view, narratives have a second-personal quality when the hearer of the story can imagine having a second-personal experience as a character within the story. Stories that provide some account of reasons God might have to allow evil within the world of the narrative place the hearer of the story within the possible world of the story, as someone who could see that those reasons might be justified. Further, Stump thinks the relatability of the story allows the hearer of the narrative to identify with the possible world enough to see that those reasons might also hold within an actual world that resembles the narrative's possible world. The theodical force of the narrative is such that it describes some possible world in which suffering is coexistent with a good God who loves us, and is directly and immediately present to us as persons, and then we see that this story resembles well the actual world.

To be able to evaluate whether theodical narratives are in fact effective when framed within the second-person standpoint, we must first get a better grasp on the purported second-personality of narratives. Given that, at least on Stump's position, the effectiveness of narrative as theodicy relates to narrative's ability to transport the hearer of the narrative second-personally within the story, it is imperative to understand commonly-agreed upon traits of the second-person standpoint. So, the remainder of this chapter will briefly compare the three main perspectives on the second-person standpoint (Darwall's in ethics, Lance and Kukla's in moral epistemology, and Stump's in philosophy of religion), will show that all three perspectives erroneously maintain that the standpoint can facilitate intersubjectivity among persons, and then will show that the second-person standpoint—as the standpoint of authority—cannot frame the intersubjective communication required for theodical narratives,[12] and so faces significant challenges to produce religious knowledge. I will conclude by demonstrating that theodical narratives in the first-person standpoint can better salvage narrative as a theodical tool, because they can foster a dialogue between atheist proponents of atrocious harm arguments and theists who emphasize that a loving God is present to us in the midst of our deepest sorrows. The work of Astell, Macaulay, and Hays can be especially instructive to guide how narratives can communicate the sense of the presence of God which contemporary theists think is a required component of theodical narratives, and can bridge the gap between theodical narratives and theodical arguments in the early modern period.

Agreement about the Second-Personal

Although the second-person standpoint is fashionable in contemporary episte-mology, ethics, and philosophy of religion, there are early prefigures to the standpoint that have impacted current scholarship. Peter Strawson's participant stance[13] suggests that an action's desirability is a wrong sort of reason for holding an agent morally accountable, because desirability does not indicate who has the authority to make a claim on an agent. There are obligations that agents execute from a detached, objective perspective, but there are also moral obligations which agents fulfill because they think of themselves as interpersonally engaged agents. Moral obligations bind those who perform actions to the people who constrain their actions. The participant stance has a continuing impact on the normativity of reasons as well as the second-person standpoint in ethics, which emphasizes authority-relations that obtain as a result of moral obligations. J.G. Fichte argued that often knowledge presupposes a mutual recognition of agents involved in activity, with the result that obligatory acts must be free. Activity is reciprocal in the sense that "we transfer into the things what in truth is only in us .... The links interchange through themselves. And their mutual joining is the form, while the activity and passivity, occurring in this joining (namely, each joins and is joined) is the content of the reciprocity. We shall call this content here the mutual relation of the interchanging links" (Fichte 1982, 144). The concept of reciprocity has been a key component of the second-person stance in con-temporary scholarship (and will be important to determining whether narrative can successfully function as theodicy). Finally, S.F. v. Pufendorf's contention[14] that obligations can be ascribed only to those who mutually trust each other and are responsible from a reciprocal standpoint—a standpoint that is possessed by the free and rational members of the moral community—looks strikingly similar to today's terms to the second-person standpoint. So, the profound impact of Pufendorf, Fichte, and Strawson on today's second-person standpoint is especially seen in (what we would call today) the reciprocity of felt obligation and the role of the authority of the other to make moral demands on us.

The leading scholars in ethics (Darwall), moral epistemology (Lance and Kukla), and philosophy of religion (Stump) who utilize the second-person standpoint agree on several constitutive aspects of the standpoint. First, all three groups accept that the moral address—the normative address of obligation—is communicated second-personally. Although they differ a bit as to the scope and content of the normative address, they all concur that moral obligations are successful in part because the agent who is obligated to act regards the obligation as stemming from a relationship between the self and another person. Darwall observes that if you were standing on someone's gouty toe, and responded to his shouts of pain, the reason you respond is because you are the person who is causing pain to another person, and recognize that continuing to stand on the toe is "something we normally assume we have the authority to demand that persons not do to one another" (Darwall 2006, 7). Second, contemporary accounts of the second-person standpoint grant that second-personal reasons depend on the *authority* of another person to make a claim. That another person is physically present is not enough to constrain action or to obligate a person to act; second-personal reasons require that the other person is justified to make a claim on another person. (Correlatively, there may be second-personal reasons that obligate whether or not a person is present. That I make a promise to you, for example, can guide my actions even when you are not around.) Lance and Kukla explain why they think these types of 'calls' on one's action derive from distinctively second-personal reasons: "Furthermore, the reason imputed by the request is inherently relational and second-personally instituted: whatever kinds of reason I had to φ in advance, your request that I φ, assuming it is entitled, now gives me a new reason to φ *for you*. And now, if I grant your request, I don't merely φ; in φing, I perform a new, normatively rich type of acting—one of 'granting'. Granting itself is a second-person transaction with its own normative outputs" (Lance and Kukla 2013, 462). That another person has an authority to make the claim is, on this perspective, a second-personal reason to answer the call and fulfill one's duty. Of course, the other person must have *de jure* authority to make a claim. In a paper that elaborates more on who has *de jure* authority, Margaret Gilbert argues (2009, 177), "Directed obligations are clearly owed to particular persons, not the world in general. If you owe me your action, I am in a position to demand that action as mine and to rebuke you when you fail to perform it." What Stump means by another having a rightful authority to make a claim is that the other is considered as a person, regardless of the extent to which there is direct contact with the person. (Our ability to conceive of characters as persons, despite characters being the sorts of things that cannot be interacted with, is a reason why Stump thinks narratives can be second-personal.)

Perhaps the most significant agreed-upon aspect of the second-person standpoint is that second-personal reasons are relational. Garrath Williams explains, "The key idea is that these relations depend on—are constituted by, in a contemporary term of art—people's sharing responsibility for one another's lives. From this sharing of responsibility arises a particular sort of authority to hold responsible … Personal relationships are forms of sustained interaction that involve a distinctively personal form of mutual concern" (Williams 2013, 351). As mentioned above, scholars disagree as to the scope of second-personal reasons. (Darwall, for example, thinks moral obligations come in the form of the second-personal address; agent-neutral reasons cannot obligate, but furnish an epistemic reason for the agent to see that there is some action for him to perform, but he would need a second-personal reason for him to assent to performing the action, (Darwall 2006, 6–7). Lance and Kukla believe moral obligations come in a variety of forms but include the second-person standpoint.) But, to the extent that scholars allow that the second-person address is one that obligates us *to others*, they also agree that the obligation is a relational one. Linda Radzik contends that Darwall and others think this obligation is relational because the agent perceives the demand of the other as the right sort of claim made by the right person to the person who is directly obligated to act upon it, and so the authority of the other is not perceived to be coercive. She writes (Radzik 2011, 584), "Notice that there is a conceptual difference between obligation and coercion. In giving someone a second-personal reason, I am not coercing her. If I am not coercing her, then I must instead be acting on the basis of an authority that she can freely and rationally accept as legitimate."

But, what type of relation is present in the second-personal address? At a minimum, scholars believe that the relation is *reciprocal*. Mutual accountability is required by the address because moral obligations bind free and rational people to act in certain ways to each other; without reciprocity, only one party would ever be obligated, and reasonable people would never accept that morality works in such a way (Radzik 2011, 585). Maximally, scholars think that the second-person standpoint moves the agent into a deeper relationship with the other person, and equal partnership between the agent and the other that transcends what we ordinarily think of by the terms "accountability" and "authority". Darwall comments, "Morality as equal accountability understands the moral point of view to be fundamentally *intersubjective*. It holds the moral perspective to be an impartially disciplined version of the second-person standpoint, in which, as anyone (or as an equal participant in the first-person plural ('we') of the moral community), one addresses someone (oneself or someone else) also as anyone (as another equal member)" (Darwall 2006, 102). Stump's 'personal interaction' criterion for second-personal experiences (Stump 2010, 75–6) underscores something akin to Darwall's intersubjectivity claim. Since second-personal experiences cannot be encapsulated propositionally, agents represent such experiences in narratives as a way to allow others to second-personally engage with the story and experience similar feelings as the agents themselves. "This is generally what we do when we tell a story," Stump explains, "A story takes a real or imagined set of second-person experiences of one sort or another and makes it available to a wider audience to share. ... The re-presenting of a second-person experience in a story thus constitutes a second-person account. It is a report of a set of second-person experiences that does not lose (at least does not lose entirely) the distinctively second-person character of the experiences" (78).

Contemporary renderings of the second-personal standpoint posit that the standpoint is relational because it builds on a mutual understanding of the agent and the other as persons, it reflects a rightful authority of the other to make a claim on the appropriate agent (i.e., one who is obligated and able to act), and grounds at least the types of moral obligations that come about from the interactions people have with each other. The constitutive elements of the second-person standpoint have their origins in early epistemology and ethics: Strawson's participant stance mirrors the *de jure* authority of the other in the second-person standpoint; Fichte's reciprocity is reflected in the mutual accountability of the agent and the other; and Pufendorf's model, in which obligations come out of what is freely and rationally agreed-upon and is expressed within the standpoint as the relational component of the second-personal address.

We recall that Stump directly ties the success of narrative as second-personal enterprise into the effectiveness of narrative as theodicy: if a narrative can provide those who engage with the story second-personally with an experience that is similar to the characters within the story, a narrative about why God allows suffering could give a plausible account as to why God might allow suffering within that particular story. Now that the commonly-agreed upon tenets of the second-person stand-point have been presented, it is possible to evaluate whether narratives could in fact do what Stump (and others) would like them to do for theodicy. In the remainder of the chapter, I will focus on the problems that impersonality presents to the second-person standpoint as the language of narrative, and will argue that those obstacles prevent narrative—as a second-person project—from being suc-cessful as theodicy. I will then suggest an alternative to a second-person account of narratives that could rescue the theodical function of narratives that is rooted in the scholarship of early modern women.

Impersonality and Second-Personality

Second-person addresses that have the authority to compel actions are vocative and imperative ("You—do this!"). But command functions are objective rather than interpersonal. We respond to the authority of the imperative because it compels us to, and we resent it when we think that the person making the claim on us is not a rightful authority. Similarly, in moral discourse, the second-person is rooted in authority, reciprocity, and communicability. Without authority, the call of the person making the moral demand falls on deaf ears.[15] Reciprocity is the component of second-personal experiences in which mutual respect is shared among all participants. Without reciprocity, felt obligations become responses to coercion, rather than as actions that stem from the proper recognition respect of another person.[16] Communicability is the aspect of second-personality in which the narrative, discourse, or command is made accessible to the listener. Without proper communication, the second-personal address breaks down. So, to have a second-personal experience, there must be an agent who has authority to interact with another person, there must be reciprocity between the agent and whomever is addressed, and the presence of each person must be properly communicated to each other.[17]

Darwall's second-personal standpoint is the standard-bearer for second-personal accounts, a fact observed by Stump (2010, 75). Darwall's stance emphasizes the authority relation for second-personality because the demands of moral obligation are always commanded, he thinks, second-personally (Darwall 2006, 6–7). Darwall (2009) sets out four irreducible second-personal notions: 1) authority to make a claim or demand; 2) a valid (authoritative) claim or demand; 3) responsibility to someone (with the relevant authority); 4) second-person reason for authority (for complying and discharging the responsibility). For Darwall, the reciprocity and communicability relations are merged into the irreducible aspects of the authority relation. (Reciprocity is found in his (3) and (4), and communicability is a component of both (2) and (4).) Without reciprocity and communicability, there is no authority relation in the second-personal standpoint, since the authority to make a valid claim depends upon the presence of another person, to ensure both that there is an obligation and that there is accountability for discharging the responsibility. Stump's own 'personal interaction' condition for second-personality in the same way combines reciprocity, communicability, and authority, since by it, the agent views the other *as a person* (for Stump, this means one who can cognize authority relations), the other is conscious, and the two engage directly and immediately (75–6).

It is not odd that scholars think of the second-person standpoint as the language of normative address, since the imperatives of morality command an agent authoritatively. If moral obligations are actions whose non-performance indicates a violation of some rule, then whenever an obligation presents itself to the agent or is prescribed to the agent, the language is second-personal: "You! Do this!" Imperatives as commands function well within the language of the second-person standpoint because the second-person standpoint is the language of authority. One of Darwall's famous examples of the second-person standpoint actually illustrates this point nicely. He imagines a military command structure in which a soldier is sanctioned by his superior officer if the soldier fails to perform the push-ups prescribed to him by the officer. Darwall contends the soldier has a second-personal reason to do the push-ups, which is that, by doing the push-ups, the soldier complies with an authoritative demand that he is accountable to perform (Darwall 2006, 248). In this example, the second-person standpoint makes sense. The soldier is commanded by a superior officer to perform the push-ups, and anyone who understands the military chain of command understands when the superior officer says, "You! Do this!" … you do it. Why? Because you were commanded to do so by a superior officer.

An important aspect of the soldier example, I think, is the impersonality of the second-personal. The 'you' of the command functions formally, rather than substantively. The scenario could easily be swapped out with more-personal endearments and the authority structure of the second-personal is preserved.

"Smith! Push-ups!" does not indicate anything more intersubjective or personal than the "You! Do this!" if you are Smith, because the only thing required of the person demanding the action is that (in this case) he demand a particular action from the agent required to perform it. Darwall actually relies upon the impersonality of the second-person standpoint when he discusses what it means to 'respect' a person (and so, for moral actions to respect the dignity of persons). He distinguishes (Darwall 1977) between *appraisal respect* (an evaluative attitude merited by a person's conduct or character) and *recognition respect* (recognition that we owe equally to everyone that is manifested in our treatment of them). The second-person requires only recognition respect—morally permissible acts recognize another person as worthy of constraining actions in certain ways. The recognition respect in "You! Do this!" functions identically as in "Smith! Push-ups!"[18]

So, in cases in which the imperative structure of morality is modeled on an impersonal, second-personal language, imperatives call us (i.e., the agents; the 'you' within the command) to perform a particular action (an action that, if not performed, would be a violation of some moral code). What is curious is the ubiquitous idea within second-person standpoint scholarship that morality's second-person call is grounded on *relationality* (at a minimum) and *intersubjectivity* (at a maximum). In his most recent scholarship, Darwall incorporates a concept of "love" into the intersubjectivity he thinks is embedded in the second-person standpoint: "[I explore] ways in which regard and respect for one another as equal persons ... is best accounted for within a moral theory that is grounded within a second-person standpoint. More specifically, I argue that central to loving and friendly relations is a form of mutual answerability that involves mutual respect" (Darwall 2013, 5). But, the language of equal, loving, and friendly relationships is indeed not one grounded primarily in the second-person, since the second-person is the language of authority. If it is true that the second-person standpoint is the language of authority (all of these scholars say that it is), then the address is essentially formal and impersonal; the only relation required of the second-personal address is an authority relation, which does not require intersubjectivity or an appraisal respect between agents. If the second-person address moves beyond the authority relation (and it must, if Darwall is right and a 'we' is created through the reciprocity condition, or, if like Stump, a "direct and immediate" "personal interaction" occurs between "persons"), it must incorporate something more (or at least, different) than what the second-personal can provide. For the address to facilitate personal relationships, to rely upon appraisal respect, and end with intersubjectivity, it is no longer formal and merely authoritative; which is to say, it is no longer second-personal. And yet, leading scholars in epistemology, ethics, and philosophy of religion contend that the second-person standpoint is the language of relationships, obligation, and intersubjectivity.

Others have observed the oddity of proclaiming the second-person standpoint to be rooted in relationality. Linda Radzik, for example, argues that those who think of the second-person standpoint as fundamentally intersubjective misunderstand second-personality in two essential ways. First, inequality is often present (and frequently required) in a second-personal address. Superiors, bosses, parents, donors, and other authorities are justified in using the second-personal address because it is the language of commands that deserve responses, and does not require respect beyond recognition respect for its morally permissible use. The second-person standpoint, as the standpoint of authority, gives voice to the obligations that are required of people who are on unequal social footing with others. Often, those authority relations are legitimately unequal in many social contexts (Radzik 2011, 585), and their directives are communicated second-personally. Another way scholars misunderstand second-personality is by suggesting that the reciprocity condition entails that moral obligations are agreements between persons. Second-person standpoint theorists concur that the authority of legitimate moral demands comes because the person who is obligated to act, "freely and rationally accepts [the demand] as legitimate" (584). But, Darwall's second-person stance has a further implication. It suggests that the reciprocity of a legitimate moral demand is derived from agential agreement, so that an act is moral at the point at which agents *agree* that someone's demand deserves attention. The seeming-subjectivity of the moral demand, then, is such that, if the agent does not stipulate that the demand of the other deserves his or her attention, it is unclear that anything morally impermissible has occurred.

Radzik's observations about the actual impersonality of the second-person standpoint hint at a further, and perhaps more debilitating, aspect of the second-person standpoint: it can foster a language of subjugation and exclusion, and can be used to silence minority voices. This is *not* to say that the second-person standpoint necessarily leads to coercion (or that oppression cannot occur in other standpoints). Rather, as the standpoint of authority, there is nothing within the second-person stance that ensures that the mutual agreement between two persons indicates something moral has occurred. Morality-by-agreement can lead, and has led, some people to perform acts that are otherwise universally-despised and has justified others in passively standing-by and not intervening when they ought. In the most egregious cases, it can result in entire people-groups being dismissed as morally considerable. (Groups who are victimized by crimes against humanity are often dismissed as being less-than-human, for example.) These results *need not* emerge from the standpoint (Darwall gives several examples in which they do not), but that they *do* emerge from the standpoint is evidence that intersubjectivity is *not* a component of the second-person standpoint.

Radzik speaks directly to the problem of intersubjectivity and standpoint, and argues that the 'second-person' standpoint really is not 'second-personal' at all. She writes,

> Moral norms are the norms of a community of moral agents, and not merely something agreed to between the two persons in the interaction in question. Although Darwall associates his theory of accountability in

relationships with Buber's (I/Thou), we are now in a position to see that the relationship that Darwall presents is not accurately represented by the pronouns I/Thou. Instead, it amount to *"Wir/Ihr"* (We/You-plural or We/Y'all) or, more accurately, by universalized plural pronouns that are not easily captured in either German or English. "All of Us" stands in relation to "All of You".

(Radzik 2011, 586)

Community's impact on the moral standpoint (whether framed first-, second-, or third-personally) seems obvious: if morality is at least about those for whom morality functions, and communities are the best expression of morality, then community will be intricately tied to how morality is framed. So, it makes sense that Darwall (and Stump) want the framework of morality—their second-person standpoint—to be grounded on the intersubjective relationships found within a moral community. Radzik's point, however, is that the second-person standpoint is *not* the standpoint of community. Darwall and Stump both seek a moral framework that is grounded in mutually responding to other people's needs. But, the second-person standpoint itself cannot deliver such a result, because it often justly requires inequality for its demands to be met, it yields actions that are agreed upon (but not necessarily moral), and (without references to other standpoints) it can be used for oppressive purposes. The "you" in relationship to the "I" is removed from the "we" that both Darwall and Stump are hoping to achieve through the use of the second-person.

The best case for Stump, and others who would use the second-person standpoint for narrative theodicy, is for a narrative to draw the narrating 'I' into a relationship with the 'you' who hears the narrative so that there is a first-person plural 'we' established (such as envisioned by Radzik), or that the 'I' can relate to the 'you' relationally in spite of the reciprocity, authority, and communicability conditions of the second-person standpoint. Stump, for her part, thinks that she gets to the relational through the second-personal in a way that most analytic philosophy cannot:

Analytic philosophy tends to leave to one side the messy and complicated issues involved in relations among persons. When analytic philosophers need to think about human interactions, they tend not to turn to complex cases drawn from real life or from the world's great literature; rather they make up short, thin stories of their own, involving Smith and Jones. ... Personal relations, however, are at the heart of certain philosophical problems. Central to the problem of suffering in all its forms is a question to which a consideration of interpersonal relations is maximally relevant: could a person who is omnipotent, omniscient, and perfectly good allow human persons to suffer as they do?

(Stump 2010, 25)

Stump is not unaware of the limitations of the second-person and narrative. She recognizes that not all narratives are second-personal, and points to stories in which the storyteller provides experiences that only include himself (80). But, Stump thinks those stories can still communicate the second-person stance as long as they represent for the hearer something relatable, "The author's presentation of the character, if it is well done, makes that character available to us in somewhat the same way the character would have been if he had in fact been directly immediately present to us. The story thus contributes to our having and learning from something like a second-person experience, only it is our experience with the character of the story" (80). This image suggests that, as long as a narrator's first-person testimony is relevant in some way to the hearer's personal experiences, the hearer could identify with what is happening in the story, and the standpoint is actually second-personal.

One picky point is worth highlighting here, because it will establish a much more significant difficulty for the second-person as the voice of theodical narrative. Placing oneself in another's story is not second-personal. It is first-personal. Seeing 'you' in my story is quite different than seeing myself in your story. To repurpose an earlier example from Stump, a potential difficulty for me in reading a novel wholly set in China (absent having ever been in China) is that I will mistake what you consider to be as culturally-rich signposts for something distinctly American—if I identify them as signposts at all. If I do successfully identify the signposts, the experience is not second-personally shared (you have been to China after all, and fell in love with the significances of the symbols represented in the novel, whereas I just read a book). You could emphatically tell me why you love the Chinese symbols, but unless I take the symbols as images to love first-personally (in which case the symbols become *mine*, or *ours*), your goal in communicating your love for China fails. If I do not have the experience as my own, it becomes at most one more item of propositional knowledge for me to recall.

The picky point of whether Stump's standpoint is really second-personal will become much more than a picky point when applied to narratives as theodical tools. The gap between the sought-after 'we' Radzik argues is the ground of morality and the 'you' of Stump's narrative is especially striking. If reciprocity, communicability, and authority are required for the second-personal standpoint, theodicies which rely upon second-person accounts (such as narratives) can only be successful if they utilize reciprocity, communicability, and authority. But, in the next section, I will show how utilizing some of these aspects of the second-person standpoint can undermine the theodical function of narrative.

Obstacles for Second-Personal Theodical Narratives

The effectiveness of narrative as theodicy depends at least upon the narrative being effectively communicated to whoever hears the story. (If, for example, you tell me a Bible story in English and I only speak Spanish, the message of your story will be lost.) Of course, there are many ways in which the communication of a theodical narrative can break down. Someone who has never suffered will more than likely miss the point of a story in which God's presence is felt in the face of suffering. If the moral of a story relies upon cultural cues, those who are not familiar with the cues will not understand the moral of the story. (Someone who does not understand the significance of a Samaritan coming to the aid of a beaten Jewish man may miss why the "Good Samaritan" is such a poignant tale.) Education can be a barrier to effectively communicating a narrative; those who have never encountered a parable or an allegory are at a disadvantage when hearing one.

But, critics of theodicy are apt to point out that subversive narrative frameworks can also impede the effective communication of a theodicy. Some atheists have questioned whether theodicy can be successful at all (not solely in narrative), because it is often removed from the lived experiences of those who suffer.[19] Consider, for example, that although the biblical stories are often about people who are not in positions of power (for example, enslaved Hebrews, or exiled Jews), the narrators (and many of the characters) of the stories were in a position of epistemic or social privilege, whether they were kings, prophets, or apostles of Christ. This privilege could be an impediment to effectively communicating a defense. Most[20] of the narratives Stump utilizes underscore this criticism. Job, considered by many biblical scholars (and Stump) to be a paradigm biblical representative of how to persevere through suffering while questioning the goodness of God, was reported to be the richest man in the kingdom (and righteous), and after his period of miserable, undeserved suffering, God restored him to even more riches (Job 42:7–17). Job's proper response to suffering, Stump suggests, makes "Job magnificent in goodness", and able to share in a special relationship with God (Stump 2010, 226). Samson, a Nazarene, was highly regarded (and rewarded) for his strength and beauty, both of which were removed from him when he sinned against God. Samson was glorified one last time in his death (Judges 16:23–31)—a glorification that does not, on Stump's model, diminish the brokenness of Samson's life (255), but amplifies the "great good" of his life (256). Abraham, of course, was originally a wealthy pagan who later turned to monotheism and was promised by God to become the patriarch of his people, a "father of nations" (Genesis 17). His suffering came from the potential loss of that promise when God commanded him to kill his son, Isaac (Genesis 22), but his hope returned when God instead offered the ram for sacrifice (Genesis 22:11–14). Stump goes so far as to say that "the suffering of Abraham's trial is redeemed not only in his flourishing through the suffering of his trial, but also in his receiving the desires of his heart" (307).[21]

In these three narratives, then, the main characters were rich leaders who temporarily suffered and were ultimately restored, whether to glory, prominence, or power. The criticism of some atheists is strong: access to knowledge can be constrained by concrete aspects of a person's situation, so any religious knowledge that could potentially be communicated through a narrative theodicy could also be limited by the hearer's epistemic and social points-of-departure. If the narratives that are meant to function as theodicy prominently feature rich and powerful people who suffer temporarily, only to be brought back into a glorified situation, they already are distanced from the lived experiences of the exploited and powerless, from those who have never been in an elevated epistemic or social position, and from those who do not see any way out of their suffering. Add to this distance a theodical explanation of the character's suffering in terms of God's love, and a type of Promethean patriarch is created, in which the narrator has a position that is so privileged and distinct from the experiences of many, that occupants outside of it must rely on (or defer to) the narrator to determine whether they can relate at all to the content of the experiences within the narrative.[22] Many of those who truly suffer from atrocious harms have no former place of glory to dream about or return to, are unable to hope for future glorification, and would scoff at their suffering being redeemable by receiving the desires of their heart, especially since the desire of many is the cessation of suffering because of atrocious harms. Stump's conclusion that "There is something incomplete about any putative solution to the problem of suffering that neglects a consideration of the things the sufferer himself has set his heart on" (307) is no doubt meant to tie into the Christian idea that God knows and cares about each person individually (100–107). But, it places a too-demanding expectation on theodicy (namely, that theodicy would have to explain each individual's own suffering not only in relation to a great good, but considered also against the backdrop of what each person truly desires). Any representative of this too-demanding narrative risks sounding tone-deaf to those who suffer from atrocious harm.[23]

These problems worsen if the experiences communicable through the narrative are, as Stump contends, second-personal. Recall that the goal of Stump's defense is to produce religious knowledge from a particular, second-personal experience of God conveyed non-propositionally through the story. So far, so good. Most who would critique narrative theodicy would say that knowledge from a particular experience or stance is a main knowledge type. Situated, experiential knowledge that is important to standpoint epistemologists, for example, is (interestingly) also that which is important to narrative theodicy: not a *knowing that*, but a knowing-from-the-stance-of-which. But, little else is agreed upon. Narratives that use the second-person are structured to teach the hearer something new, in a non-propositional form, about "the sense of [another] as a person" (53). Stump's vision is for humans to be able to experience the (authoritative but loving) presence of God through a second-personal experience of him. Standpoint critics could raise two objections for the second-person as a framework for the narratives which are meant to share this vision—the first from the form of the narrative, and the second from the situation of the narrative's characters. As has been demonstrated, the second-person standpoint is the standpoint of authority (which allows it to command some things, like moral imperatives, consistently). The structure of a second-personal narrative can prevent the hearer from engaging with the story.

Adult children who were abused by their fathers, for example, may be repulsed by a narrative depicting God as Father, especially if the framework is second-personal in the way Stump's Job narrative suggests (i.e., the transcendent God maps onto the abusive Father, 'I', who relates to the subservient, damaged Job interlocutor, 'you'). Further, if the characters of the story are situated in epistemically inaccessible power or authority positions, the primary content of the narrative may be outside the scope of experiences of many who suffer—a result that can further alienate those who are oppressed.[24] And such a result would mean that the narratives could estrange the very people theodicy is meant to persuade.

There are a handful of potential responses that second-person standpoint theorists like Stump could provide. First, they might deny that biblical narratives are written from a point of privilege that excludes most sufferers. (In fact, one could think of the person of Christ as someone who suffered tremendously—in order to relate to the lowly—as evidence for the relatability of Scriptural narrative.) This response misses, however, the theodical purpose that is proposed for narrative: it is not enough to convince a critic that there are biblical narratives of suffering that are relatable, but the narratives must be relatable *and* effectively communicate a defense of divine perfection in the face of human suffering. It is possible to accept that biblical narratives could be relatable and still reject that they explain second-personally God's goodness and love. Another reply might be to draw the intended audience of the narrative quite narrowly, so that the narratives communicate second-personally only to those who can relate to the stories, and the presence of God is experienced in a new way to whoever has epistemic access to the story. This is, it seems, quite close to Stump's view.[25] A main worry with this response is that it capitulates to the criticism. It agrees that there are a number of skeptics with regard to theodicy who will simply not be reached by the story, because of their skeptical views. Independent of the worry that this reply allows the criticism to stand, it also suggests that theodicy (and theodical narratives) primarily benefit—and engage—those who already believe. Further, accepting the criticism removes the possibility of disagreement between the atheist and theist, because it precludes the atheist from being an interlocutor with the theist who tells the story. And, if theists really are just telling stories to each other, then no true defense occurs.

A Better Standpoint for Theodical Narrative

the First-Person Plural

It is unfortunate that in *every instance* in which Stump discusses the first-person standpoint, she refers only to the first-person singular, because by rejecting the first-person plural along with the first-person as the standpoint of theodical narrative, she misses an opportunity to frame narratives successfully against the atrocious harm criticism. She rejects the first-person altogether as the standpoint of the experiences she wants narratives to communicate (those 'direct and immediate' encounters of personhood):

> The way in which I have formulated what Mary learns—what it is like to be touched by someone else, and so on—may suggest to someone that Mary learns things just about herself, and that she learns them in virtue of having new first-person experiences. It seems, then, that whatever Mary learns can be explained adequately in terms of a first-person account. But this is clearly wrong-headed ... What is new for her, what she learns, has to do with her personal interaction with another person. What is new for Mary is a second-personal experience.
>
> *(Stump 2010, 52–3)*

Stump supplants the first-person with the second-person, which she believes can bring us into relationship and can facilitate religious knowledge. Recall that Stump wants narrative to provide morally sufficient reasons for God to allow suffering, and she thinks that the way narratives can do this is to bring us into relationship with God, or into the presence of God. She writes (113), "It is one thing for God to be present always and everywhere with direct and unmediated causal and cognitive connection to everything but hidden from human view, and it is another thing entirely for God to be present to a human person in the stronger sense of presence." If narratives can introduce the hearer to God, the hearer is better able (like Job) to feel God's presence in spite of, and perhaps in the midst of, suffering.

The 'strong sense' of presence that can be facilitated through narrative does not occur when a hearer picks out (or relates to) a formal 'you' in a story, and may not occur when she objectively is able to identify with the characters in a story. If Stump is right, and an effective story allows the hearer to place herself in the story, the hearer's experience is indeed first personal, but not exclusively in the first-personal singular sense Stump rejects for Mary. Rather, if the hearer can be directly and immediately present to God and others as a result of engaging with a narrative, the 'relationship' Stump actually describes is a first-personal plural relationship – a 'we'. She wants for us what she thinks Job has—a special relationship which "would have opened Job's eyes to a coupling between commitment to God, on the one hand, and cosmic (rather than worldly) prosperity, on the other" (224). But, the authority relationship upon which the second-personal often depends is not indicative of the 'strong sense' of presence Stump seeks for those who gain experiential knowledge through a narrative, and is not framed in the 'we'.

The aspirant relationship between humanity and God is in one instance compared by Stump with Martin Buber's 'I-Thou'. She quotes Buber (1970, 129), "The essential element in our relationship to God has been sought in a feeling that has been called a feeling of dependence ... the one-sided emphasis on this factor leads to a misunderstanding of the character of the perfect relationship … feelings merely accompany the fact of the relationship which after all is established not in the soul but between an I and a You" (73). Buber's I-Thou, however, does not present the same "You" as distinct from the 'I' of the second-person standpoint, because Buber's I-Thou imagines a new relationship that is neither first-person singular nor second-person singular, but is a conjunction of the two. For Buber, a person has experiences as an 'I' (of course[26]), along with shared experiences with and of other people, "but it is as We, ever again as We" that we develop within the world (Buber 1970, 120).

Isn't it the 'we' that second-point standpoint theorists really are after, in spite of philosophy's trendy infatuation with the second-person standpoint? By substituting only "first-person plural" with "second-person", the following quote from Darwall suggests exactly this:

> I argue that the modern conceptions of morality and human rights are grounded in the idea of equal *first-person plural* authority—the notion that we share a common basic standing or authority to make claims and demands of each other and hold one another mutually accountable. In calling these modern moral concepts "*first-person plural*", I mean that they implicitly refer, in a way that other ethical and normative concepts do not, to claims and demands that must be capable of being addressed *in the first-person plural*. I argue that it is part of the very idea of a moral (claim) right that the right holder has the authority to make the claim of the person against whom the right is held and hold him accountable for compliance. When we hold people accountable, whether others or ourselves, we take a *first person plural* perspective on them and implicitly relate *to* them in a way that is different than when we view them in an "objective" or third-personal way.
>
> *(Darwall 2013, 1)*

Whereas the 'you' in the second-person can be an objective relation (though distinct from the third-personal), the emphasis on the first-person plural shows the relational quality Darwall wants by "relat[ing] *to* them in a way that is different". The relational 'we' resists objectifying the participants of the 'we', because the agent (in part, anyway) identifies herself with those to whom she relates.

This is not to say that the first-person plural can always stand in place of the second-person. The second-person standpoint is, after all, the standpoint of moral authority. Stump is convincing, for instance, when she argues that God sees Job and addresses Job's criticisms second-personally[27] because God's invocation of himself as Creator places God as the ultimate authority. God's use of the 'you' in Job 38 perfectly reflects the authority relation of the second-person, "Then the LORD spoke to Job out of the storm. He said, 'Who is this that obscures my plans with words without knowledge? Brace yourself like a man; I will question you, and you shall answer me.'" Further, when Stump discusses the 'minimal personal presence' required for someone to have a second-personal experience, she is clearly right: Paula's second-person experience of Jerome is simply that she is aware of Jerome (Stump 2010, 116–17). But, as argued above, the second-person moves to the first-person plural when the standpoint concerns itself with the intersubjective, relational aspects between agents. Such a shift seems consistent with Stump's own perspective, "In my view, for mentally fully functional adult human beings, full-fledged dyadic joint attention is required for significant, as distinct from minimal, personal presence" (117). What is problematic is that Stump thinks that this full-fledged dyadic joint attention is best framed second-personally, and that narratives are best suited for theodicy when they use the second-person standpoint.

I think (following Radzik) that the interpersonal, relational goals for Stump (and Darwall, and Lance and Kukla) are better achieved if we instead model the potential standpoint for theodical narratives upon the first-person plural. Turning to the first-person plural creates the framework for a discussion of the possibility of Stump's 'strong sense' of the presence of God in our lives. This presence, like Buber's vision, allows for a reciprocal relationship in which agents answer the calls (moral, practical and spiritual) made upon them. Given that narratives have a goal of relating their characters and their content to hearers, hearers already use the first-person singular or plural standpoints to identify with the story. Keith Yandell (2001, 259) suggests that when a hearer identifies with a narrative, she interprets (and thereby makes) her autobiography part of the new story—she sees the narrative as affecting who she is and how she might behave. It follows that if she engages with a story in which the characters are interrelated (as a 'we'), she regards the story as an experience she could share with other members of her community (i.e., the 'we').

Making the narrative accessible to various situated knowers is the potential obstacle that also faces the first-person standpoint in narrative. How can an agent identify with the community of believers in a biblical account, for example, if she is not already within the community? How can an agent experience the love of God through a narrative if she already blames God for her extreme suffering? It has to be admitted that the problem of the situated knower is a problem for any standpoint, whether first-, second-, or third-personal. Narratives have a better chance at communicating to hearers, however, by utilizing the first-person. The first-person is the language of identity, and narratives that use the first-person are better able to facilitate self-identification with the story. To succeed as theodicy for hearers that are not already believers, narratives that use the first-person will have to use relatable concepts, situations, and characters. This might mean rejecting some narratives as potentially efficacious defenses. The story of Job, for example, is a salve for believers for a number of reasons, but may also not be suited for theodicy. (Its primary answer to Job's undeserved suffering is that it was consistent with God's will; the linguistic framework between God and Job is authoritative rather than intersubjective; and it dissuades members of humanity from questioning why suffering occurs in the world.)

It might also mean turning to other biblical narratives for theodicy, for their relatability and for their use of the first-person, even if they are narratives that might otherwise be overlooked. Prime candidates might include: Jesus healing the bleeding woman (Mark 5:21–30, which so movingly describes how she was ostracized and brought into relation with Christ), his meeting with the woman at Jacob's well (John 4, with whom he was not supposed to talk, and who cared for her despite her alienation and despicability), and Christ's interactions with the leprous (see, for example, Luke 17:11–19, in which Jesus brings lepers—most notably a twice-ostracized Samaritan, who suffered because of his genetics and his disease—back into community). Although the authors of these stories might have epistemic privilege (their epistemic privilege, however, I take to be positive, because their friendship with Jesus gave them authority to tell their tale rather than a power that distances the reader from the story), these stories indicate Christological relationships that were offensive to the power-elite of the day but that the oppressed could latch onto: healing sinners, touching the unclean, rebuking the rich and powerful, dining with prostitutes, reaching out to tax collectors, etc., were all actions that were, at the time when written, perceived as morally contemptible (see, for example, Luke 7:36–50) and yet they resonate with contemporary sufferers. The risks Jesus took to include the suffering among those he cared for might go far in the canon of theodical narrative.

The story of Christ's own oppression might be the best example of a theodical narrative that is relatable first-personally. Philippians 2 indicates that humanity's unity with Christ—identification with him and his story—is facilitated and made possible because he "made himself nothing, taking the very form of a slave". Christ's *kenosis* (the emptying of himself) allowed him to be "a man of sorrows, acquainted with grief" (Isaiah 53:3), and made him a paradigm of subjugation. By hearing that Jesus identified with those who suffered—and on their behalf—those who are alienated might also identify with Christ's lament to "let this cup pass from me" (Matthew 26:39), and this narrative can foster dialogue about the reasons Christ had to suffer. If Jesus, in his anguish, was allowed to ask, "My God, my God, why have you forsaken me?" (Matthew 27:46), ordinary people who feel abandoned by God are enabled to ask (and approach answers to) the same question, as a result of engaging with the narrative.

It is true that some hearers will not identify with these narratives. But the reason will not be that a second-person framework distanced them from the narrative. Rather, there may not be enough points of contact between the narrative and the hearer's own set of experiences. Or, the hearer may be able to relate to the narrative but may deny that the relevant components are enough to provide morally justifiable reasons for God to allow suffering. But at least in the latter instance, the theist is actually in a position to engage the hearer in a conversation about what constitutes morally justifiable reasons. The hearer can reject the idea that she is a participant in that story—but she at least is able to determine whether she *wants to be*, rather than being excluded as someone who *could be*. Herein resides the ultimate benefit of the first-person plural over the second-person for theodical narrative. The first-person plural invites those who are alienated to hear the biblical narrative, and so can engage them in dialogue as to whether the theodical message succeeds. It does so while at the same time integrating what standpoint theorists from Darwall to Stump want from the second-person: intersubjectivity, love, attention, and respect.

Narratives and Situatedness in the Early Modern Period

Now that the possibility of theodical narrative has been revived through the use of the first-person, we can approach the possibility that narratives in the early modern period serve a theodical purpose. For the women theists this book is focusing on, doubting the nature of the divine threatens either to make the believer blame God for evil, or to deny the existence of evil itself. But this disjunction fails to remedy the difficulty that political injustice is at odds with the conception of 'God'. (And, as Astell observes, depending upon the powerful for guidance in shaping one's beliefs can have dangerous consequences, "For if any Histories were anciently written by Women, Time and the Malice of Men have effectively conspired to suppress them" (Astell 1696, 23). Macaulay (1775, 26) similarly warns that "the want of power is the only limitation to the exertion of human selfishness," – and is best evidenced in the subjugation by the educated of those who do not have access.) The only conclusion that could consistently be made from asserting that all evil is necessary or illusory is a deistic one, in which God has independent existence from creation and is by nature unrelated to (and so, uncaring about) what happens in creation. What is needed is a theistic defense of divine perfection that does not deny the existence of evil, the necessity of the possibility of evil, nor the concrete consequences of freely chosen evil in the world. Macaulay, for her part, argues that such arguments are necessary to discount popular attempts to account for the phenomenon of evil as a type of universal good. Such a belief is immoral, is fallacious because it limits either the power or the benevolence of the Deity, and it leads the prosperous to have contempt for those who are more unfortunate, "as not coming in the nature of things within the compass of God's mercy and benevolence" (Macaulay 1790, 417). Macaulay's belief that moral evil is politically concrete actually puts her in a unique position to defend—through different reasons—the place of God amidst moral evil in the world.

It has already been noted that these women were largely excluded from writing philosophy, and out of necessity so much of their political, social, and theological commentary was written in the guise of other bits of literature and various forms of narrative. Academia is learning the mistake of confusing this scholarship with mere storytelling. Susan Wiseman (2006, 27) argues that, "it is not simply the case that politics is absorbed as if from outside into 'women's networks', or that women's letters, unlike men's, were not understood as political discourse. Far from women's political writings and imaginings existing solely at the level of relationships which can be understood as preceding political consciousness, political language and ideas are articulated in a range of places". One of those prominent places for Astell to explore philosophical difficulties was in the form of poetry, which, "ultimately enables her to invert the worldly hierarchies that exclude women; she thus confronts the problem of gender inequality by shifting her reader's attention from an earthly existence in which women are disadvantaged to a spiritual one in which such disadvantages are eradicated" (Pickard 2007, 115). By embracing the relatability of the narrative voice, the reader/listener could be empowered to *respond* to the narrative—whether positively or negatively is at this point irrelevant, because the point is *that* there is engagement with the narrative. If the narrative can be engaged, it can create the conditions for 'confrontations' of the systems of injustice (those systems, we recall, that are the basis of the atrocious harms of horrendous evil). Once confronted, for Astell, justice becomes viable.

But, the possibility of an effective confrontation (that is, one that engages all of the relevant members) seems to *require* the ability to successfully communicate what is known, and for many women in the early modern period, that ability was squelched—in many cases, in order to continue to subjugate them.[28] Hays lamented the position of the uneducated, "of all bondage, mental bondage is surely the most fatal; the absurd despotism which has hitherto, with more than gothic barbarity, enslaved the female mind," (Hays 1798, 61) and Astell contrasts those who are educated to most other women:

> who so their Purse was full and their outside plausible, mattered not much the poverty and narrowness of their minds, have taught them perhaps to repeat their Catechism and a few good Sentences, to read a Chapter and *say* their Prayers, though perhaps with as little Understanding as a Parrot, and fancied that this was Charm enough to secure them against the temptations of the present world and to waft them to a better; and so through want of use and by misapplying their Thoughts to trifles and impertinencies, they've perhaps almost lost those excellent Capacities which probably were afforded them by nature for the highest things.
>
> *(Astell 1697, II.17)*

The challenge for many forms of narrative (even Christian ones, according to Astell, Macaulay, and Hays), is that they really are void of content when they are not understood (and so, they can be misapplied). Astell is clear here that women are meant to engage at the highest level with argumentation but that all those who are kept from an education are at a persistent disadvantage to understand any truth about the world. She altogether scoffs at those who are in power and claim epistemic advantage in gaining understanding, "For a Man ought no more to value himself upon being Wiser than a Woman if he owe his Advantage to a better Education, and greater means of Information, than he ought to boast of his Courage, for beating a Man, when his Hands were bound" (Astell 1696, 20).

Astell's resentment towards those in power ran deep, given that she saw "ignorant and morally inferior men" in positions of theological and political power, and the only reasons provided for their superiority were that women were necessarily denied the possibility of power and gain because they were women (Ruether 1998, 134–5). So, difficulties in communicating spiritual truth include access to education (to better relate to narratives whose goal is identification with a story) and the ability to obtain positions in which women would be able to communicate knowledge once they possess it.

One way to overcome the limitations of power and access to education which can suppress knowledge and its communication is to use reason to focus on the goods described in Chapter 2. Each of these women believed that the oppressed has equal *natural* access to knowledge (whether theological or otherwise), although they admit that those who are oppressed could suffer more by seeking to break out of the system of harm. Hays encourages women that disrupting the system of harm to tap into truth that is naturally accessible can be virtuous, "'verily God is good', is the language of reason and of nature; and besides, had there been no disorder, there could scarcely have been any virtue, the whole rational creation would have been asleep" (Hays 1793, 167).[29] Macaulay argues that those who do not attempt to break out of ignorance are reduced down to an animalistic existence, which can perpetuate atrocious harm, "[God] requires not of us a slavish reverence on the principle of fear … and to those who shut their eyes … and willfully continue in the dark gloom of skeptical perverseness, that they do not seem to have been set by their reasoning faculties so far above the brute animals in life as to deserve not to be leveled with them at their death" (Macaulay 1783, 276–7). Despite being excluded from power structures in politics, religion, and intelligentsia, women can use their reason, both to push against those systems of injustice, and to better access and communicate truth—and what better evidence that such a consequence is possible than these writings, which use narrative to compel action?

One final note on narrative and knowledge for these scholars: they used the language of identity both to relate with and compel their readers. Macaulay, for example, understands the educational limitations of women in Great Britain, but still writes as though she is included among the group of women who needed to be motivated to act—'we' are among the 'us' who ought not to respond out of fear and who ought to cultivate a knowledge of natural laws as well as divine goodness, so that 'we' do not succumb to a "depravity of our natures" that overcome those in power (Macaulay 1783, 393). Hays, conversely, uses disparate pronouns to distinguish the oppressed—her audience "these teach *us* that a Being of infinite power and boundless benevolence could not have created intelligent creatures without intending their ultimate benefit"—from those in power, "on account of *their* limited capacities … *they* are liable to much evil and woe" (Hays 1793, 183, italics mine). Even Astell, who sought to be accepted by the male thinkers of her day as a philosopher and commentator on social and political issues, but was recognized mainly for her writings on marriage and women's education, uses stark comparisons in her writing to show her female audience she identified with them, and they could identify with her work, "To proceed therefore if we be naturally defective, the Defect must be either in Soul or Body. In the Soul it can't be, if what I have heard some learned Men maintain, be true, that all Souls are equal, and alike, and that consequently there is no distinction as Male and Female Souls; that there are no innate Ideas, but that all the Notions we have are derived from our External Senses, either immediately, or by reflection," to which she concludes, "Neither can it be in the Body, for there is no difference in the Organization of those Parts, which have any relation to, or influence over the Minds."[30] Each of these scholars recognized that their narratives were only successful to the degree to which they could relate to their audience. Although their civil, philosophical, and theological tasks were all-the-more difficult because they had to appeal to the men in power while motivating a range of educated women, their projects all depend on developing a community of thinkers who could buy in to their narratives, and to their arguments. Though such an endeavor is complicated, their position mirrors the dilemma of contemporary theodicy: for these scholars, they had to effectively communicate a message to motivate action, and so could not alienate their audience; for theodicy, the narrative must effectively communicate its message, and so cannot be divorced from the experiences and perspective of its audience—which means that it ought not use language that is rooted in an authority relation.

Whereas Chapter 3 bridges contemporary analytic philosophy of religion with the narrative work of women in the early modern period and demonstrates the possibility of doing so through the voice of identification and community, Chapter 4 will demonstrate that although none of these women explicitly sets out to do theodicy, each defends God against blame for pernicious evil as they attempt to minimize political and moral injustices against women. The theodical project of these women—to draw a line from concrete suffering to each person's own transformative actions in the world—resonates with some contemporary philosophy of religion, which recasts those who are oppressed, especially, as those impacted most by the communication of divine love through redemption. I will argue that there are three primary theodical arguments within their canon: *Virtue Accounts* (moral arguments that focus on continually improving the moral landscape for the oppressed, discussed especially by Hays and Astell, but also Cavendish); *Natural Balance Accounts*, defenses of God that are grounded in the role good plays in the created order, rather than a best of all possible worlds view—Astell especially provides arguments that are distinct from Leibniz); and *Transmutation Accounts* (theodicy that focuses on personal efficacy in eradicating evil, which is a primary focus of Hays and Macaulay). The chapter will conclude with disagreements between the scholars on each of the arguments, but especially the eschatological account. Some (Hays, for example) vehemently reject the idea that individuals suffer only for an omnipotent God to instantiate an all-things-considered good, and Macaulay maintained that a perfect God could not mandate the suffering of the most needy and innocent. These scholars provide distinctive contributions to the philosophy of religion, then, while relying upon a situated notion of suffering.

Notes

1 Nicholas Wolterstorff 2001.
2 Eleanore Stump 2001 and 2010.
3 Card makes this point in both of her books, but also see (for example) Eric Russert Kraemer (2009), Robin May Schott (2009), and Alison Jaggar (2007).
4 Following Linda Radzik (2011).
5 As well as second-person standpoint theorists Stephen Darwall (2006) and Mark Lance and Rebecca Kukla (2013), which more deeply discusses the second-person as introduced in their 'Yo!' and 'Lo!': The Pragmatic Topography of the Space of Reasons (Lance and Kukla 2009).
6 In (for example), Davidson (1982) and (1992).
7 In various, but most recently, The Therapy of Desire: Theory and Practice in Hellenistic Ethics, (Nussbaum 2013), in which she writes that this methodology, "while committed to logical reasoning, and to the marks of good reasoning such as clarity, consistency, rigor, and breadth of scope, will often need to search for techniques that are more complicated and indirect, more psychologically engaging, than those of conventional deductive or dialectical argument … all in the service of bringing the pupil's whole life into the investigative process" (35).
8 I take the 'theodical function' of narrative to refer either to a story's ability to provide for some defense of, or demonstration that, divine perfection is consistent with the presence of evil in the world.
9 Given that Stump is the best example of the effort, this chapter will concentrate its discussion of narrative theodicy on her work, but the observations within it could be directed towards other theodical narratives that rely upon a second-person standpoint.
10 Though an evaluation of the distinction is outside the scope of this book, Stump names the differences in knowledge as that between 'Dominican' (knowledge-that) and 'Franciscan' (knowledge beyond knowledge-that). This naming does serve well her purpose of advancing Thomistic theodicy in (201ff). For the remainder of the chapter, references to Stump will be to (Stump 2010).
11 See Vince Vitale (2013), for a nice treatment of this thought experiment.
12 The reciprocity constraint is that second-person claims are understood both by the person making the claim and the person required to respond to the claim. The communicability constraint is that obligations are, either implicitly or explicitly, communicated by a person in authority to a person in a subjected position who must respond to the claim.
13 See, for example, Strawson 1985, 34–7.
14 Darwall, for one, acknowledges his indebtedness to Pufendorf. A nice example of Pufendorf's sense of mutual obligation can be seen, for example, in On the Law of Nature and of Nations (Pufendorf 1995); VII.3.1, 2.10.
15 Perhaps culpably, of course. Anyone who has a teenager knows there are times when the "you" should have been heard, and was communicated properly, and yet simply wasn't given attention. But this example actually indicates why the authority component of second-personality is important: without authority, the agent making the claim has a monologue, rather than an interaction. Correlatively, if a listener does not engage with the narrative (as will be shown, this can happen for multifarious reasons), the narrative is unsuccessful at communicating its truths; the narrator just as well could speak to herself.

16 Radzik (2011) and Darwall (2006) both take up the distinction between coercion and response from respect (though they diverge on the implication of the distinction).

17 This communication does not have to be verbal, and in fact, the physical presence of another person is not required to have a second-person experience (which explains, for Stump, why narratives can facilitate second-personal experiences) (2010), 119.

18 If we would like the address to contain more familiarity with the agent—so, appraisal respect beyond recognition respect—then we move outside the scope of the second-personal address.

19 See, for example, Mattias Gockel (2009)—; Jill Hernandez (2013); A. Morgan (2008); and Patrick Roney (2009).

20 The last instance invoked by Stump is that of Mary of Bethany, sister to Martha and Lazarus, who was scorned for sitting at the feet of Jesus. Stump thinks Mary of Bethany is an exemplar of a person who suffers shame and heartbreak through the shaming by her sister and then the death of her brother. Though different from the other three characters (Mary of Bethany is not obviously wealthy and does not have social power), I don't include a discussion of her here. Although her story is, of course, told by a man (John), her suffering is not the same as those in Stump's other narratives for two reasons: first, because her grief results from standard certainties of real-life relationships (e.g., sibling strife and death of loved ones), and second, because Stump includes controversial claims as aspects of Mary's story to bolster the interpersonal aspects of her suffering, such as that Mary of Bethany perhaps was the anonymous, despised woman who anoints Jesus's feet in Luke's gospel.

21 It is noteworthy that Stump's defense of Thomistic theodicy depends upon providing morally sufficient reasons for suffering on the basis that "suffering is the best or only means in the circumstances for the sufferer to have what he himself cares about" (416).

22 Daniel W. Conway's (1997) "*Circulus Vitiosus Deus?* The Dialectical Logic of Feminist Standpoint Theory," is especially helpful here.

23 The atrocious harm criticism is relevant here—it would be difficult even to consider how to tell, for example, families impacted by genocidal rape that God has a great good in mind *as well as* the deepest desires of the victims' hearts.

24 This criticism is based on the most widely-agreed upon tenets of standpoint theory, and does not require the rejection of objective, or propositional, knowledge. The most radical proponents of standpoint theory argue against the objectivity of any knowledge, and that all knowledge is situated. (See, for example, Sandra Harding (1991, 126): "Knowledge emerges for the oppressed through the struggles they wage against their oppressors. It is because women have struggled against male supremacy that research starting from their lives can be made to yield up clearer and more nearly complete visions of social reality than are available only from the perspective of men's side of these struggles". Of course, analytic standpoint epistemologists also contend, rather non-controversially, that some aspects of experiential knowledge depend upon the situation in which a knower finds him-or-herself; a 'situated knower': Robert Westmoreland (1999); Don Ihde (2012); Sarah Clark Miller (2009); Kristina Rolin (2006); and Justin Steinberg (2014), among others.

25 She is aware of the difficulty. She writes, "This desideratum for solutions to the problem of suffering will, of course, strike most people as utopian, if not lunatic, because in our world, the heartbrokenness caused by suffering is only slightly less obvious than suffering itself" (307). Of Job's story, she writes, "an explanation of Job's suffering that is in the form of a second-person account will be disappointing to some readers or hearers of the story, however satisfying it might be to Job" (225).

26 Even some second-person standpoint theorists admit to the ineliminability of the first-person perspective. See Lance and Kukla (2009), 2.4. Others have written on the ineliminability of this standpoint, see especially David Enoch (2010).

27 Stump's further stance that God's love, regard, and concern for Job are second-personal relations is contestable.

28 Of these men, Astell writes, "This is our Case; for Men being Sensible as well of the Abilities of Mind in our Sex, as of the strength of Body in their own, began to grow Jealous that we, who in the Infancy of the World were their Equals and Partners in Dominion, might in the Process of Time, by Subtlety and Stratagem become their Superiors; and therefore in good time to make use of Force (the origin of Power) to compel us to a Subjection, Nature never meant" (Astell 1696, 21).

29 Jane Hodson, in "Women Write the Rights of Woman: the Sexual Politics of the Personal Pronoun in the 1790s," touches on the significance of Mary Hays's use of the second-personal to her theology, and indicates that the more Buberian sense of 'Thou' is a formal invocation for use when addressing God, whereas the less formal 'you' is reserved for persons, "As with Radcliffe's use of *ye*, the use of archaic pronouns here appears to invoke a religious register: the address is 'thou busy priestess of vanity'. Indeed, Hays also uses seven instances of *thou/thee/thy* to address God directly. The remaining two instances of the archaic second-person singular pronoun are used to chastise the 'pampered race' of wealthy families (1798: 244). Every other second-person pronoun (11 *ye*, 47 *you*, and 15 *your*) addresses male readers specifically. For example, she writes, 'to **you** fathers, brothers, husbands, sons, and lovers, I submit the following pages' (1798, iii), 'They are indeed directed to **you** oh man!' (1798, 28), and, 'Ah, ye abetters of hypocrisy! ye self-imposers! **Ye** slaves to surface!' (1798, 123). Hays's direct and repeated address to men is perhaps to be expected given her title" (Hodson 2007, 296).

30 Astell (1696), 11–12. Astell does here pay homage to Locke, "whose Essay on Human Understanding makes large amends for the want of all others in that kind," (1696), 54.

4

THEODICY OF EARLY
MODERN WOMEN

Whereas Chapter 3 bridged contemporary analytic philosophy of religion with the theodical narrative work of women in the early modern period, Chapter 4 demonstrates that early modern women provide at least three genres of theodical arguments that are unique in various ways, that will form the structure of the chapter: *Virtue Accounts* (arguments that focus on continually improving the moral landscape for the oppressed); *Natural Balance Accounts* (defenses of God that are grounded in the role good plays in the created order, rather than a best of all possible worlds view); and *Transmuted Accounts* (theodicy that focuses on personal efficacy in eradicating evil[1]). Although none of these women explicitly set out to do theodicy, each defends God against blame for pernicious evil as they attempt to minimize political and moral injustices against women. The theodical project of these women—to draw a line from concrete suffering to each person's own transformative actions in the world—resonates with some contemporary philosophy of religion, which recasts those who are oppressed, especially, as those impacted most by the communication of divine love through redemption. In an oblique way, all of the accounts are a variation of the transmuted account, since each underscores the primacy of good, and the importance of moral action in being fulfilled, in spite of evil in the world.[2] There are disagreements between the scholars on each of the arguments, but especially on whether they depend upon some version of an eschatological justification for the presence of evil in the world. Some (Hays[3], for example) vehemently reject the idea that individuals suffer only for an omnipotent God to instantiate an all-things-considered good,[4] and others (Macaulay, for example) specifically argue that the suffering of the most needy and innocent could not be necessitated by a perfect God.[5] These scholars provide distinctive contributions to the philosophy of religion, then, while relying upon a situated notion of suffering.

The Need for Theodicy

The concreteness of the early modern approach to evil belies a pragmatic and moral point for these thinkers as theists: there are lived experiences of suffering and evil that must be made consistent with a loving, relational God. It is difficult to defend God's dual role in preserving justice and divine love. If God cares that we suffer, who will be responsible for inflicting it? How can there be justice if the innocent bears the punishment of the guilty, and how is justice administered if responsibility for divine suffering is transferred from humankind to God?[6]

Just as the philosophical work of Hays, Macaulay, Astell, Wollstonecraft, and Cavendish provides an account of evil that, if written today would fall under the scope of the atrocity paradigm, so too many of their ponderings about the consistency of evil and God in the world should be considered 'theodicy'[7]: concrete moral evil is part of the created moral order of God that does not impinge on divine omniscience, omnibenevolence, or omnipotence. Their arguments are frequently distinct from those offered by male philosophers of the period; in fact, although they would not deny altogether Leibniz's best of all possible worlds argument in *Theodicy*, their work indicates that traditional theodicy is insufficient for a number of reasons. First, of course, Chapter 2 demonstrated that their conception of evil is distinct from what is typically used in traditional theodicies like Leibniz's. 'Moral evil' as these women thought of it is inseparable from concrete suffering in society and in the home, and so any theodical arguments they would give would relate to atrocious harm. Second, Chapter 3 showed that the discourse on theodicy ought to include a notion of evil that is readily relatable to those who suffer, if theodicy's purposes include engaging the theist and the atheist in dialogue, and salvaging divine perfection (including God's relational qualities, like omnibenevolence) for those who actually suffer. In twenty-first-century parlance: culpable, preventable atrocities in the world pose a threat to divine perfection, especially divine benevolence.

But the threat to divine benevolence is of special concern to these women in the early modern period. All of them believe that God is good, and so cannot bring into existence anything except which corresponds to his goodness. If God is a creator, then, what God creates must be consistent with his goodness. (Of course, it does not follow from this that all of creation must *remain good*, if indeed creation is separate from God, which these thinkers also believe is true. Anything that is created, even if it is created good, is susceptible to perversion if it is the result of free will.) Similar to today's theists, some of these writers would qualify an investigation into God's goodness with our limited, human rationality. Macaulay raises the general question (although she invariably provides several answers) as to whether our limited rationality could comprehend the foundations of divine justice, "If our ideas of moral perfection are only modes of thinking, adapted to our human state, and framed by human intelligence; or, if of divine origin, engrafted by power on the mind of man, how can we found any hopes on what we call the justice and benevolence of God?" (Macaulay 1790, 360). Hays moves away from a general concern about our rational abilities to the specific worry about how our perspective of God's actions in the world is finitely constrained. Our experiences of suffering, our perspective on events, and even our pronouncements on the divine are all filtered through a finite temporal lens. But God and his attributes are outside of time, just as this life is the first step of an infinite series for us (Hays 1793, 179). Created beings are not always aware of the eternality of things, and our reflections of experiences are limited by our reason and senses. But if we could think of our experiences longitudinally, and not within the limits of the body, we might better see how evil fits within the system, within the course of the whole. The picture Hays paints is one that differs from, for example, Spinoza. We are not part of God, but part of God's creation and God sees us distinctly from himself—and yet, he has the advantage of knowing what will become of us. She notes that even if we are now dead (in our sin, as Christians posit) or will eventually physically die, "God, who sees into futurity regards us" as though we "were already raised from the dead, and speaks of us" as if we "then stood in the same relation to him, that we ever did, or should do" (Hays 1793, 162–63). Humans experience time, but God, "who does not himself change," has a different perspective.

Take, for example, the way theists tend to think of the gap between death and the afterlife, as either a long interlude in which nothing happens or as a wholly unique set of perceptual experiences circumscribed by the same constants of space and time required by experiences in a finite body. Some would argue that the theist's commitment to an afterlife muddies their view of atrocity, because it permits the theist to lazily attribute some later-to-be-realized paradise as a justifying reason to do nothing while others suffer. They might point to Astell's text for evidence. Astell values the eternal life of the believer over our temporal welfare (Goldie 2007, 80), "Self-preservation … is not our cardinal aspiration. Or, rather, not our ordinarily considered, for it is the preservation of our spiritual rather than our bodily self that we ought to seek," given that self-preservation, "does not consist in the preservation of the person or composite but in preserving the mind from evil, the mind which is truly the self … It is this self-preservation and no other, that is fundamental sacred and unalterable law" (Astell 1705a, §312, 305).[8]

Hays's work can help to assuage the worry of those who think that not knowing answers to difficult questions makes seeking the answers a meaningless quest. Hays would disagree with Astell as to whether there is a qualitative difference between the afterlife and this world—she thinks instead that the afterlife is contiguous with this one, simply another stage in our development in which our being will be fulfilled, consistent with God's moral attributes. That makes moral evil finitely proscribed in time, so that any evil in the world—even atrocious evils—cannot indefinitely pervade human experience. But, Hays would agree with Astell that focusing on the afterlife can obfuscate the fact that evil exists in this world, right now. An answer is needed as to how it is that no evil or free act, or human system, could counteract God's ultimate beneficent intent for the world.[9] But, a belief in the afterlife is not required to engage in theodicy and with the work of these scholars (even Astell). We can accept the qualification that we are limited rational creatures who at times grasp for answers to deep existential questions while also, at the same time, continue to grasp for those answers. It might be the case that we would not find the *ultimate* answer as to why God permits suffering, but that does not make the exercise of attempting to find an answer empty. Instead, seeking an answer is part of participating in the atrocity paradigm's call to fight horrendous evil. Yet for those who undergo the harm of atrocious evils, the phenomenological experience of daily suffering clouds the ability to see the world through the picture of divine intent. If God creates the conditions under which moral evil can thrive, those who suffer the harm of evil—especially those who are believers—must understand how it is that God and evil are consistent.

To respond to the consistency worry, much of what is now known as 'traditional' theodicy frequently relies upon the idea that human free will is a better overall good for humanity than any harmful consequences that could emerge from freely chosen immoral actions. Leibniz, of course, made his case for the free will defense in *Theodicy*. And, female scholars of the period were not inured to the free will defense. In fact, to say that these scholars provide unique defenses of divine perfection in light of evil in the world is not to say that in some ways they do not also mirror closely traditional defenses. Many of them echo reasons consistent with other theists about the reasons God might allow evil in the world. Mary Astell, for example, in private correspondence with John Norris, wondered about whether it could have been possible for God to create humans without the passions, or whether God could prevent suffering by limiting human freedom. Ultimately, she denies the latter, since rationality is the specific difference of free creatures, so we are set apart naturally as those who have "in their very Natures to Choose their Actions, and to determine their Wills to that Choice by such Principles and Reasonings as their Understandings are furnished with" (Astell 1697, II, 26–7). The fact that humans act irrationally, unreasonably, and immorally underscores divine providence. God provides humans with reason to properly inform the will, and when they exercise the will, humans themselves demonstrate God's benevolence to the human race. For Astell, without reason to educate the will and act as a moral check on animalistic desires, humans would be slaves to the passions, but we have evidence of divine perfection through the free use of reason,

[God] would not have us enslaved to any Appetite, or so taken up with any Created Good whatever, as not to be able to maintain the Empire of our Reason and Freedom of our Will and to quit it when we see occasion. And this is all that the Rules of Self-Denial and Mortification tend to so far as they are Rational, they mean no more than the procuring us a Power and Disposition to do that which we come now in the last place to recommend, which is to sanctify our very Infirmities, to make even the disorderly Commotions of our Spirits an occasion of producing Holy Passions.

(Astell 1697, II, 258)

So, although evil is in the world, God ordained human freedom to work in concert with reason to function as a natural moral constraint against evil. Hays agrees with Astell that freedom is evidence for divine benevolence, even if humans use their freedom to act immorally. She thinks that only a benevolent and omnipotent God could harmonize the natural and moral laws of the universe with the ignorance, despotism, and cruelty that those who suffer experience as a result of free human action. The one is not overcome by the other, and to those who would suggest that God is blamable for the humanly-inspired evil in the world, and that such evil could outweigh divine benevolence, Hays rebuts, "Do you reproach me with ascribing evil to God? I answer, that it is seeming evil, which will ultimately terminate in the greatest possible good; and in return ask, from what source do you deduce this partial disorder?" (Hays 1793, 167). Human freedom, rather than trumping the goodness of God, is the completion of the plan for creation that God had for us since the beginning of time. God creates a world that is metaphysically limited, that is ordered with physical and moral laws that dictate the equality of all rational beings, and that is governed by the free will of those beings.

As with many free will defenses, a critic could argue that such a position places Astell and Hays in an ugly moral situation—one in which evil is necessary in order for humans to enjoy the benefits of living in a divinely-ordered world. The aesthetic conclusion (that suffering is required to experience goodness) seems to follow from the proposition that goodness in the world is contingent upon free will (and its likely immoral practical consequences). But Astell, Hays (and Macaulay as well) reject the thesis that evil is necessary in order to better know the good. Macaulay claims that the aesthetic argument for evil:

is so far from being the only comfort that Omnipotence is willing or able to bestow, that the Almighty has condescended to reveal to us his benevolent intentions. He requires not of us a slavish reverence on the principle of fear, but invites us to cultivate that knowledge of his goodness which is so well calculated to inspire love; and to those who shut their eyes from the prospect of a blessed futurity, and willfully continue in the dark gloom of skeptical perverseness, that they do not seem to have been set by their reasoning faculties so far above the brute animals in life as to deserve not to be leveled with them at their death

(Macaulay 1783, 276–277).

Both Astell and Hays agree that living in a created natural order does not require human suffering. If freedom is necessary for the best sorts of human action (that is, the free sort), then when human agents freely choose to act in the best way, they are better able to experience the blessing of living within God's created order. Living with a free will ensures that we can use that will, either in accord with reason (and so, beneficially) or against reason (and so, to perpetuate suffering). Hays confirms that reason helps us to understand the implications for our free actions. She writes, "It is true we are not angels! Yet if upon the whole of our existence (of which perhaps the present life is but the infancy) happiness predominates, we have reason to be thankful for the gift; and 'verily God is good,' is the language of reason and of nature; and besides, had there been no disorder, there could scarcely have been any virtue, the whole rational creation would have been asleep" (Hays 1793, 179).[10]

The tension between understanding why free will is a component of a morally good world (a world that also contains evil) is one of the general aspects of the scholarship of early modern women that maps onto the work of their male counterparts. But this shouldn't be a surprise. The problems of evil and free will really are existentially crucial questions, regardless of a person's theistic commitment. What might be a surprise is that a number of these women did not hide that they questioned to what degree implicating God for evil's existence in the world is a helpful exercise. As noted in Chapter 2, even Cavendish found that it would be irrational to believe that God's existence could happily coincide with poverty and suffering (Cavendish 1655, 29–30). Macaulay's theism, on one hand, leads her to condemn those as scoffers who would suggest that God could intervene more to limit evil. For her, to say that God can prevent, limit, or eradicate political abuses of power in the human system would demand from the Divine "such a superintending providence, and such an exact distribution of reward and punishment, as to have formed a kind of theoretical government" (Macaulay 1790, 388). And yet, even though she warns against being a scoffer, Macaulay still poses the question, "if the benevolence of God equally extends to all his creatures, why is instinct sufficiently strong in the brute to prevent his falling into any evil which is not brought upon him by external force; and why is reason so impotent in man as to render him almost on every occasion the author of his own misery?" (1790, 8–9). Wollstonecraft thought that theism was a "necessary support" required to live in a world rife[11] with "human weakness" but also believed that theism was not required to live a free, moral life, "But an acquaintance with the nature of man and virtue, with just sentiments on the attributes would be sufficient, without a voice from heaven, to lead some to virtue" (Wollstonecraft 1798a, 186).

We should, at a minimum, take comfort from the tension evident within these writings, because it indicates an authentic struggle with the problem of evil—which, at root, is what the atrocity paradigm compels theists to admit. If the problem of evil is not just a logical problem, then it also is a personal one. To witness serious scholars—scholars who also experienced marginalization for being women—engage in a struggle over the problem of evil suggests that their scholarship takes evil to be a felt phenomenon in the world, and so inextricably tied up with how we interact with each other. To treat it otherwise is to remove it from the human experience. Correlatively, if the problem of evil is about the human experience, theistic responses to it ought in some way to involve that experience. On this point, the scholarship of early modern women is noteworthy. There are at least three different, and unique, accounts of divine perfection in light of the problem of evil that are given by these women, and each of them is tied to the phenomenal experiences of being human, related to each other and the Divine. Virtue accounts evaluate the problem of evil along with considerations of completion and virtue; natural balance accounts provide an all-things-considered perspective that does not require that this is the best-of-all-possible worlds; and transmuted accounts discuss (what I will call) the transmutation of horrendous evils into something qualitatively different and can create the possibility of something good. Keeping in mind that the conception of 'evil' these women are working with depends upon concrete – and, as I have argued in Chapter 2— atrocious harms, their theodicies are significant because they bridge the contemporary atheist's conception of evil with the theist's desire to make consistent the co-existence of God and evil in the world.

Virtue Accounts

Although the aesthetic conclusion—that evil is required for good to be in the world—can be avoided, some of these women do argue that morality and moral predicates require the will to be exercised from among a range of possible actions. Such a view makes moral praise and blame depend upon the will. (The qualification is important, since it does not make *good* require evil, rather, a will that is not compelled.) Especially for Macaulay, Hays, and Astell, exercising human choice to pursue human happiness—when what is sought is consistent with reason—reveals divine goodness and cultivates moral virtue, and pursuing moral ends can function as a defense of that goodness in spite of evil in the world. Evil comes when immoral people seek immoral ends for their own individual satisfaction (a satisfaction that these scholars would find irrational), and this evil often emerges socially in the guise of political and domestic injustice—and pits the overall social good against the individual's own desires. When the quest for individual happiness deviates from virtue and leads to political and social despotism, theists can be left wondering where the justice of God is. One shared aspect of virtue accounts is that they respond to this worry in part by committing to human agency, the development of which produces moral good *as a reaction to* evil. Although God could not adjust the intentions of free humans to always respect the moral law (such an action would alter the definition of 'freedom'", see Macaulay 1790, 470), by his foreknowledge and benevolence, God put in place a system of morality under which people can thwart the predictable, denigrating consequences of evil human choices by choosing differently. As the system of morality set in motion by God can counteract the disorder of immorality, virtue matures in people in spite of the suffering that they experience, and (as Hays explains), "misery calls forth benevolence, suffering fortitude, tyranny patriotism, necessity exertion, etc" (Hays 1793, 180).

Emphasizing virtue development moves the theodical conversation away from the metaphysical worry over whether God could efficiently cause moral evil (as Leibniz is compelled to deny), and onto whether God's creative power could facilitate consistently good motivation and action within a system of human morality. The moral perfection of God leads him to create moral beings that choose among alternate possible actions, and his goodness in creating the conditions under which goodness can be a part of the human moral order extends to particular individuals as well as the collective good. Macaulay argues that humans are able to draw closer to God in spite of evil because of this systemic benevolence, "so instead of adopting that trite observation, 'partial evil is universal good', it contends that the Lord and giver of all good gifts, to whose omnipotence every difficulty gives way, has so benignly and so wisely arranged the established laws of nature" (Macaulay 1790, 479). By emphasizing that the moral law is an established part of the natural order, Macaulay is in a better place to conclude that God's bene-volence remains (even when humans actually use their free will to commit evil actions) because the existence of moral evil is evidence that evil people have wills that are improperly motivated. Evil does not mitigate either the existence of God or the strength of reason (Macaulay 1783, 6–11), because the presence of evil shows that God created people with the ability to choose improper ends—and when they do, that they act against reason in favor of bad intentions. For Macaulay, moral evil is not initiated in flawed reasoning, since if it was, the source of moral evil would be a created defect. As natural beings, humans have imperfect reason (but reason is metaphysically flawed, rather than morally flawed). Humans are created with limited reason, but also with volition that enables them to choose (after using reason to discern the right from the wrong) proper action. Macaulay's argument is as follows (1790, 460): If God prescribes the moral law to his creation but creates people with natural defects which limit their ability to understand morality's requirements, then we must conclude that God is irrational or immoral—either he establishes a goal he knows is unattainable or he games the system in a way that prevents humans from following the law. But a perfect God is neither irrational nor immoral. Rather, the moral system he put into place creates the possibility for humans to choose what is good. His perfection (and so, his moral goodness) ensures that the system is rational and is the overall best within the natural order, but does not guarantee that humans (or even, *most* humans) will choose to act morally. In a system of morality that depends upon the exercise of a will between alternate possible actions, moral evil comes from human free will.

A *better* world, the atheist could contend, could at least be one in which God interferes with human motivation. We could conceive of a world, for example, in which God alters human motivation only in the cases in which God sees that atrocious harm will occur from a given act. Humans would be free to choose between alternate actions, except when the outcome is horrendous evil. There are two different responses that could be given by Macaulay (to different degrees of success). The first is that even if it is evidentially true that most people generally would exercise choices that lead to misery, this is not proof that more misery than good is produced from human action. Perhaps instead the nature of good is so qualitatively different than misery that its existence cannot be overridden by any human action. (Since Macaulay's goal is to show that freely chosen evil is consistent with a divinely-established created moral order, evidence of atrocious harm is not evidence that God does not exist.) The second response Macaulay might give deserves more attention because it frames other treatments of virtue in the period. If God adjusted human motives—even to block the temptation to be motivated by an action that could produce atrocious harm—there would be no experience for people to be motivated to choose what is virtuous (Macaulay 1790, 481). The premise that an all-powerful God could constrain a person who intends atrocious harm mistakes the component life experiences that contribute to a person having bad intentions which, for Macaulay include, "a bad disposition, a bad education, early acquired habits of the unfavorable kind, strong passions, pampered appetites, inattention to a rational interest, and above all an ignorance in the art of disciplining the mind" and these "do all of them act with such a prevalent hostility against the virtue of mankind, as often to create a necessity for perverse volitions and correspondent actions" (1790, 483–4). For God to interfere (even anecdotally) with human motivation, he ultimately would have to determine the full course of a human's life, since there are a number of experiences which inform the will when a person acts.

Hays articulates a theory of virtue that is consistent with Macaulay's second response. Today we might say that for Hays, *consequentially*, the best expression of human freedom is when people use their reason to choose the moral act from among alternate possible actions. Absent the ability to choose from among options that are moral and immoral, humans would not really be free to be moral. The category of 'virtue' itself seems to depend upon the ability to choose from among actions that are not virtuous. Hays suggests this when she writes, "For though I cannot perhaps express myself, with philosophical precision and propriety; yet I shall be understood when I say, that I hold liberty to be in the moral world, what the very air which we breathe is to animal and vegetable life. In each case excellence is possible with a small, or a moderate degree. Without any, physical, and moral death must ensue" (Hays 1793, 106). The ability to act virtuously is rationally grounded, conveys dignity to the person in whom virtue develops, and demonstrates the equal stature of men and women. If men and women were not equal in their ability to reason from among alternate possible actions, God would not expect equal virtue from both men and women, but since both genders are expected to aim towards moral completion ("the desirable point therefore in all cases surely is that, where, as much freedom is enjoyed as is required, to bring forth every degree of possible perfection" (1798, 106)), they must be equal in their reason and in their capacity for free action (1796, 196). So, all of our action—domestic, social, political, and religious—is meant to aim towards virtue.

Macaulay's and Hays's emphasis on the system of morality as a response to the problem of evil nicely frames a conversation about virtue accounts in the scholarship of early modern women. Morality is part of the created order, so that both good and evil actions are proof of divine benevolence (since both demonstrate God's goodness in creating the conditions under which humans can freely choose among actions). Since God could not remain fully benevolent and interfere with human motivation, the development of virtue in a created moral order can be the avenue through which humans battle those who intend evil. For those who seek virtue—and all the more, for those who do so while suffering—sorrow and disappointment can result when those who are evil flourish and those who are virtuous live in misery. But continuing to choose what is right over what is expedient can function to "correct the depravity of our natures" so that, gradually, the person who endures suffering but chooses the virtuous can reflect a divine disposition. (It is important to note here that these women are *not* advocating suffering for virtue's sake. Macaulay, for example, repudiates as an "absurdity" the opinion that we should undergo more pain in order to become more virtuous and that a person who becomes perfect by suffering is morally laudable. God, after all, is perfect without suffering (Macaulay 1790, 500). She also disputes the idea that God would allow the "villain" to "finish his course in a triumphant career of success" and yet "punish others of his frail, yet comparatively virtuous creatures, with the anguish which ever be annexed to the keen sensations produced by temporal calamity, remorse, and self disapprobation" (1790, 393).) Rather, virtue can be the moral agent's rebuke against the immorality chosen by others—and for the believer, the practice of morality helps positively impact a world made possible by divine benevolence (1790, 399). The divinely-designed system of morality includes this reformative aspect, so that there will be those who are positively changed by virtue, and their actions will work to better the world.

This desire to better ourselves and the world is actually intrinsic to our humanity, according to Mary Astell, and explains why we do seek virtue, and for those who don't, why they *ought* to. All rational persons were created with a desire to "advance and perfect" their being and when people freely choose "worthy and becoming action", they demonstrate "the grace of God" (Astell 1697, I.20).[12] People struggle with animalistic desires, but pursue "worthy and becoming action" towards the goals of *living well* and *living freely*, reaching for the perfection of the self "as much as may be" (1697, II.201). So, we seek virtue naturally and rationally, and following its path leads to a state of flourishing (even if we endure suffering). Corrine Harol argues that by "portraying the human condition as torn between the desires of the body and truths of the understanding, Astell makes a case for learning as a key to morality" rather than suggesting (as some of her contemporaries did[13]) that people often ignore bodily pleasures and seek out the good.

Although seeking virtue is rational and natural, Astell thinks that we too often are distracted by the body (especially when things are not going well). We are built to aim for perfection, and if we spent time properly reflecting we would do a better job at putting bodily wants in their place, questions about God's role in the world, and the goodness within creation, would be better informed:

> Did we in the last place contemplate the Author of our Being, *from* whom we Derive and *to* whom we owe our *All;* and instead of prying saucily into his Essence, (an insufferable presumption in Creatures who are ignorant of their own) or pretending to know more of him than he has thought fit to communicate in his Word, and in that Idea of Infinite Perfection which he has given us, Frequently, Seriously and Humbly Meditate on what he has been pleased to unveil. Did we but employ so much of our Time and Thoughts on these things as we do on our Sins and Vanities, we should not be long in discerning the good effects.
>
> *(Astell 1697, II.230)*

Astell's contention that proper reflection gives us a better understanding of our relationship to a creative God and provides us with the ability to reach for "Infinite Perfection" articulated by Christian theology is not reducible to the notion that theism conveys special knowledge of virtue. Rather, Astell thinks that Christian philosophy cannot "so plainly and fully resolve all difficulties" and contains obscurities that arise "chiefly from the necessary limitation of human nature, and imperfection of our present state, which will not allow us to see any otherwise than through a Glass darkly, as we are able to bear it" (Astell 1709, 115). But she does think that Christian philosophy answers some general questions "more clearly than other Philosophy does or can", although sometimes answering these questions "is too hard a task for our titans" (1709, 115).

Even if ultimately *solving* the problem of evil is an insurmountable task for anyone, an advantage theism gives the thinker is a path to the completion of one's character that is rooted in a *telos* that differs from those who seek to dominate and oppress others, as discussed in Chapter 2. There, it was demonstrated that, for Macaulay, Hays, Astell, Cavendish, and Wollstonecraft, although our actions are meant to contribute to making us virtuous, those in power often become corrupted and create more suffering as a result. And so we might wonder whether, in a system of punishments and rewards, the moral people end up with virtue and the immoral end up lording power over others. But, the absence of virtue that comes from freely choosing badly can be used in a virtue defense of divine perfection against the problem of evil. Humanity, in spite of its created metaphysical limitations, is yet designed to pursue the highest goods through free human actions. Further, the ability to cultivate virtue is tied up with the important moral changes required in a person's life, and the fortitude to make the changes necessary to perform the virtuous action. Choosing what is virtuous rather than what is expedient, or while being tempted to perform actions that would harm others, creates the possibility for gradational virtue development. Hays's position is that virtue is able to "take root" and produce "lasting improvement" in someone's character when it is learned over the course of one's life (Hays 1798, 106). If virtue were easily achievable, or if there weren't harmful alternate possible actions, our actions would not reflect the best expressions of our freedom. For Macaulay, Astell, and Hays, the best representation of human freedom is the right act chosen from other (potentially prudentially rewarding, immoral) actions.

To say that virtue best expresses the created natural order is not to say that prudentially rewarding actions are always immoral, or that what is moral is always against self-interest, or that we can't freely choose whatever is pragmatically rewarding. By necessity of the goal-orientated nature of action, our acts often permissibly do tend toward the expedient. And they frequently are motivated by self-interest rather than an interest in morality or virtue. The love of the self is the source of most moral evil for a number of these thinkers[14] (Astell believes self-love leads to an emphasis of the bodily over the spiritual; Macaulay thinks self-love leads to a desire for political power; for Hays, self-love is at odds with reason because it motivates us to think of the personal impact our actions have rather than the corporate utility; and Wollstonecraft derides self-love as something that can infect the "mass of mankind" and even "make liberty a convenient handle for mock patriotism" (Wollstonecraft 1792, 24)). But when the expedient and pragmatic are at odds with right action, when we choose what is right, these scholars tend to agree that we most fully experience what it means to be free.

The function of this argument as theodicy is unique, and unlike any other that is included in the typical canon of early modern philosophy. Rather than argue that free will is the best defense against the problem of evil—that evil is a logical category that necessarily follows from God choosing the best world, and the best world is one that contains human free will—these scholars argue that virtue and moral categories require alternate actions. Alternate actions that best express virtue include immoral, vicious acts. Further, the key distinctive feature of humans as moral beings is their ability to freely choose right actions from among pragmatically beneficial wrong actions. If God is interested in creating the best world (and if he is perfect, he is interested in creating the best world), the world he creates must be one in which there are actual opportunities for humans to choose evil. Real opportunities to choose evil only exist in a world in which humans turn away from the evil alternate possibilities for action which tempt them when they choose what is right. Free will is at its best when it is tested and leads the agent to what is right. (Even Wollstonecraft, who does not give an exemplary representation of a virtue account, still held that a woman's ability to be moral despite suffering permits her to "apprehend and identify with the divine" uniquely, and doing so "was so fundamental to women's sense of ethical worth, and so far-reaching in its egalitarian implications, that it can properly be described as one of the founding impulses of feminism" (Taylor 2003, 102).[15]) It is not enough, then, on these scholars' account for God to create beings with freedom of will—he must also create a world in which there is actual, concrete evil—and not merely its potential. For Hays, the "ultimate benefit" of being a created, limited, intelligent creature that exists "liable to much evil and woe" is to rectify the sinful tendencies that threaten our own mortal happiness (Hays 1798, 183–84). God's power is made evident in that he limits the human ability for self-destruction, and God's benevolence is demonstrated in the continued human pursuit of seeking to become godly through self-perfection. The perfecting of the self, correlatively, is only possible through the practice of moral virtue—which itself cannot exist in the human moral system without the possibility for moral evil in the world.

Natural Balance Accounts

There is a genre of theodical arguments within the canon of early modern female scholarship that at first glance looks similar to the best possible worlds account provided by Leibniz. Leibniz argues that since God must, out of moral necessity, create only the best, the actual world is the best out of any logically possible world, and any evil in it is permitted by God because preventing that evil would create more overall harm than the evil itself. (In fact, when we look at the way the world works, we ought to assume that God does intervene in the natural order whenever such intervention does not interfere with human freedom, and as long as it sustains the best of all possible worlds.) Although we experience particular instances of evil temporally, all events are part of a larger sequence of goods, and in the end, God is the ultimate mathematician. Good, when weighed against the evil in the world, at the end of time will be found to have outweighed all of the evil suffered.

Most of the women writing in this period would not disagree with Leibniz that God creates what is in the final assessment a good world (although one notable exception will be noted below). Nothing can override the benevolence of God, even freely chosen moral evil. Mary Hays warns any who think that human choices could mitigate divine perfection, "Is there any power capable of counteracting the benevolent designs of the Deity? In the delicate situation in which you place yourself: be cautious how you proceed, lest by robbing the Supreme Being of his attributes, by which alone we can form any idea of his nature, you incur the suspicion of Atheism" (Hays 1793, 167–68). As was shown above, these thinkers agree that God cannot intervene in human free will and stay true to his divine nature. To argue that God would have to prevent evil by impinging on alternate possible courses of action (or on human desire for particular ends) is to say that God must violate his natural perfection to produce the best, although the best possible world must be one in which God remains God. This disrupts the balance of natural order as much as it would if God determined all individual human action—to require that God violate his perfection is to mandate that God be something other than God. Cavendish would go one step further and say that a created order in which there is human freedom would contain natural irregularities, which could include moral evil and other possibilities for error.[16]

But, there are significant differences between Leibniz's best of all possible worlds and the thinner version envisioned by many of these women—of a world created by God, in which people are ultimately responsible for the good and evil contained within the world. Their versions collectively are better grouped under the umbrella-term '*natural balance*' theodical accounts. Natural balance theodicies do not claim that good, at the end of the day, will balance out evil (since evil and good actions are equally chosen by humans as a result of the system of freedom given by God[17] whether there is a quantitative balance of goods and evils depends upon which actions humans choose), but that the ability to choose good is a naturally balanced part of a created order, and that its qualities are a necessary component of God choosing what is best. God's duties do not include making sure that every mild pain has some greater good attached to it, since it is sufficient to preserve divine benevolence that the wisdom with which God created ultimately produces the possibility for humans to always choose the good. And if we take—as most theists do—an individual's life as one temporal block within an eternal time sequence, most of the scholars in the period believe that goodness will be the dominant predicate that could be ascribed to the whole.

Hays presents a strong vision of a natural balance argument for divine goodness. A perfect being would provide for the possibility of goodness by constructing a system in which the greatest general good (and mostly, the best individual goods) are produced (Hays 1793, 178). Human choices can seem to undermine the goodness of God, but God forsees that, too, and the same system that can undermine goodness can also undermine the consequences of evil into something good. She writes,

> The principle of Nature, like all the other operations of an all-wise Providence, tends to universal good, though it may be perverted to partial, or temporary evil …. It may be indeed selfish, in the worst sense of the term; or it may be trained to find its happiness in communicating happiness to all around it, by channels, which will return it an hundred fold, in its own bosom.
>
> *(Hays 1798, 224)*

The natural balance account need not altogether deny, then, that God has created a world in which there is more good than evil, as long as the content of God's foreknowledge includes all human action. God's benevolent wisdom provides for humans to use their passions and freedom in an individually and collectively good way, even if we are epistemically limited to predict how each instance of good and evil can be weighed against each other. The fact that we are not perfectly rational only means that we might not understand how God's goodness will be evident in the midst of atrocity.

But if God is perfect, good must exist independent of evil (a product of human choice). The natural balance within which God has provided a way for good to thrive indicates that divine justice will be upheld in the world. Mary Astell makes the case that God's justice is evident (and will continue to be evident), in spite of human evil: "Indignation and Wrath, Anguish and Tribulation … which cannot but be Equitable, since it is their Choice, the natural Fruit, and the necessary Effect of their own Doings. God can as well not Be, as not be Just; as must be allowed by every one who has any tolerable and consistent Notion of the Divine Nature. Therefore since Justice has not its Effect at Present it must infallibly have it Hereafter" (Astell 1709, 120). Astell's suggestion here is that although God's justice might not be obvious to all people now, a necessary component to divine perfection is divine justice. Her stance that suffering is equitable because it results from freely-chosen human action is meant to be tempered against the justice of God—those who suffer can take some comfort from knowing that "God can as well not Be, as not be Just" (Astell 1709, 120).

(It would be simple to fault Astell for suggesting that suffering is equitable because it results from free will. How can her statement that "the Goodness of GOD is the only Reason why He does us Good" be made consistent with her opinion stated just two sentences later that, "all the Evil that we do is absolutely and entirely from ourselves, and by consequence we draw upon our own Heads all the Evil that we suffer" (Astell 1705a, 129)? Although it *might* be that the simple reading is correct, and Astell must be ignoring the suffering of the righteous— perhaps the suffering of Christ as the ultimate counterexample—another reading is possible, and more consistent with her conception of divine justice. The best answer must be that Astell is thinking of the system in which human goods and evils are possible—and wholly distinct from divine goodness. "Equitable" in the 1709 passage must refer to corporate, rather than individual, suffering. It has already been shown that Astell recognizes that there is *disproportionate* suffering in the world, so Astell does not think that all who suffer do so because they have sinned, nor does she think that those who are righteous or believers will not suffer. Rather, the reason there are terms that separate those who are good from those who are evil is because God is just—without those designations, all human choices would be the same, with the result that there would no longer be a category of 'morality'. She writes,

> And if a Wise, Just and Holy Goodness, be better than a tame and careless Easiness … then cannot the Great Lord and Governor of all Things, whose Knowledge and Power are Infinite as Himself, remain an idle Spectator of the Wickedness of the Sons of Men, nor forbear to make a Distinction sooner or later, between the Righteous and the Wicked, the Holy and the Profane
>
> *(Astell 1709, 119)*

Some proof for the benevolence and justice of God, then, is that God recognizes the actions of the virtuous as morally distinct—and better—than those who are vicious. Absent a system of morality, all actions are arbitrary, and if all actions are arbitrary morally so is the suffering we undergo, as well as the triumphs we experience. So, it isn't that human suffering is payback for choosing unwisely. Instead, moral goodness naturally results in spiritual fulfillment, "*This is the Will of God, even your Sanctification*, says the Apostle, there being no way to be Happy but by being Perfect, and no way to Perfection but by being *Holy as God is Holy*," whereas those who are evil suffer "the necessary and intolerable Effects of degenerating from the dignity of our Nature" (Astell 1705a, 99–100).)

Macaulay's work can also contribute importantly to natural balance theodical accounts. Similar to Astell and Hays, Macaulay would agree that God creates in the best way, and so creates a world which contains evil as a result of free, rational agency along with freely chosen good actions. Also like the others, Macaulay believes that the righteous are subject to experiencing harm, and that—as far as God can without manipulating the natural order or by impeding human motives and will—God builds into the natural order corrective measures to prevent further evil from being produced. She agrees that God would create more harm by preventing or limiting evil by altering the decision-making processes humans use when weighing morally relevant considerations, and would create the most harm by changing people's minds for them—since by doing so he might destroy every principle of rational action by which even the evil or the apathetic are meant to act (Macaulay 1790, 419). Macaulay contends as well that divine perfection is not threatened by permitting moral evil, and that the structure of morality and of the natural order mirrors divine wisdom in the physical world. Humans experience this natural order in individual segments, and as their personal lives culminate towards their natural end, Macaulay thinks that people will be able to see that God's benevolence and omnipotence was perfectly interwoven into the natural order so that evil experienced is a mix in "the draught of life to produce good, and that good not being universally experienced in this life, is to be expected in a future state of existence" (Macaulay 1790, 387). Evil, then, can only be properly understood within the fuller story of creation. Just as there is a balance between natural forces and velocity, just as there is reaction for every action, and just as there is an unchanging amount of matter in the physical world, so too is there an agreement within the moral system between suffering and peace. Just as God permits a certain "necessary agreement and disagreement in the nature of things", divine justice disallows "the portion of any created being to drink the cup of felicity without a certain proportion of evil proceeding from that equal balance of power enjoyed by opposite principles" (Macaulay 1783, 24).[18]

Where Macaulay differs significantly from her early modern female contemporaries is that her natural balance defense of divine perfection does not assume, as Leibniz's argument explicitly states, that all things will work out well. Macaulay does think that our finite and temporal sufferings are encased within a system that is good. But, the goodness of the system really is just that: a goodness of the created system, and not (necessarily) some good that outweighs evil. If goodness comes from the system, then all are able to benefit (whether theists or not). She concludes, "It has been advanced by almost all of the Christian writers, that repentance for sins is not enjoined in any system of paganism; but repentance for sins seems to be so congenial to human sentiment that it is difficult to believe that it should not have a place in every system of religion" (Macaulay 1790, 447). Macaulay thinks of the balance of good and evil (so, of 'sin' and 'repentance' or a turn away from sin) as a systemic part of the created moral order that all people can benefit from or suffer under. The process of choosing wrongly and repairing our wrong choices is part of the created, human moral system, and the system is organized according to rational rule, and functions over time holistically. One result of how Macaulay frames the system of morality (and, consequently, the conclusion that things might not always work out swimmingly for the believer who is part of the moral order) is that she denies that evil exists for evil's sake. Evil instead is a part of the system, just as reformation is part of the system that can transform and heal people who are harmed by those who choose evil. For theodicy, the result has to be that conceptualizing evil without a nod to the concrete misses the existential significance of living in a world with pain and suffering.[19]

Transmuted Accounts

Chapter 1 argued that atrocity paradigm scholars reject traditional theodicy in part because of its inability to account for systemic evils that perpetuate atrocious harm. Contemporary feminist atheists are particularly worried about theodicies which require some 'redemptive' version of suffering, such that the justification for undergoing atrocious harm is that the harm will, at some unforeseen and later time, lead to a good. Redemption is eschatologically hoped for, then, by the theists as an ideal that is only complete when there is a divine reckoning of the moral scales. Leibniz, for example, thought that the biblical account of the fall of man was actually "a *felix culpa* (fortunate fault)" because it led to the Atonement[20] and that "the redemption of the human race could not have taken place in a better way."[21] Humanity can only proximate "the greatest possible nearness" to the Creator, and so, can only ultimately fulfill God's plan for creation, "through an expiation of the sins of humanity, carried out in the worthiest way possible" (Antognazza 2008, 84)—all of which is impossible without evil. But, 'redemption' for scholars like Astell, Macaulay, Hays, Wollstonecraft, and even Cavendish, refers to the transformation of civil society en route to individual spiritual restoration and is not dependent upon this being the best state of affairs. Redemption is realized, "not primarily in an otherworldly escape from the body and the finite world, but by transforming the world and society into personal and social relations of justice and peace between all humans. This is the true message of Christ and the gospel" (Ruether 1998, 6–7). So, human action helps transform social, religious, and legal systems that perpetuate suffering and denigrate human dignity, and theodicy that ties the divine concurrence of evil to spiritual, eschatological redemption still carries a burden to also explain how justice can be accessed or experienced in day to day life without sacrificing those who are already at the margins. Most atheists, of course, reject as possible theodicy's ability to account for concrete, atrocious harms without some yet-to-be-determined redemptive good.

Those early modern women whom we focus on here would almost invariably agree that good's existence in the world ought not be dependent upon the presence of evil in the world—and many contemporary redemptive accounts seem to generate their success from the fact that without evil, we would not experience such goods as salvation. But for these women, to say that good depends upon evil is akin to suggesting that the person who perpetuates atrocious harm is closer to moral perfection because his first-hand knowledge of evil gives him a leg-up on understanding the good. (The biblical retort that comes to mind is Paul's exhortation in Romans 6, "Shall we go on sinning so that grace may increase?"). Rather than requiring the presence of evil for good to take root, in order to flourish—here, while we are members of an earthly society (and independent of a consideration as to whether we will be members of a transcendent, heavenly society)—all people ought to collectively and collaboratively seek justice, and in the absence of incarnate examples of Godliness, we ought to become our own examples of wellbeing—and overcome our own tendencies towards evil.

Theists need not duck from the fact that suffering and atrocity persist in the world. As has already been demonstrated, it is consistent with these women's beliefs that the moral process that is put into place to ensure freely chosen moral action also creates the conditions under which atrocity takes root. But with the same token, a system is also in place to create the conditions under which moral good, altruism, healing, and (even) redemption are possible. This is true for all, whether theist or atheist. Just as there are none who could live a life free from the shadow of suffering, so too there are none who are excluded from the scope of transmuted good. Chapter 1 established that the conception of 'good' at work in the transmuted goods account is not one in which all things will go well, but it is instead contrasted with the atrocity paradigm's sense of 'atrocity'. Transmuted goods could have been otherwise—they are the products of human choice and interaction, just as atrocious harms are. They are culpable, so that we hold individuals to account when they bring them to be. They are ultimately praiseworthy, since the process of transmutation alters the person who experiences them (just as an atrocious harm alters the person who suffers it). Transmutation is the process that alters the real harm experienced by the individual, and makes it as a phenomenon something other than what atrocity is meant to be (essentially debilitating and degrading). But, transmutation is also not synonymous with redemption. Redemption is a theistic term, and experience of those who believe, so that their sins are no longer held against them by God. By its nature, then, redemption is exclusive. It functions in part so that believers can live without the fear of a final, ultimate destruction for those who do not, in the end, find the knowledge necessary to live a moral life. But, the system of transmutation (even though, if you are a theist, you will believe the system is put into place by God), functions independent of theistic commitment. It provides for otherwise-unexplainable expressions of dignity[22] after experiences of atrocity. Lives alter—against reason and evidence—after atrocities have been suffered. It is true that there are some people who suffer who will not experience transmuted goods—but the system is not to blame for this (people are) just as people are to blame for the atrocity paradigm. It is also true, of course, that there are concrete instances of evil that are not transmuted, and these seem readily explainable as predictable results of the harm suffered.

But just as the point of the atrocity paradigm is to identify and then eradicate atrocious harms, so too the point of a system of transmuted goods is to identify and promote those goods. The harms and goods within the larger, global moral system mitigate each other, but neither justifies the other. (Transmuted goods are goods despite atrocity, and since nothing can justify the presence and persistence of atrocious harms in the world, their presence stands as a stain independent of good.) Nothing within the nature of atrocious harms admits of good as a predictable result from atrocity, given that horrendous evils diminish the good of someone's life. And yet, there are transmuted goods that alter the lives of individuals who have suffered atrocious harm, and derive from a system of human action that works to mitigate the harmful impact of atrocity. Cooperative effort is one way in which transmuted goods are brought about—but the vision and participation involved in such a project require tangible, and often social and political goods since transmutation must work on something atrocious to yield a transmuted good. It has already been shown that these scholars agree that the system God put into place allows for the free exercise of the will, and a result of this system can be the degradation of other social systems that depend upon the natural moral system. An institution in which the powerful, (and, in that time and now) predominantly white men rule the earth and stamp down the natural and equal rights of all rational beings is a perversion of the good use of the will God wants for us (Hays 1793, 168–9) and subsequently creates a need in those who suffer to be whole.

Whereas redemptive accounts suggest that those who suffer are (in some cases, at least) better able to be blessed by God with redemptive blessings, that they can become better people as a result of those blessings, transmuted accounts need not make this claim. Even though there are indeed aspects of a redemptive account in the scholarship of early modern women,[23] a closer read suggests an account that is something very much like the system of transmutation I have argued for in Chapter 1. Take Hays's suggestion, presented in Chapter 2, that suffering can have a "reification" impact, in which some evils lend themselves to a later benefit for the believer (Hays 1793, 183), "And these teach us that … though on account of their limited capacities in this first stage of their existence, they are liable to much evil and woe, yet these very sufferings may have a reifying tendency, and may be links in a chain of causes and effects, that will eventually terminate in the highest felicity." Whereas "the first stage of their existence" along with the eventual termination in felicity could suggest a redemptive account of evil, it also could justify a sense of transmutation. Evil is part of the natural order, similar to causality, and good is also part of that system. Transmuted goods change the person who suffers so that they become something other than the atrocious harm would suggest. In later work (Hays 1798, 179–8), Hays argues that the ability to experience ultimate and complete felicity can only be attained by our individual and collective responses to moral evil in the world, which indicates something different than the traditional Christian conception of redemption, by which impact of the believer's suffering is quieted and made complete by the suffering of Christ. Rather, participation in the moral order over the course of any life can alter the consequences of oppression and injustice.

To have a theodical function, of course, the transmuted account must offer something as a demonstration that God always intends and acts according to the most rational, best ends, and that atrocious harm is consistent with God willing and creating the world that we inhabit. This task is particularly difficult in relation to women's suffering, since many think (historically and today) that women have distinct metaphysical disadvantages when compared to men (some even think men are stronger physically, intellectually, and morally[24]). But, the goods that are emphasized by these early modern women are a demonstration of a divine, systemic plan for humans to thwart the evil that others can perpetrate. Bear in mind, for example, that most of these scholars argued at length for access to education for women (an issue still relevant today, and for which women around the globe still suffer atrocity). Whereas a redemptive account could imply that women need only look forward to some future divine justice for their oppression, these early modern female scholars argue for improved access to knowledge and subsequent protection of civil liberties for women *today*, because knowledge is the divine fail-safe designed to enable any individual to overcome the appeal of acting immorally, and for communities to collectively fight those in power who seek to oppress. Knowledge (and its function in morality) is meant by God to be the direct and natural vehicle to promote love and virtue, to improve the mind, and to correct the heart, and so God has provided knowledge as a corrective moral tool to fight against atrocity and to protect what is beautiful and good. Those who seek to oppress by limiting access to knowledge are fearful that their own power will be subverted if the oppressed gain knowledge. Even in Wollstonecraft's *Mary, a Fiction* (Wollstonecraft 1788), the key theme of the story is that systemic injustices built on social rank and perpetuated through sexual power and the suppression of educational rights are continual moral struggles against which women must fight.[25]

But, God cannot be to blame when evil men choose to circumvent what God intends for good. This theme is present throughout the scholarship of early modern women, and often presented in the 'system' language invoked here for transmuted goods as a response to atrocity. Consider Wollstonecraft's conception of the 'natural', which is "normatively linked with reason", even when symbolizing "what is fearsome and controlled" (Frazer 2008, 44). For Wollstonecraft, divine perfection demands that there is no evil that is unaccounted for (Wollstonecraft 1792, 14–15) and that reason is a natural function given to us by God to help us emulate divine perfection by discerning good from evil, and to choose the right. William Richey argues that Wollstonecraft denies that evil is the *felix culpa* that produces a future good, but is a necessary part of a world in which humans "lift themselves closer and thereby accomplish his will" (Richey 1994, 35).

The transmuted goods account of theodicy is unique to the genre at least in its characterization of the phenomenal, felt-impact of suffering. The sufferer who, as a result of the nature of atrocious harms, ought to be indelibly and unalterably negatively impacted by horrendous evil, is altered so that even though the atrocious harm was undeniably suffered and its consequences felt, the negative impact is transmuted in the sufferer. The sufferer becomes something other than what the atrocity intends for her. The transmuted goods account is different from the more ecumenically-accepted Romans 8:28 version in which "All things work out together for good to those who love God and are called according to his purpose," and is distinct from traditional theodicy's view that good and evil are binaries which can be added together to form a sum that is in the end good. Instead, just as the atheist contends that good, meaningful lives are ineradicably, negatively altered by atrocity, this account contends that transmutation can transform those who suffer from atrocious consequences into something qualitatively different than what resulted from the atrocity. That the transmutation occurs is itself a net positive, since atrocity by its definition negatively affects an agent by taking away the ability to create and sustain a meaningful life, and transmuted goods result in a life in which meaning (and, even, flourishing) can occur.

This possibility for meaning stands as a direct challenge to the atrocity paradigm atheist's stance that a system of atrocities stands as evidence against the existence of God. In Chapter 1, I argued that the theist can (and should) admit that there are atrocities which are culpable, blamable, and the result of human action. But, the theist also is in a better position to explain what atrocity paradigm atheists are unable to: meaningful, even impactful lives, can emerge out of atrocity and sometimes only as a result of atrocity.

There are plentiful examples in which atrocity indelibly strips away the possibility for meaning within a person's life—that is the essence of what it means for a person to suffer a horrendous evil. And, the atrocious harms suffered are not those that can be trumped by, overridden with, or made acceptable because of some greater good. There are no goods that justify atrocious harm. But there are also countless examples of people (independent of theistic belief) who emerge out of atrocity in ways that could not be accounted for on the basis of the atrocity paradigm. Their lives provide evidence of transmutation by goods that have allowed them not only to retain their own dignity, but to, in ineradicably positive ways, act and speak for others who suffer in the world. At the risk of minimizing the enormity of the numbers of those who come out of atrocity and experience transmuted goods, reminding ourselves of even a few well-known instances can be instructive. Nelson Mandela, San Zaw Htway, Aung San Suu Kyi, Liu Xiaobo, and Karla Charvatova were political prisoners who suffered atrocious harms and emerged to ultimately change the world indelibly for the better. Sojourner Truth, Frederick Douglass, Srinivasa Ramanujan, Mother Teresa, Dobri Dobrev, and Irena Sendlerowa endured through systemically-perpetuated harms such as slavery and abject poverty to fight against those same harms. Annunciata Nyiratamba, Malala Yousafzai, Lilane Umubyeyi, Yvonne Kabanyana, Megan Paterson, Italia Méndez, and Loretta Rosales all suffered tremendously, and yet became advocates for victims of heinous gender-based crimes, including torture and genocidal rape. Each of these individuals experienced atrocity and had reason to capitulate to their atrocity and eke out lives devoid of the dignity that was stripped from them. Instead, their lives became living symbols to others, that meaning can emerge despite atrocious harm.

It is this shift that the female scholars in the early modern period seem to have presaged in their theodical writings. Their focus was on a theodicy away from eschatology in which, at the end of days all suffering will be trumped by a resultant good, and towards the transmutation of lived experiences of suffering into something *different*. [26] Astell, for example, has been criticized for arguing that suffering can be celebrated if it enables spiritual growth (Pickard 2007, 125) but she uses the concept of growth to encourage women (especially) to attain eminently good lives apart from their domestic misery. Astell "locates conflict between subjects and the social spaces in which unreflective and unrestrained self-interest will inevitably exclude some from access to the social privileges that others enjoy," which justifies her condemnation of the social oppression of women and "its vexed dependence on a repressive model of desire", but also posits a "good in general" that women can attain through education and right reason (Harol 2007, 97). Hays, for her part, argues that to truly motivate the change needed to overcome suffering, there must be a *resolution* in which all agents (regardless of theistic commitment) engage in a holistic, completed existence. She writes, "Are we then (horrible thought!) to attribute the final destruction of the impenitent to God? Such a final destruction is no part of my creed; from the infinite goodness of the Parent of the universe, I expect the ultimate resolution of all his intelligent offspring, when purified and refined by sufferings" (Hays 1793, 169). Comparatively, Macaulay believes that our own creative acts ultimately culminate in our *choices*, which can transmute the experiences of the sufferer. "It is also observable," she notes,

> that though the voice of revelation does not condescend to enter into the nice distinctions of metaphysical reasoning, and talks only of freedom in a popular sense, viz., the freedom of action correspondent to volition, yet it everywhere presents motives to the human mind, as the only impellers of volition and in all the dispensations of Providence in regard to human

sufferings, which we observe to take place in the human system, they are commonly attended with the salutary effects of reformation.

(Macaulay 1783, 259)

Macaulay's contribution on this point is significant, since she emphasizes the systemic nature of freely-chosen atrocities and goods. Macaulay is convinced that suffering and change away from it results from the creative agency of the human person. This agency which can transmute our experiences also resonates with Margaret Cavendish's work. Although it is true that of the female scholars here, Cavendish provides the thinnest evaluation of divine culpability for evil, her writings focus on positive, transformative human creation. This response is largely due to her skepticism about whether we can know the nature of God, rather than skepticism about whether God exists. She argues, "No part of nature can or does conceive the essence of God, or what God is in himself; but it conceives only, that there is a divine being which is supernatural" (Cavendish 1666b, 17). That God exists is not something to be skeptical about, since the natural order is a created one, but we ought to hesitate to claim to reason about things that are outside the scope of the created natural order. It is false to infer from her skepticism, however, that Cavendish entirely avoids the problem that evil poses to divine perfection. Instead, it would be absurd on her view to think that God foreordained a world in which evil could run rampant, unchecked, against humanity. Doing so would suggest that God would permit Satan, "to have such a familiar conjunction, and make such contracts with Man, as to empower him to do mischief and hurt to others, or to foretell things to come, and the like" (Cavendish 1664, 227), which Cavendish rejects as nonsense. Rather, in a nod to theodicy, she posits:

> God's Mercy would not Permit or suffer Man to Damn himself, for that would be to Make Man to that End, Knowing it before, as Fore-seeing it, and if he gave Man a Free-Will, that were to give away one of his Attributes, and so to make Man Great, and himself Less, and only to empower Man to Damn himself; … this would not Express Justice so much as severity, if not Cruelty, as first, to Fore-See the Evil, then to make the Creature, and at last to Suffer that Evil, and Damn the Creature of the Evil; neither, said she, can that Rational Part that God hath given me, perceive how it can stand with his Goodness and Mercy, or his Wisdom and Glory, to Suffer more Devils, than to Make Saints.
>
> *(Cavendish 1664/1997, 234–5)*

There are several theodical moments in this passage. First, Cavendish argues that divine omnibenevolence would prevent finite human sins to condemn anyone to eternal damnation. She juxtaposes the benevolence of God—characterized here as mercy and justice—against concrete evils suffered as cruelty and suffering. (Of course, there is a hint at a free will defense as well, but that is strongly overshadowed by an appeal to divine goodness.) It is irrational, Cavendish's character asserts, to conceive of a good and fully wise God who would create humans who could eternally condemn themselves, just as it is irrational to conceive of a good God who could predestine his creation to suffer. An upshot to this interesting bit of philosophy of religion is that Cavendish thinks that what we can know of God indicates that he would be more interested in fostering the moral development of his creation rather than continually weighing whether the suffering within it is outweighed by a good. This isn't enough to demonstrate that God's existence can be consistent with evil in the world, but it is enough to provide a reason for why it might be. Even more, that reason fits in with the transmuted account—God has provided a system for human action that, through education (and, for her, proper governance), can lead to a different world.

If we are ignorant of divine essence (as Cavendish (1664, 107) believes we are), how could Cavendish consistently advocate for a moral response (both for humans, who must work towards moral improvement, and for God, who must limit evil in the world) to the problem of evil? The answer more than likely resides in Cavendish's conception of faith, which can ground some substantial claims about God's nature (Cavendish 1664, 210–11), as well as God's creation. "So, she believes," Karen Detlefsen writes (2009, 430), "in accordance with faith because it is in keeping with Church and Scriptural authority, that God is immaterial, divinely infinite, and perfect (1664, 186–7) …. Yet more regularly, and quite constantly in her mature works, Cavendish says that God is the author not only of nature's perceptive, knowing capacity and therefore of nature's freedom, but also of nature's self-moving power."

Considering God as the author of nature's system of capacities, freedom, and ability to self-move leads Cavendish to stop short of concluding that God is the author of moral evil. God creates the system in which humans freely act, and his power does not rule the minute details of everyday life "like as one wheel in a clock turns all the rest" (Cavendish 1666a, 212). Detlefsen describes the relationship Cavendish sees between nature and God as "interaction through rational suggestion" (Detlefsen 2009, 439). Recall from Chapter 2 that on Cavendish's account, suffering occurs either because of epistemic error about what our obligations are or because of erroneous desires. If God's perfection functions as a moral compass for created beings, then the presence of evil in the world is countered by reforming bad actions (that come, for Cavendish, from some false thinking). Reforming evil requires that individuals who perform evil actions, "be improved through good education, gainful employment, and exposure to models of virtue" (Boyle, 2006, 260).[27]

Cavendish thus adds support to a transmuted goods account in which reformation is realized by transforming evil minds within peaceful society, rather than some heavenly escape from the trappings of the body. Humanity's original goodness can be masked by intellectual paternalism, but when we do the difficult work of opening access to free intellectual pursuits, oppression changes from the inside out. Rather than depend upon an otherworldly eschatology for redemption—which is an object of theistic faith—our focus can be on widening the scope for those who fit under the umbrella of the intellectually considerable. Reason affords us the ability to change the intellectual suppression of others which perpetuates suffering, "Each opinion in natural philosophy may be judged as sociable and irenic or unsociable and bellicose. In Cavendish's scheme, philosophical civility is guaranteed by intellectual governance, a regulatory function she attributes to institutions that foster heterogeneity" (Barnes 2009, 54).

Thus far, then, the theodicies offered by women in the early modern period differ both from their point of departure (i.e., from concrete rather than abstract evil) and their teleological goal (i.e., the transformation of lived experiences rather than a purely eschatological redemption for those who suffer), although they ultimately affirm the conclusion of traditional theodicies of the period, that the existence of God is not inconsistent with suffering. But their conclusion that God and suffering can consistently coexist depends upon a system of morality in which all people can mitigate the suffering that evil brings about by transforming their own actions. One of the most significant differences in their theodicies compared to traditional theodicy, however, is shared by a number of writers[28]: that all people will invariably be redeemed, and that those who practice virtue, self-perfection, and good lives despite suffering are better positioned than others to experience spiritual goods.

Universal Redemption

At many points, the scholarship of early modern women (which we ought to consider theodicy) is distinct from an Orthodox Christian conception of good and evil as balanced in the world, especially given that many of them subscribe to a universalist conception of ultimate redemption. All people ought to emerge out of suffering, and all people will eventually respond positively to the moral law. Some (like Hays 1793, 169) specifically reject the idea of an eternal hell for non-believers in similar fashion to Hume, who denied that finite sins could be punished infinitely by an all-good and loving God. This—the life that we live—is the first and imperfect stage of existence, and can prepare us to stand in the presence of God. Eternity functions in part to demonstrate God's omnipresence through all stages of existence. Unjustified or unexplained suffering would be evidence against the existence of God. But Hays thinks that all people will eventually be brought to justice, and then will turn towards the Good of God. She writes,

> For it must be allowed, that even a just and virtuous purpose, ought not to be brought about by means unworthy of the end. And it would be impious to suppose, it is even against reason and daily experience to imagine, that every purpose or end, just and virtuous in itself, is not to be effected, by means equally so. If the reverse of this were true, how imperfect, and how unworthy of the great Author of all good and all perfection, were the moral

government of this sublunary world! If the reverse of this were true, though we could not easily bring ourselves to believe that the work of creation was formed by chance, we might well be justified in supposing it governed, by that blind principle.

(Hays 1798, 157)

Macaulay also warns against redemption only for the elect (Macaulay 1790, 2–3), "Almost every sect of Christians, to spur on the lazy virtue of their votaries, have represented the rigorous justice of God in a light which confines his benevolence to a narrow sphere of action; and whilst he is represented as devoting an eternity of torments for the far greater number of the human race, the gates of paradise are barred to all but the elect. Tremendous thought!" But, those who suffer share an affinity with the crucified Jesus Christ, and as a result, Hays thinks that they are less likely to sin.[29] The possibility of redeeming one's immoral choices is itself restorative, and preserves something created good—the human spirit. "God, who sees into futurity, regards [us] as if we were already raised from the dead and speaks of us as if we stood in the same relation to him. And surely, it is not more difficult for the Supreme Being to renovate us again, to restore to the mind its consciousness, and to the body its form and vigor, than to preserve the spirit from becoming extinct" (Hays 1793, 160–1).

Nor are the wicked exempt, either from the impact of evil or its potential to be redeemed. "Christianity alone affords any stability to our hopes of a future resurrection," Hays argues, "we must believe (it should seem to me) in the final restitution of all things, though for a period, both here and hereafter the wicked will suffer the consequences of their guilt, till refined and rectified by sufferings, they are fitted for a system of perfect purity and order" (Hays 1793, 180). Those who use their power to exploit others ignore their responsibility to seek a virtuous life, and the scales will eventually be balanced, which can cause pain. Although Hays goes so far as to warn women (specifically) against paying back evil for evil, she also recognizes that women typically "acquiesce in suffering the most manifest injustice, from prudence and necessity, rather than from conscious inability and decided inferiority" (Hays 1798, 135) and they should refrain from doing so because such activity undermines redemptive moral work,

I cannot however in conscience recommend to our sex, the wretched casuistry of excusing their own neglect of duty, from the example of others. If we are once sincerely persuaded that the percepts of our Savior are drawn from a divine source, and adapted to human nature, with a tender compassion for its imperfections and sufferings, and that as such they are best calculated of all to produce happiness—mortal and immortal—If we are once sincerely persuaded of all this, though we see others abandon this great standard of duty, it ought not—nor it cannot indeed then—greatly affect our conduct.

(Hays 1798, 255)

A contemporary critique could be leveled here at Hays and Macaulay—and has often been leveled at Cavendish[30]—that encouraging women to "do their duty" is a way of perpetuating abuses and so could not be reflective of a loving, powerful God. This critique would have more teeth if these writers were purporting that women should just remember their place and submit as Christ did. (Remember that even Cavendish's arguments were built on the ability of women to have intellectual—and so active, social, political, educational—freedom.) For Hays, women are recommended to be virtuous as a way to repudiate oppression, and to understand that in the created order, all are equal. "In the Christian system, as delivered by its divine founder, there is not I believe I may boldly say, a single sentence that even can be tortured into a meaning, against the liberty, equality, or consequence of Woman; reason goes hand in hand with religion in opposing the claims of the one sex, to a right of subjecting the other" (Hays 1798, 27). Wollstonecraft would agree—and in fact, sees the prospect of heaven as setting up an argument against the oppression of women. Barbara Taylor notes that, for Wollstonecraft,

> If the human soul were not immortal—if our brief existence invariably terminated at death—then female oppression, however censurable in itself, would be only one more of those infinite woes which make up our lot in this vale of tears …. it is the prospect of life beyond all such mortal contrivances which makes women's sufferings as a sex wholly reprehensible— for in enslaving women on earth men have also been denying them heaven
>
> *(Taylor 2003, 106)*

The reformative function of theodicy is strengthened for Hays when seen in the purview of the emptied Christ, who serves as collateral for all of our own spirits' completion and evidence of a redemptive theory of evil:

> The Universal Parent of mankind commissioned Jesus Christ to incite men to the practice of virtue by the assurance of his mercy to the penitent, and of his purpose to raise to immortal life all the virtuous and the good; but to inflict an adequate punishment on the wicked. In proof of this he wrought many miracles, and after a public execution, rose again from the dead; as an example of the promised resurrection.
>
> *(Hays 1793, 187)*

Contrary to some theodicies of the period, our restoration is not something that only believers will experience (and will experience after death), but is happening right now, in varying degrees, in everyone. Those who recognize their own participation in redeeming evil can work to effect change in the world, and so to be a physical representation of social change.

Points of Difference and Overall Contribution

There are several points to remember when thinking about the theodical arguments given by these early modern women. Their theistic beliefs differ in sometimes drastic ways. They disagree as to how salvation is achieved—in fact whether it needs to be—and they give sometimes different accounts as to the existence, nature, and extent of eternal punishment. Cavendish, for example, suggests that the human soul is finite (since it is material), and yet discusses the soul's salvation in relationship to Christ (whom she thinks must have a material and a divine soul[31]) as something "which I leave you to the Church" (Cavendish 1664, 224). Astell, on the other hand, is unequivocally theistically Christian, "are all liable to Condemnation, unless they believe in the Messiah, who by his own Blood hath obtained eternal Redemption for us, putting away Sin by the Sacrifice of himself. And as the Messiah was once offered to bear the Sins of many, so unto them that look for Him shall he appear the second time without Sin unto Salvation" (Astell 1705a, 60). Wollstonecraft argues for a weaker position in which, "The justice of God can be vindicated by a belief in a future state—but a continuation of being vindicates it as clearly as the positive system of rewards and punishments by evil educing good for the individual and not for the imaginary whole. The happiness of the whole must arise from the happiness of the constituent parts, or the world is not a state of trial but a school" (Wollstonecraft 1798a, Note 20, 187).

They do not always provide consistent views on evil, and perhaps most insufficiently, on the necessity of evil. Astell, for example, argues that "we must then allow a *Providence* as well as a Deity, one is as necessary as the other in order to the Solution of the Phenomena of the Universe; which can no more Subsist a moment, than it could at first Be, without the Omnipotent Power and Efficacy of its Divine Cause" (Astell 1709, 119) which, when juxtaposed against evil's presence in the world requires some argumentation. Macaulay places her defenses in a similar difficulty when she writes (1790, 360), "And if there is no portion of moral or natural evil in this world, but what is necessary in the nature of things— if existence is to be esteemed a blessing, however burdened with pain and misery—if the perfect benevolence of God is necessarily limited in its effects by an impotence of power," although she quickly dismisses the possibility that God concurs with evil in the world, "It is these injudicious defenders of the ways of Providence, who have unintentionally enlarged those narrow limits in which skepticism has hitherto ranged to an extent which threatens the annihilation of every found principle in morals and religion."

And finally, that their perspectives are so distinct means contemporary scholars who are looking for a unified theory of early modern, female, philosophy of religion will ultimately be dissatisfied. Not only are their arguments often embedded within a wide array of literary media, but since they are not intended for the purpose of theodicy, they were not written to be an integral part of a metaphysical system. Yet, the theodical force of their collective ideas is undeniable. They believe evil is concretely experienced, and mitigates at least our experiences of a divinely perfect being (and for some, threatens the existence of a perfect God). They attribute (what we would now call) horrendous evil to human action, typically within oppressive systems of power. And, they also provide some answers to the question of how God could consistently concur with human evil in the world, and these responses differ in important ways from the theodicies that their male con-temporaries offer. Rather than doing moral math about whether every individual harm is counteracted by an individual good—math which the atheist thinks stands against theism—some focus on the role virtue plays in overcoming evil, some focus on good as a naturally balanced part of creation, and some identify the system of human morality as a divinely instituted part of the world that can transmute evil experiences. Not only is their work significant historically (for the fact that women were doing theodicies in the early modern period) and philo-sophically (both for their use of a concrete sense of evil and unique defenses of divine perfection in light of it) but it impacts the contemporary philosophy of religion landscape. Their work helps bring into focus a dialogue that atheists should be having with theists, but for which theists have currently been quite reticent to engage: can theodicy account for atrocious harm?

Thus far, I have argued that the reasons for which the rare theodicies of these women are important are, first, for having been made and, second, for their relation with current atrocity paradigm atheism. Whether their arguments succeed as theodicy has not been discussed. In the final chapter, I will address this issue, along with a number of other potential criticisms that face the project.

Notes

1 In other work, I have called these 'redemptive' accounts (see Hernandez 2014), but I have changed my thinking about these accounts, and so what I am calling them, for a handful of reasons. First, 'redemption' at least on the face of things is already-theistic language, and it seems that accounts of the coexistence of God and evil should not depend upon a concept that itself connotes divine existence. Second, my opinion on whether these thinkers have redemption itself in mind has changed, given that, while redemption is possible (from a theistic perspective), as a theistic act, that occurs after conversion. Rather, for more of these women who work with something like *trans-formational* accounts, it seems that the idea is that we as humans participate in creating good as a contrast to the evil in the world. Such a prospect does not logically entail the redemption of particular—or systemic—harms. But the concept of 'transmutation' is entailed by that prospect.

2 Even when providing other arguments for the existence of God, the writers rely upon a background concept of a morally good God who wants good things for creation. Consider Mary Astell's own version of the teleological argument, which draws from the aesthetically good and ordered aspects of creation to an inference about the existence of a good and well-ordered God, "If there is no God, be pleased, gentlemen, for the sake of those who would reason like men, as well as for the benefit of the good people who desire only to laugh and be at ease, to shew us how and from whence the world had its being?… Your self-moving atoms and their lucky Jumble into such a beautiful form as that of the universe, is yet more ridiculous. Show us then some

New and Better way of Accounting for our own Being, and the origin of the world, if you reject that of an infinitely perfect and self-existing mind, the maker and governor of all Things. But be satisfied that whatever it be to which you ascribe self-existence, unless this eternal mind, and something must necessarily exist or else not anything could be, you will not only run into all the difficulties that you would seem to avoid but into other so great, so contrary to the Common Principles of Reason, that no man of tolerable judgment will be able to endure them" (Astell 1709, 116).

3 An interesting historical note is that Mary Hays, a Unitarian, was reviled by some of her contemporaries for her theological commitments. Gina Luria (1974) argues that "for personal reasons, Samuel Taylor Coleridge denounced Mary Hays in a letter to Robert Southey, describing her as 'a thing, ugly & petticoated' who 'seeks to ex-syllogize a God with cold-blooded Precisions…& run Religion through with an Icicle'," although, Luria observes, "this evaluation of Hays which posterity has sustained, many of her contemporaries (including Southey) dissented" (13–14).

4 Hays denies that there is an all-things-considered good because of the essentially good nature of God. God concurs with evil only because of it is a part of the system of human morality, not because all of the goods in the world were weighed against all of the evils, good would win out, "If good would not ultimately arise from any kind or degree of evil, natural or moral, a good Being would not *permit* it: and if good would necessarily arise from it, he would be justified in *appointing it*, being the proper and necessary means to a valuable end" (Hays 1793, 190).

5 Macaulay, for her part, condemns theodicies that must rely on some future good in order to make consistent divine perfection and evil, "These are the melancholy visions of, perhaps, the greater part of the religious world, whilst to the eye of the modern philosopher, God is infinite only in his natural attributes; and because they cannot find a more satisfactory reason for the introduction of moral and natural evil, they limit the power and the benevolence of God, to a size which exactly squares with the objects of sense" (Macaulay 1790, 2). She calls those who would question the coexistence of God and evil "Scoffers," who would have to maintain that for God to prevent, limit, or eradicate political abuses of power in the human system, he would have to invoke "such a superintending providence, and such an exact distribution of reward and punishment, as to have formed a kind of theoretical government" (1790, 388). Imagine what the Scoffer expects of God: to create humans with a desire for power while at the same time wresting it away from them; to protect all innocent creatures; to punish all people who perform evil acts and at the same time reward all those who deserve merit; to care for the natural order so human life is preserved and also prevent humans from hurting natural systems; to marry the human need for power with superior intellectual excellences; and to foster the moral development of humans through the just application of the moral law. In this *de facto* theocracy, God would be in charge of the universal good as well as held responsible for the consequences that come from each individual's choices within the system—and all the while, God would have to perpetuate the illusion that humans make their own choices and are morally accountable for them.

6 This point is made by Michael Walker (1988), 183.

7 Their work provides, maximally, demonstrations of divine perfection in light of evil, and minimally, defenses or reasons for the coexistence of God and evil in the world.

8 Much has been made of the fact that Astell explicitly takes up Locke's work on self-preservation in this section. See, for example, Goldie (2007), 79–80, Broad and Green (2009), 273, and Springborg (2005), 195.

9 A genuine question of "Why be moral?" might apply here, but the defenses (especially the transmuted account) will address some of that worry.

10 Other free will views might be more difficult to identify. Karen Green and Shannon Weekes, for example, argue that Macaulay's thoughts on free will are ambiguous, and probably a response to political stimuli and the impact of John Locke. See Green and

Weekes (2013). We know at least that Macaulay holds human agents morally responsible on the basis of human free will, since she argues that a free will is what constitutes the very essence of rational agency (Macaulay 1783, 257–8) and that (as was shown in Chapter 2), when the will responds to immoral motives, it often seeks to benefit the self, which then can result in social and political injustice.

11 Taylor and Knott (2005) point out that although some scholars think that Wollstonecraft as a humanist is hostile, or in the least indifferent to, religion (13), "So it is startling, on looking closely at the *Rights of Woman*, to find that it contains at least fifty discussions of religious themes, ranging from brief statements on one or other doctrinal point to extended analyses of women's place within a divinely-ordered moral universe. Nor are these discussions in any sense peripheral to the main message of the text. If Wollstonecraft's faith becomes a dead letter to us, then so does much of her feminism, so closely are they harnessed together."

12 Interestingly, Astell's belief that reason is the basis of moral sentiment leads her to argue that women's access to education ought not to be limited: "And therefore to be ambitious of perfections is no fault, tho' to assume the Glory of our Excellencys to our selves, or to Glory in such as we really have not, are. And were Women's haughtiness expressed in disdaining to do a mean and evil thing, wou'd they pride themselves in somewhat truly perfective of a Rational nature, there were no hurt in it. But then they ought not to be denied the means of examining and judging what is so … If by reason of a false Light, or undue Medium, they choose amiss, theirs is the loss, but the Crime is the Deceivers" (Astell 1697, I.20–21).

13 Such as John Norris. See Harol (2007), 91.

14 Cavendish (perhaps not surprisingly) is the odd-woman out in her conception of self-love. In an article that demonstrates Cavendish's dual-sense of 'soul' (i.e., the natural soul and the divine soul), Deborah Boyle argues that the natural soul has no use for self-love, which for Cavendish is "the strongest Motion of the Mind," and so, the strongest motion of the natural (corporeal) soul. Boyle argues (2006, 260): "Cavendish's theory also gives considerable weight to self-interest. For example, in *Sociable Letters* she refers to 'Pure Self-love, which is the Root or Foundation of the Love of God and all Moral Virtues' (1664, 163). *Worlds Olio* goes even further: 'Self-love is the ground from which springs all Indeavours and Industry, Noble Qualities, Honourable Actions, Friendships, Charity, and Piety, and is the cause of all Passions, Affections, Vices and Virtues; for we do nothing, or think not of any thing, but hath a reference to our selves in one kind or other… .' (1655, 155)."

15 Amartya Sen (2005, 4) hints at this when he points out that "the full title of Mary Wollstonecraft's book, *A Vindication of the Rights of Woman: With Strictures on Political and Moral Subjects*, makes clear that her approach takes human rights well beyond the limits of legal action and invokes political and moral engagement."

16 Brandie Siegfried and Lisa Sanderson 2014, 10.

17 Of course, some of these thinkers are not averse to the idea that good will counterbalance favorably against evil when the tally is totaled. Astell, for example, writes, "Good Christians are indeed the truest *Epicures*, because they have the most tasteful and highest Enjoyment of the greatest Good. For GOD is too Kind and Bountiful to deny us any Pleasure befitting our Nature; he does not require us to relinquish Pleasure, but only to exchange the Gross and Insipid for the Pure and Relishing, the Pleasures of a Brute for those of a Man" (Astell 1697, II.258). This passage suggests that Astell believes in an all-things-considered greatest good for theists, but at least with the caveat that she could consider the experience theists have *of God* as the highest good any one could partake.

18 See, especially Macaulay (1783, 73ff.), for more on the relation between divine justice and the moral law, which for Macaulay does not reflect a puritanical sense of getting what one deserves, but instead a more Platonic sense of justice (i.e., balance, proportion) in the created order.

19 There are feminists who would disagree, certainly, with Macaulay's argument. They might contend, perhaps, using Macaulay's reasoning that oppressive paternalistic regimes could continue their abuses of political power with the promise that their antics are necessary for the ultimate betterment of the world. Macaulay is not arguing that political injustices are justified because invariably they'll end up strengthening the character of the person who suffers because of them. Instead, if we did not experience the consequences of moral evil, virtues like patience, forgiveness, integrity, etc. would also not be part of our phenomenological cache. (See Hernandez 2013.)

20 The 'Atonement' refers to Christ's substitutionary suffering for the remission of sin.

21 Maria Rosa Antognazza, 2008, 18 and 84. It is important to note that Antognazza argues that Leibniz takes a non-kenotic view of the Atonement, one in which Christ's divine nature is "hidden" behind a veil of human nature in the Incarnated Christ (87).

22 There are many positive expressions of dignity, but they can include hope rather than hopelessness, making future plans rather than staying stagnant, the creative impulse rather than apathy, love rather than a myopic focus on hate, and forgiveness rather than bitterness.

23 I have argued for this interpretation in Hernandez (2013), 184f).

24 Hays specifically addresses these points throughout her work, but especially in Hays 1798 (58ff and 105), in which she compares the plight of women to circus animals, who have to learn their roles, are taught tricks that go against their nature, and look happy doing it.

25 Hanley (2013) makes this point, especially from pp. 12–37.

26 'Better' ought not to be used, as it assumes an eschatological justification for suffering.

27 Unsurprisingly, Cavendish thinks moral transformation can result from a *proper* authoritative structure within government, "Thus the role of government is not merely to control those with 'rude and wild natures' but to transform them" (Boyle 2006, 260).

28 Astell offers a traditionally Christian account of redemption for the elect, though she underscores the idea that all are in need of redemption, "Who offered one sacrifice for sins, and by that one offering, hath perfected for ever them that are Sanctified; hath purged our Sins, and given us Redemption through his blood. And being thus purified from the Guilt and Stain, we are then, and not otherwise capable of making use of God's grace to save us from the power and dominion, and consequently from the evil effects of Sin. For all being Sinners and Transgressors of the Law, and so unjust; are all liable to Condemnation, unless they believe in the Messiah, who by his own Blood hath obtained eternal Redemption for us, putting away Sin by the Sacrifice of himself" (Astell 1705a, 60). Against those who do not believe, and who (as a result) do not perfect the virtues, Astell writes, "And those who will not be cured are the Persons who bring a reproach upon his Divine Art; for how is it that Religion improves Nature, but by teaching us to subdue those passions it does not extinguish?" (1705a, 380).

29 At (1793) 211–12, Hays writes, "The gospel also teaches that 'whom the Almighty loveth, he chasteneth'. May we not conclude from hence, that as gold is tried in the fire, so the human character is perfected by sufferings; and those from whom the dross is separated in this first stage of existence, are assuredly nearer to that state of pure and perfect enjoyment, where our faculties will no longer be enigmatical, and where these glorious faculties, here too frequently only inlets to pain, will find their proper gratification? Whether we reason from experience, observation, or analogy, every conclusion goes to prove, that this world is a state of discipline and progression and can never be, 'The final issue of the works of God, forever rising with the rising mind'".

30 See, for example, Boyle (2013), 526–30.

31 Siegfried and Sanderson point this out in their (2014), 103–5.

5

CHALLENGES FOR THEODICY FROM ATROCITY

There are a number of ways that this book could succeed—whether as a reclamation project, as a new contribution to the philosophy of religion, as a unique theistic engagement with a major contemporary ethical perspective, as an addendum to the history of the early modern period in philosophy, etc. For each plausible avenue of success, there is a correlative way for the book to fail. I have not, after all, provided a work whose sole focus is to rediscover early modern women as philosophers of religion. None of them explicitly write theodicy, and many of them have a social and political end for their writings, rather than a philosophically theological one.[1] The book is similarly not focused solely on the philosophy of religion, and experts in the field may fault my efforts here as a historical rather than philosophical enterprise. My interest in showing these women as philosophers (and good philosophers of religion) may be unpersuasive to those who want them to be discussing the modalities of perfect beings across possible worlds, or to have rigorous theodical arguments distinctive from defenses. Atrocity paradigm atheists will have various ways at hand to dismiss my endeavor: from my attempt to reclaim evil back for the theists to my desire to draw the paradigm into conversation with theism; from whether the examples I use in Chapter 2 actually are historically-situated atrocities to whether it is appropriate to apply the atrocity paradigm retroactively; from my implementation of standpoint theory to engage with theodical narratives, to whether transmutation just is a redecorated version of a redemptive defense of God. And, surely, there is ample fodder for historians in philosophy to dislike the work, not the least of which is that it does not provide an exhaustive textual treatment of any single thinker on any topic, and employs interpretive moves that some will reject.

The purpose of this chapter is to anticipate the criticisms that directly relate to the potential success of the project's goals towards which I have aimed: to bring contemporary atrocity paradigm scholarship into dialogue with theism through the unique theodical discourse found in the rich philosophical writing of early modern women. Although it is pragmatically impossible to discuss the wide range of reasons scholars from across the disciplines could have for thinking the book falls short, I will here integrate my responses to potential criticisms into what the book has purported to do, and will then forecast the benefits of my argument and some new directions for it.

One worry can be quickly dispatched, and was briefly mentioned in Chapter 2: that building theodicy around a concrete sense of evil is an attempt to 'gender' evil, and evil is something that cannot be gendered. There is nothing within the arguments posed in this book, or within the texts upon which the book draws, which suggests evil can or ought (and, correlatively, 'cannot' or 'ought not') to be gendered. Other scholars, especially in theology, have done a superlative job at drawing out the parameters for, and implications of, a gendered conception of evil.[2] For better or worse (each reader will decide), this book makes no claim on such a project. Rather, I have drawn upon the senses of 'evil' that are debated upon by leading philosophers of religion and contemporary ethicists, and have steered away from making metaphysically rich claims about facticity and evil.

A different, though related, worry includes a general problem with standpoint theory and Chapter 3: that grounding theodicy either in someone's lived experiences, or grounding the ability to access knowledge in situated epistemic factors—undermines the objectivity required for knowledge claims. This is an interesting potential difficulty, and one that this chapter will address more thoroughly. Additionally, I will respond to other predictable minor criticisms: that it is anachronistic to discuss 'standpoint' or 'atrocity' in the early modern period; that these scholars are not really philosophers or doing serious philosophy or doing theodicy; that their theodicies really are reconstructions of Leibniz's; and that their theodicies do not succeed. To this last claim, I will argue that there are several ways that these theodicies can succeed. First, it is a philosophical discovery of import on its own if these women are actually making contributions to theodicy. Further, these arguments are successful *at least to the extent* that they answer the contemporary atheist's contention that theodicy is divorced from concrete, atrocious harms. If they make contact with the atrocity paradigm, they are already enabling a conversation with contemporary atheism—a conversation that is precluded by most versions of theodicy today. Finally, I will provide reasons to encourage further discourse on the theodical arguments provided within the book. Such reasons will provide a point of departure for many to enter into the debate.

The "What Counts" Criticism

A critic might worry that there aren't strong enough parameters provided in this book to delineate types of evils. There are injustices that daily pervade real life which result from oppressive systems of power, lessen the ability of someone to live a meaningful life, and limit a group's or individual's potential for flourishing. How are these different from atrocities? Further, how ought economic inequalities that are endemic to a given region or political system be distinguished from horrors which are intended to eradicate or enslave entire groups of people? It seems that if theodicy is concerned about the concrete, it should have some criteria in place to distinguish among concrete atrocious harms. Finally, if my view divides concrete particular harms from concrete atrocious harms, then it ought also to map out what the essential characteristics of atrocity are.

On one hand, the allure of the criticism is understandable. The wartime rape of infants in the Congo seems significantly morally different than the suffering of a community that does not have access to clean water, or from economic inequalities that perpetuate racial or gender disparities. More generally, there seems to be something right about thinking that particular systems lead to particular instances of injustice, to varying degrees of suffering. So, the atrocities of war are strikingly abhorrent in a way that atrocities of a peaceful (though unjust) system might not be. Atrocity paradigm scholars have noted how arduous the task of delineating atrocious harms can be, especially if a crucial element of atrocity is its *intolerability*. What is intolerable for one person may be tolerable for another, and many oppressed people have survived through horrendous evil by finding tolerable aspects of their lived experiences to hang on to. (The intolerability of an experience has led Card, for example, to contentiously argue that certain fundamental social institutions, such as American and European systems of marriage and mother-hood, are intolerable and potentially evil.[3]) Although there is disagreement about what counts as intolerable experiences, Ann Cudd helpfully points out, "What counts as a tolerable existence? If it is to be judged by the subjective experience of the victim, then misogyny itself is typically tolerable—women rarely complain about their treatment, even when their status is grossly unequal to that of men, and they are subject to material and psychological deprivation."[4] So, the subjectivity of the feelings associated with atrocity can pose an obstacle to considering what counts in the category, but also has led some atrocity paradigm scholars (like Cudd) to argue that Card's perspective needs to be supplemented with more rigorous clarifying conditions for the scope of atrocity, rather than indicating "merely oppressive inequality," (Cudd 2009, 100). And, interestingly, early modern women also recognized that providing an exhaustive list of the horrors we perpetrate on each other might be outside of our ability, "To detail human misery in all its various shapes is not in the power of any individual: so complicated and numerous are the ills of this life, and so various its misfortunes, that we need not have recourse to the airy regions of fiction and romance to find out objects of distress, to portray the woes of our fellow creatures" (Radcliffe 1799, 404).

But, on the other hand, it is unclear that categorizing particular harms as atrocious or otherwise is a necessary endeavor for my project, and seems indeed to be counterproductive. Although it is important to understand the nature of atrocity (the significant aspects are the atrocity's systematicity and that it denigrates the ability to express human dignity) to be able to characterize harms as atrocious or otherwise, a benefit of my model is that I do not need to explain or justify any particular harm. That any single harm is an atrocity just means that it results from a human system that permits and maintains atrocious harm, and that system requires a theodical response. There are various moral meanings to the varieties of atrocities, and each doubtless elicits different appropriate emotional responses and calls to action. But, the atrocity paradigm as a system is what has not yet been addressed by theists. Rather than providing an unabridged list of atrocities, in Chapter 2 I demonstrated instead that early modern women were concerned about the same sorts of atrocities that concern contemporary atrocity paradigm scholars. The idea is to show agreement with atrocity paradigm scholars on the fact that there are evils that ought to be treated differently than individual harms and to agree with those who arrange the paradigm to confront our understanding of how evil relates to human agency that comes out of moral and political systems (Lara 2001, 2). Whether a particular harm is atrocious depends upon the system that generates it and the harm that it creates (and I have focused on evils which are systemic, pernicious, and denigrating), and *that* it is a horrendous evil is enough to generate a human moral obligation to respond to it. That obligation, and the goods that come as a result, sufficiently challenge the atrocity paradigm's contention that atrocious harms are unanswerable by the theist.

Some might take a different tack and contend instead that the project of identifying some evils as horrendous itself leads to particularizing evils *too much*. This criticism is Janus-headed: there are theists who will resist the concretization of evil for the purposes of discussing the problem of evil, and others will argue that (in order to be discussed by theism) atrocity must be a definition without particularity. Each head of the criticism is grounded on the same worry—that discussing particular atrocities disqualifies the theist from engaging with the difficulty because the problem of evil is logical. Of course, there will be theists who will remain unconvinced by the atrocity paradigm, or any other evidential problem of evil, and will engage in some foot-stomping about the problem of evil being solely a logical problem. I cannot hope to persuade the foot-stompers from an evidential standpoint—if, after all, you remain convinced that each individual evil will be justified and outweighed by some later, greater good then you will not be convinced that the atrocity paradigm is anything except a revamped version of the evidential problem of evil. But, I can at least hope to convince theists that they are not yet in the same philosophical room as the atheist, and that (at best) when they reject concrete evil out of hand they relegate their most persuasive theodicies to the annals of well-worded monologues. Surely the theist would like to have their theodicy directed towards someone who takes the problem of evil as a serious threat to the belief that God exists. If the theist agrees that theodicy should be aimed at those who see evil as problematic, then she will understand that most people think God ought to care enough to prevent suffering that they (and those for whom they care) undergo. If the theist can take that step, then they undoubtedly will want to be in dialogue with the atrocity paradigm atheist—who, at the end of the day, shares a commitment with many theists to do whatever possible to limit real life, daily suffering.

The "Why Be Moral?" Criticism

A main unifying thread to the early modern female scholars that I have incorporated in this book is that a person's journey out of suffering and towards meaningful, virtuous living is not something that only believers will experience (and will experience after death), but can happen right now, in varying degrees, for everyone. Those who recognize their own participation in eradicating atrocities and demand better in the world can effect change in the world, and so can personally be tangible, impactful conduits of social and moral change. But this shared emphasis of these thinkers also leads to a potentially damaging criticism. To say that we all, in varying degrees, have moral (virtuous) and existential (transmuted) reasons to participate in making the world around us a better place (especially if we have experienced atrocious harm) might suggest that we need not hold others accountable for perpetuating atrocious harm, nor that we ought to condemn oppressive acts (since all people are part of a human moral order regardless of whether particular evils outnumber or seem to outweigh particular goods). If we accept the early modern women's position that we all participate in systems of good and evil, and also capitulate to those who believe that, evidentially, actual evils in fact outweigh, outnumber, and are not justified by goods in the world, then is there moral motivation to do good? Perpetrators of evil could, after all, continue their abuses with the promise that their antics are necessary for the project of redemption to occur. Of course, as indicated in Chapter 2, theists could contribute to the problem by suggesting that human evil is justified as long as those who suffer serve as sacrificial lambs to redemption.

Although there are some atheists who would disagree with any sort of redemptive theodicy for its potential to fall into this difficulty, none of the scholars featured in this book argue that injustice is justified on the basis of whether it eventually strengthens the character of the person who suffers. Nor has it been argued that atrocities are necessary in order for there to be goods. (The presence of systems of atrocity and transmutation would not require the instantiation of any specific atrocious harm or transmuted good.) But, given that these occurrences are part of the cache of human experiences and permitted by God, theists are still faced with the question, "Why be moral?" Lynne Arnault (2003, 163) frames the difficulty away from the question of redemptive suffering, "victory cannot always be snatched from the jaws of cruelty, no matter how long the story goes on, and that insistence on this consolatory construction is sometimes morally problematic … just as there is no universal form of suffering, there is no universal way in which redemptive longing takes place." On one hand, atrocity paradigm atheists have a less 'morally problematic' way to answer the question since they deny moral justification for suffering. If humans are the source of moral praise or blame for human action, they are morally obligated to create and sustain systems which contribute to human well-being rather than suffering. There is no eschatology or transcendent moral thinking to fall back upon. But, on the other hand, the view I have constructed would agree with the atheist that humans are the source of moral praise and blame for human action, since humans are responsible for participating in atrocity or transmutation. My model is not at odds with the atrocity paradigm on whether and to what extent humans are responsible morally for the kinds and amounts of harm in the world, and indeed I agree with the atrocity paradigm that the problem of evil should function to address human action. (My account is also consistent with other theists. Marilyn Adams, for example, writes, "I agree with Tooley that the abstract problem of evil—while not uncontroversial—is of marginal theoretical interest. It is the *concrete* version that captures our attention because of the depth of its correlative existential and pragmatic implications" (Adams 1999, 14).)

The departure between the atrocity paradigm and the version I have argued for here is the moral explanation for moving beyond atrocity and towards performing right actions. Although a thoroughgoing sense of the right is currently absent from atrocity paradigm scholarship, the paradigm emphasizes actions that go beyond the morally benign. Good actions are those that fight against evil (Tirrell 2009, 35), and so represent our continued attempts to defeat suffering which results from atrocity. Maria Pia Lara argues for 'collective reflection' in which a community recovers their past *critically* through "an extensive exercise of collective self-examination" (Lara 2009, 207–208). Democratic systems are more amenable to the type of reflection she would like, because they tend to provide individual rights, judicial impartiality, and legal responsibility for law breakers (208). Once a system has provided for a complete collective reflection, Lara argues, "social transformation becomes both possible and necessary"—the main goal of which is for a society to break away from oppressive power structures (209). It is insufficient for action, then, to aim towards moral neutrality. As we think and act corporately to take down oppressive systems, justice requires that our "goal is justifiable when set up against the harm suffered" by those who have endured an atrocity (Veltman and Norlock 2009, 14).

Early modern women—while embracing a notion of right action that works to upend injustice—recast those who are oppressed as objects of divine love, sometimes especially in places seemingly bereft of it. Their approach, then, neither tramples the oppressed en route to a greater good nor requires of right action that it trump or best suffering. Rather, that an action is right is sufficient for the action to stand opposed to atrocious harm. An advantage to this perspective is that it makes positive actions accessible to all people, regardless of their proximity to democracy, social transformation, or minimally, to a just government. The message of women like Hays, Astell, Macaulay, and Wollstonecraft[5] is that we all ought to participate in creative, transforming actions in order to alleviate suffering wherever we are.

The result, if we choose, is that institutions are transformed, rights are expanded, and voice is given to those who lack it politically or socially. The theodical project of these women—to draw a line from concrete suffering to our own actions—affirms the atrocity paradigm's emphasis on human culpability for atrocity but underscores the curious problem of justice for God as a victim of suffering. Whereas Card accepts Nietzsche's criticism of Christianity, that God would have "been nobler" to take on the guilt of the world rather than have humans bear an "eternal debt of gratitude" for salvation (Card 1996, 25), Macaulay (for example) argues that God does indeed bear the guilt of human action, and so is aligned with us in our pursuit of right action:

> How came the beneficent giver of so many rich and valuable gifts, to suffer mental and bodily disease; how came he to suffer guilt, remorse, and all the numerous train of evils which accompany sin and death? Thus to deform his works and to mingle themselves in such a manner with all the benefits he has bestowed on his creatures, as to render it a doubtful question among some … is a question which continually occurs, but which continually deludes the anxious curiosity of the inquisitive enquirer.
>
> *(Macaulay 1783, 23)*

Although the question, "Why be moral?" can be posed to any ethical theory, the work of early modern women provides an answer that is consistent with the atrocity paradigm, but moves it forward to embrace all permissible action, in an effort for any individual to emulate the divine nature.

The Standpoint Worry

Another potential criticism stems from a general problem with standpoint theory—that grounding theodicy in someone's lived experiences, or tying the ability to access knowledge to particular facts surrounding one's unique epistemic position—undermines the objectivity required for knowledge claims. In Chapters 3 and 4, I embraced only the most agreed-upon tenets of standpoint theory in relation to narrative theodicy that remains consistent with the analytic standpoint's commitment to objective knowledge: that some aspects of experiential knowledge depend on a 'situated knower'. Although standpoint theory's criticisms of objectivity have been met with censure, it hardly can be disputed that there are knowers who come to whatever is objectively true by way of being situated particularly by gender, race, class, religion, sexual orientation (etc.). And while standpoint theory's articulation of what counts as properly grounded epistemic evidence is controversial (Intemann 2010, 784), standpoint theorists have effectively shown that how one is situated epistemically impacts how a knower can access evidence for, and weigh, the most objective of propositions (even those in science).[6] Further, although the low-hanging fruit of standpoint theory is a contention that all knowledge is socially situated, it would be difficult for critics to deny the more basic and significant tenet of feminist standpoint theory, that no epistemic standpoint must rely on others to determine the objective content of one's experiences. If the critic must agree that there is no epistemic privilege so great that any other standpoint must rely upon it for knowledge, the impact on the problem of evil becomes palpable. Admitting that there are situated knowers locates the problem of evil on the level of the concrete, to explaining an individual's suffering. Basic aspects of standpoint theory, then, can help theists such as Astell, Hays, and Macaulay, shift their inquiry away from the logical problem, to the consideration of the effect that living through experiences of suffering has on making sense of a world in which evil is ubiquitous and sightings of God are rare.[7]

The appeal to standpoint when thinking about the problem of evil is, then, an appeal to the concrete, which is an advantage for theists who want to engage atrocity paradigm atheists. If only those who have epistemic privilege tell the stories about God and evil, then those who are oppressed—that is, those for whom theodicy really is meant to function—are silenced. But if the stories are told from the standpoint of the oppressed, and philosophers stand ready at the gate, then personal encounters with evil might be able to be augmented with the production of hope. Standpoint theory's commitment to the impact of the subjective (even if universal[8]) on knowledge can help philosophers organize and explain the experiences of the oppressed in the language of those who suffer. Though each person has privileged epistemic space to their own experiences, oppression binds those who fight against suppressive privilege in a similar voice. Each individual group shares some social facticity beyond their oppression—whether their gender, their class, their religion, their race, etc., which can produce explanatory assumptions and theories.[9]

Standpoint, then, can importantly serve to help the sufferer communicate with those who are willing (in the least) to stand outside of the perspective of someone who has not suffered similarly. Other evils are detached from our individual, personal experiences, and yet because of the obvious and relatable suffering produced by them, ought to be identifiable as problems to be solved by atheists and theists alike. These atrocities do not require a special epistemic privilege to be understood as evils. When Angelina Jolie speaks out against rape as a weapon of war, it is not because she knows what it is like to be raped in wartime but because she knows what it is like to be a woman and a mother who could imagine living where rape is weapon of war.[10] The standpoint theorist can recognize what is propositionally true (here, Jolie's contention that rape need not be a weapon of war), then can look beyond the facticity of the objective to the subjective meaning of that proposition: there are suffering women whose plight is unheard, those who can effect change in the world have epistemic privilege, those who have epistemic privilege (in this case, a rich, white Hollywood starlet) can also step outside the privilege to align with the oppressed. Given that no special epistemic access is required to understand that living as a wartime rape victim is an atrocious harm, we are justified in blaming those whose actions continue to permit genocidal rape in war-torn areas as well as those who have the ability to prevent or limit this suffering and look away—and are ourselves blamable when our actions do nothing to disrupt the systems of atrocity that created the suffering in the first place.

The Theist Worry over Eliminating the Redemptive Account

Just as atheists might worry that I've presented a redemptive account, such that certain goods require the presence of certain atrocities (a conclusion I've debunked, above), theists might worry that, by eliminating a redemptive account from theodicy, I cannot make sense of certain goods. The version I have put forward in this book is that redemptive accounts are not required for early modern female theodicy, and that a result of their theodical work is that a theist can consistently maintain that there is, evidentially, more evil than good in the world, and that there are atrocities which are not justified by other goods. Plantinga, for example, might contend that I could not make sense of the good of Christ's atonement without evil, and that since Christ's atonement is the highest kind of good a human can experience, it is a good that requires the presence of evil. (Without the actuality of sin, there would not be a need for atonement.) Redemption itself, for that matter, seems nonsensical without fallenness.

There are a litany of treatments, versions, and criticisms of Plantinga's redemptive account, and I do not intend to present one here—mostly because I do not think that what I have offered is in competition with, or depends upon, Plantinga's famous argument. Whenever a person takes on a new line of study, new terminology is introduced and sometimes, that new terminology brings with it new methodologies for approaching the world. It seems to me that the Christian faith (and so, arguments that link directly to it, such as Plantinga's redemptive account) is one such study. 'Redemption', 'atonement', 'sanctification', etc. all are terms that do not make sense without a Christian worldview. Once within a Christian standpoint they go a long way to help a believer explain their experiences to other believers, and indeed, to motivate particular action. But, to the degree that epistemic privilege can prevent a rich person from being able to effectively communicate with a poor person their own experiences of suffering, so too, utilizing exclusively Christian terms to justify universal experiences such as suffering demonstrates an epistemic privilege that disconnects the theist from the atheist. If the Christian thinks that evil is justified only by taking on a Christian standpoint by using terms that only a Christian finds meaningful, then she cannot begin a dialogue with the atheist who believes that evil is not justified writ large.

That is not to say to theists that a redemptive account of suffering does not succeed. (I'm not engaging in that argument one way or the other.) Rather, redemptive accounts can be an additional way to explain particular theistic experiences with others who have a shared theistic commitment or interest. For example, whereas Wollstonecraft, Hays, and Macaulay could argue that all people benefit from acting morally and combating injustice (and are morally blame-worthy when they don't), a Christian theist could take their arguments a step farther and say that the ultimate goal of acting morally and combating injustice is to aim towards Christ-like perfection. What I have offered here is neither an explicit affirmation nor rejection of this position, although it is a broadly theistic response that can engage in a conversation with atheism. A theist could maintain both the early modern women's thesis that all people benefit from acting morally and combating injustice, and the specifically Christian theist's stance that it also aids in becoming Christ-like. My model does not require special epistemic access or standpoint, unlike the specifically Christian theist's view.

Of course, that could lead to a worry by both the atheist and the theist, that I have not offered a response to the atrocity paradigm that is specifically theist, and so I have failed to bring atrocity and theodicy into dialogue. There are several responses to this worry. First, it is true that the transmuted goods paradigm I have suggested here is not specifically Christian or theist. I take this to be an advantage of it. I have argued, stemming from the work of early modern women, that transmutation can be conceptualized as part of a created moral order, in which there are goods that can morally transmute atrocious harm. If you reject the view that there is a created moral order, you need not reject transmuted goods or a system of transmutation as long as you think there is a moral order. The system is meant, after all, to be consistent enough with the atrocity paradigm that atheists could enter into debate about whether it is a plausible system. But I also argue that transmuted goods provide something that the atrocity paradigm scholar has a difficult time explaining—those who have undergone an atrocity can go on to live meaningful, dignified, lives. My argument is that the theodicy of some early modern women explains goods, and specifically transmuted goods, in a way that the atrocity paradigm cannot, given the atrocity paradigm's commitment to the inexcusable and indelible undermining of human dignity that occurs in an atrocity. So, theistic proponents of a system of transmutation have an explanatory advantage when it comes to goods and evils, rather than evils *simpliciter*.

Importantly, the responses of theodicies of early modern women to the pro-blem of divine benevolence provide a picture of suffering that is more amenable to those who want a stronger theistic or, specifically Christian, response to suf-fering: women (historically, those who suffered disproportionately) are directly related to the crucified Christ (who was without blame, and yet suffered by, *contra* Card and Nietzsche, carrying human guilt). Marilyn McCord Adams (2006, 274) encapsulates the relation, "God sacrifices humankind by setting us up for horrors. God defeats horrors by sacrificing God's own self. But sacrifice requires material stuff, and divinity is immaterial. To make this offering, God must become Incarnate, the Word (or some other Divine person) must be made flesh". Rather than representing Christ as the powerful King and Ultimate Conqueror within another System of Human Power, early modern women offer a healthy distortion of power, so that women can relate to a Divine who chooses to be with us, rather than transcend. The theodicies of early modern women share the community-focus of the atrocity paradigm, with the goal of being empowered (rather than *overpowered)* in moments of everyday life.[11] The community-focus, which atrocity paradigm scholars suggest can break cycles of atrocity endemic to particular power structures, actively denies the continued subversion of women at the hands of religious practice. The central image of the suffering servant as having a redemptive value is itself inconsistent with the radical political message women like Wollstonecraft and Macaulay promulgated. Instead, the suffering of the oppressed is meant to be alleviated by those who recognize what our reaction to atrocity is meant to be, and if we suffer oppression, we are meant to fight against it. (Just as the *end* of Christ's suffering is *power*—power over sin, temptation, loss, suffering, evil, and death—and Christ stood in solidarity with suffering people—we are meant to be empowered.)

Although Mary Astell offers the most traditionally-Christian perspective out of all the early modern women studied, she also argues that the benefit of Christian theistic belief is that identification sufferers have with the passion of Christ, his suffering and then, his empowerment. The passion offers the single most significant evidence of the goal of theodicy: rescuing divine benevolence in the face of suffering of God's creation. Astell writes:

> GOD has been pleas'd to manifest His Love to us in a most amazing manner, by the Incarnation and Death of His Son…. The Manifestations of the SON of GOD in the Flesh, as it is the greatest evidence that cou'd be given, both of the evil of Sin and GOD's infinite hatred of it; and also of His infinite Love to Mankind and readiness to Pardon them: So it is a *Sensible* Argument, and what the most *Simple* and *Illiterate* may understand
>
> *(Astell 1705a, 125).*

The image of God provided by theodicies of women like Astell is drastically different than that suggested by atheists. God participates in the system of atrocity by serving as substitute for human guilt, but also by relating to us through the participation in suffering, and experiences the ultimate transmutation. To the extent that this "greatest evidence" fulfills our spiritual needs, we are called to meet others (whether we are or feel afflicted) at the point of their need. "This divine kenosis [*emptying*] lays the foundation for our own. Our renunciation is to be a mirror of this divine self-emptying: by remaining hungry, by looking instead of eating, we reflect back to God and to a broken humanity the infinite kenosis that God has displayed for all" (Holmes and Farley 2011, 169).[12]

The mirror of human to divine suffering that leads to the completion of need has led some theists to use images that many atrocity paradigm scholars would reject, whether because the images are too anthropomorphic or because the images represent power structures that cause suffering. Although contemporary conservative churches often rely upon the New Testament adage of God as

Father (a symbol directly rejected by some[13]), early modern women (particularly Macaulay and Hays) take solace from oppression in the image of God as Parent. Rather than create further distance, the representation is meant to draw us closer in, "The uniform voice of revelation everywhere proclaims God the universal Parent of creation. By this appellation, I would describe a relation more tender than what we commonly annex to our ideas of the author of nature" (Macaulay 1790, 2). The tenderness within the parent image provides a healthy familial relation, but also relates back to the treatment of the problem of evil.

Hays, for her part, argues that to truly motivate the change needed to overcome suffering, there must be a *resolution* in which all agents (regardless of theistic commitment) participate in a holistic, completed existence. She writes, "Are we then (horrible thought!) to attribute the final destruction of the impenitent to God? Such a final destruction is no part of my creed; from the infinite goodness of the Parent of the universe, I expect the ultimate resolution of all his intelligent offspring, when purified and refined by sufferings" (Hays 1793, 169). The 'resolution' (purification, refining, transmutation) of atrocity completes the action of creation. If theists want to engage in a more richly theological depiction of theodical narrative, the terms they can use to incorporate a wide range of noumenal experiences can be centered upon the mutual suffering of God and humans, along with the continued presence of God in the midst of suffering—that God also *remains* to carry the weight of evil, to commend us in our journey towards virtue, and to respond to us as fulfillment of the creative act.

Such a stance directly repudiates any contention (such as that held by Althaus-Reid 2006, 37–8), in which power is never really shared in suffering. Christ did not merely play at suffering, and those who are oppressed do not merely spin hyperbolic tales of suffering. Power and strength can be found in the intersection of divine and human suffering. What other evidence of divine benevolence would be required? Of course, the atheist might still worry that there is a problem of logical consistency if God suffers as a result of a system over which he ought to have knowledge, ability, and love to prevent. Rosemary Ruether puts the problem this way, "yet surely evil exists, and is the central theological problem. How can it be reconciled with this revelation of unmixed divine goodness in which all creation participates as its true 'ground of being'?" (Ruether 1998, 107).

The divine benevolence worry maps onto the earlier criticism—one that could be leveled at Hays, Astell, and Macaulay—and has been directly leveled at Cavendish[14]—that encouraging women to "do their duty" is a way of perpetuating abuses and so could not be reflective of a loving, powerful God. This critique would have more teeth if these early modern women were arguing for women to simply remember their place and submit as Christ did. (Remember that Cavendish's arguments too were built on the ability of women to have intellectual—and so active, social, political, educational—freedom.) Instead, we are recommended to be virtuous as a way to repudiate oppression, and to understand that in the created natural order, all are equal. "In the Christian system, as delivered by its divine founder, there is not I believe I may boldly say, a single sentence that even can be tortured into a meaning, against the liberty, equality, or consequence of Woman; reason goes hand in hand with religion in opposing the claims of the one sex, to a right of subjecting the other" (Hays 1798, 27).

For these early modern female scholars, then, divine justice is enacted by the instantiation of a human moral order as a part of the entire created system, whose completion is in our perfection. This is not to say that those who suffer are on the fast-track to redemption. (Rather, those who suffer could choose actions that do not work towards redemption.) But, those who choose to act creatively can preserve the natural goodness of the human spirit, which is a way to conceptualize God and suffering in a different light. These women confirm, then, the necessity of moral and spiritual transformation, but also rely upon a situated notion of evil that is parallel to the contemporary atrocity paradigm. The minimum result is that their work, which moves from concrete, situated evil to a defense of divine existence, ought to be considered philosophy of religion. Perhaps, too, the maximum result is a theodicy whose end—participative morality—is available to all, independent of theistic belief. The accessibility of theodicy underscores the normative force of early modern female philosophy of religion. The moral law is embedded into the created order, organized according to the rules of reason, and functions for all people. Moral improvement is available to everybody, and has the ability to transform institutions of evil—and, indeed, we are morally blameworthy when our actions don't work to overcome evil. Theodicy that ignores concrete evil misses an opportunity to dialogue with those who suffer the phenomenological significance of living in a world ravaged by evil.

Challenges from Early Modern Philosophy

In the same way that ethicists and philosophers of religion might have worries about this project, early modern philosophers could raise two main criticisms, concerning my treatment of the writings of early modern women and to the substance of their theodicy. When borrowing from disparate thinkers from the late 1600s to the early 1800s and from writings as diverse as political pamphlets and novellas, some might wonder as to whether there is a unified enough sense of atrocity and theodicy in these thinkers. Although in-depth treatments of specific thinkers on a particular issue might do a better job of making clear the extent to which each scholar mentioned in this book is doing philosophy of religion in interesting ways, I have provided a unified depiction of their theistic endeavors—in spite of their otherwise disparate commitments or methodologies. Each thinker presents moral evil as ultimately concrete, and a result of institutional harm, and so, their work is aligned with the contemporary atrocity paradigm model in ethics. That is not to say, of course, that these scholars thought of their work as theodicy (as I have indicated earlier), nor that their views reduce to an early version of the atrocity paradigm's conception of evil (although their ideas map on nicely, I haven't argued that they are identical), and historians will understand that I have attempted to construct more out of their arguments than they originally intended to say. (Some of the most compelling questions in philosophy and religion come to us in this way.) My hope is that I have preserved the legal purpose of these women's writings (when applicable, to win civil and political liberties, especially for women), but with the amplified goal of showing, first, that their writings demonstrate a concrete notion of evil similar to today's atrocity paradigm, and second, that they provide several unique theodical arguments although they conceive of evil concretely.

These women provided an explanation for physical and moral laws that served to justify their impression that the rights of all people were guaranteed but threatened by moral evil within human systems. For atrocity paradigm theorists, criticizing the institutions that perpetuate harms aids us in transforming the beliefs and values that keep the institutions in power (Lara 2004, 190). Correlatively for early modern women, the source of suffering is human action (rather than some logical, necessary consequence of a created order brought on by God; see Hays 1793, 168) and fighting against oppression and the "innumerable mistakes, both philosophical and moral" can create a space for freedom for those who suffer, "Free thinking, and free speaking, are the virtue and the characteristics of a rational being: there can be no argument which militates against them in one instance, but what equally militates against them in all; every principle must be doubted, before it will be examined and proved" (Hays 1796, 7). Atrocity paradigm theorists emphasize that fighting against some evils requires the disaggregation of systemic harms, and, correspondingly, early modern women contend that people ought to overturn the institutions that suppress individual rights. Their theodicy then argues that God's designed purpose for humanity is realized when there is an equal responsibility under equal law for all people, so that those who are in power must strive "to restore to woman that freedom, which the God of nature seems manifestly to have intended, for every living creature!" (Hays 1798, 105). The concrete sense of injustice and immanently human goals for theodicy are indeed unique for theodicy of the early modern period.

But do their views rise to the level of theodicy? I believe so, but perhaps not to the analytic philosopher of religion. Theodicians have made sharp distinctions among what I have labeled "theodical arguments". Marilyn Adams explains these distinctions:

> *Total refutations* boldly deny that evils are even *prima facie* evidence against God's existence because God's ways are so much higher than ours that we would not expect to be aware of Divine reasons for their permission if there were any. *Defenses* trot out armies of possible reasons why God might permit such evils, contending that even if we don't know the actual reasons, the greater the number of apparently available reasons, the less obviously

pointless are the evils in question. *Theodicies* suggest actual reasons, whether on grounds of reason or common sense.

(Adams 1999, 14–5)

While I haven't argued that early modern women provide refutations of the problem of evil—it is unclear that total refutations invite dialogue—some might contend that my treatment rises only to the level of a defense and not a theodicy. I am not devoted to proving that the theodicies of early modern women offer actual rather than possible reasons for God to allow evil, although it seems to me that if they function as plausible reasons, they have actually succeeded to respond to the atrocity paradigm. The arguments have, at the end, placed these early modern women to directly contend with the atrocity paradigm, which rejects theodicy as a project because it is fully divorced from suffering that ensues from atrocious harms.

The substance of the theodicies provided should also be attractive to scholars of early modern philosophy and religion, because they are unique to the time period.[15] Although I have noted similarities with Leibniz's theodicy where they exist (especially as they agree that human free will is necessary to explain moral terms and to make sense of the moral order), the theodicies are distinct both in terms of the concrete examples of evil they utilize and in how they make evil consistent with this created world. As a whole, early modern women are not committed to this being the best possible world (in fact, none of the theodicies presented in Chapter 4 rely on this being the best world, because this world could and should be better than it is), they are not promoting a conception of good that outweighs evil (for the natural balance account of theodicy, if evil outweighs good, it is because we have not been virtuous and participated in transmutation), and they focus on the moral cultivation of the individual (finite beings have more advantages available as they approach nearer to the excellences towards which they strive).

What some might find as an attractive quality, others might worry about, and as mentioned in Chapter 4, a number of these women offer theodicies which are consistent with universal redemption. Of course, the theodicies offered by these scholars can be separated from a pronouncement that all people will be saved, especially since all of the theodical arguments I have presented center around the positive moral action we perform, rather than a doctrine of specifically Christian salvation. It seems to me that a stronger criticism of the theodicies is that they do not provide a reason why virtue or morality or perfection or goodness could not be obtained without atrocities. Atheists might then contend that a divinely perfect creative being would create humans with what is needed to live a good life without requiring that they suffer from horrendous evils. There could be a world that contains particular concrete harm, without also containing atrocious (dignity-reducing) harm, and such a world would be a better world. If God wanted to create, and had to create the best but also wanted to create a world with human free will, the better world is the world without systemic, atrocious harm.

But such a criticism does not relate to the theodicies I have provided, since those from early modern women do not require that this is the best of worlds which God could have created, and (as I showed in Chapter 1), the presence of atrocious harms in the world is insufficient to show that a world with concrete, but not atrocious, harms is better than this world. The question posed by the presence of atrocious harms instead should really center on whether God is omnibenevolent. If God's power is ultimately shown through the created order, the lingering question remains as to whether God intends an outweighing good for those he created. That *is* a question addressed by the theodicy of early modern women. If God is bound by his nature to do what is best and good, then God intends for all creatures to experience the greatest fulfillment that their natures are capable of receiving. That does not mean, however, that created beings will experience more good than evil. Traditional theology's message of eschatological justice[16]—and temporary (even if, daily) suffering of the oppressed at the hands of those who benefit—simply cannot be reconciled with the God of Christian Scripture. If God is perfect and loving, God's created order would not mandate the suffering of the most needy and innocent. Such gratuitous evil is inconsistent with the goodness and power of the divine. Mary Hays observes, "Such a system, however, we may be permitted to say, is not founded on natural justice, and of course can never be supported by reason or by Christianity. Unstable therefore in its very nature, it is always tottering to its base and perhaps we would not risk much by predicting its complete and final overthrow" (Hays 1798, 156). The obstacle facing theists may actually be less about evil and God, but more about our commitment to an idea that individuals suffer only for an omnipotent God to instantiate an all-things-considered good. Early modern women have shown that God's intention for us is demonstrated by the created moral order—a system of right and wrong freely chosen by humans, who are built to navigate and, most significantly, control the system. Critics of this theodicy who focus on divine benevolence would have to show that God's goodness would be better demonstrated either by not instituting a moral order or by wresting control of the system in order to produce better, or more, particular goods.

There are many (theist and atheist alike) who agree that if God did exist, such a being must be just. Preserving dignity, creating meaning, and reducing suffering in the world are human enterprises, but if the theist is correct, she would have to explain how divine justice is necessary if there is universal (or, nearly universal) human meaning-making. (This is more the case, for example, in the Middle East, in which ancient articulations of 'God' contribute to a contemporary sense that divine power—as for any powerful ruler—is evidenced through his justice. This stands in contrast with the predominantly American emphasis of equating God with love.) If all people can participate in developing virtue and can access transmuted goods (which can change the nature of atrocious harms suffered), then what is the role for divine justice for evil? Similar to the question of 'why be moral?' this question focuses on a divine moral motivation for God to set things right in creation, specifically through retributive punishment. I suggest, though I won't argue for it here, that the atrocity paradigm's rejection of God is strengthened in part by the theist's retributive arguments for divine justice. For example, David Hume's worry that an infinite God could not punish finitely created beings infinitely for finite transgressions resonates with contemporary atheists. (Card writes, "The holy Christian God, unlike the noble Greek gods, plunged His children further into debt, by the same token preventing their ever paying it off" (Card 1996, 125).) There are other theistic responses that would be a good place to start (though to what extent they are consistent with early modern female scholarship would be an interesting inquiry). Marilyn Adams argues for a doctrine of "impanation" (real presence) of the emptied Christ as a way to think about divine justice for divine *and* human suffering: "Calvary's ironic reversal repeats itself. Biting and chomping our salvation confers immeasurable dignity, insofar as impanation turns the hostile act of eating into an act of intimacy with God" (Adams 2006, 311). The suffering of the oppressed is taken up by Christ—he 'eats, defeats, and destroys' our personal ruin—although the further question remains as to whether impanation is sufficient to consistently explain the early modern women's position that Christ's passion was for all (for perpetrators of atrocity and sufferers from atrocity).

Transmuted Goods and Personal Disappointment

Whether the theodical arguments succeed depends in part on to what extent the systematicity condition of the atrocity paradigm holds. Whereas more recent developments in atrocity paradigm scholarship focus on the structural, or systematicity, requirements of institutional harm, earlier work focused on the fact that atrocious harms were culpable. (Card's 2002 work defined the rules that govern institutionalized atrocities, and her 2010 book articulates the parameters of collective responsibility for atrocities.) Scholars, then, who adhere to the earlier version of Card's atrocity paradigm, might reject my reading of the paradigm, as being dependent upon structural or systemic frameworks which create and sustain horrendous evil. I would concur with them, that we ought also to focus on eradicating evil actions that create suffering without the aid of some structural framework. But, I disagree with the rejection of the systematicity condition. Even non-Cardian treatments of atrocities, such as those given by Lara, Adams, and (to a lesser extent) Stump, are evidence that a wide range of perspectives agree that part of what distinguishes an atrocity from a lesser harm is that atrocities are institutionally perpetuated.

Just as there may be questions over the systematicity condition of the atrocity paradigm, I anticipate questions over transmuted goods. Similar to the concepts 'atrocities' or 'theodicies', early modern women do not, of course, utilize 'transmutation' or 'transmuted goods', but certainly that really is beside the point. Rather, I coined the term to describe a theodical response that appears in the scholarship of these women but which also meets a significant need for theists in responding to atrocities. The atrocity paradigm provides the framework for what can be thought of as transmuted goods, and transmuted goods are designed to incorporate the same essential components of atrocities, yet with inverse results. The derivation of transmuted elements from nuclear events is a forceful image for the tranmuted good model, since atrocious harms suffered are a type of cataclysmic experience to the person who experiences them. And, in the same way that there are questions (which were addressed earlier in this chapter) over what counts as an atrocity, so too there will be questions over what counts as a transmuted good. Although I am not here committed to delineating the entire scope of transmuted goods, it should be made clear *what* types of things can be transmuted. The framework I have sketched out here, which will require more future work, is that *atrocious harms* are the sorts of things that become transmuted goods within, or for, a person. If atrocities denigrate human dignity, transmutation occurs at the level of the atrocity so that the harm—and so the person whose dignity was diminished—is transmuted into something other than a harm.

Are atrocities by nature transmutable? (If so, someone might contend that they really aren't atrocities at all—oppressors might say something to the effect that they really are rainbows in disguise of tornados or some such nonsense.) Chemical elements which transmute do not *by their nature* transmute. They transmute as a result of a nuclear reaction—a catastrophic physical event that happens external to the element which fundamentally changes the compound into a different element. Similarly, atrocious harms do not by their nature transmute into a good. (Rather, by their nature, they exert life-changing damage, are inexcusable and ought to have been otherwise.) It is the presence of the good that otherwise alters the atrocity. In physics, transmutation can occur instantaneously, or happen over time, and so too the change exerted by the transmuted good or goods could be quick, or could occur longitudinally.

As I suggested in Chapter 4, there are key benefits to a theory of transmuted goods. Transmutation offers a justification of early modern female scholarship on theodicy and also explains certain benign and positive events in the lives of people who suffer that the atrocity paradigm has a difficult time explaining. Further, transmuted goods free the theist from previously compelling theological commitments—specifically, that this is the best of all possible worlds, and that all instances of evil are morally justified. A theist like Leibniz could consistently accept that there are transmuted goods and still maintain that this is the best possible world (say, the best world is one in which there is an off-setting system of moral goods and evils, even if all individual evils are not in fact off-set by goods). But, my account explains how theists like Macaulay, Hays, Cavendish, and Wollstonecraft provide a theodicy while also believing that this would have been (and should be) otherwise. And theists could agree that, along with these scholars and contemporary atheists alike, it appears evidentially as though evil outnumbers or outweighs good in the world; or, in the very least, that we cannot know that it doesn't. The burden of theists to have to maintain the moral math of individual evils against particular goods is lifted by focusing on goods that transmute, and places the burden on the atheist to explain the sorts of transformative consequences that transmuted goods evidence in the life of the person who experiences them.

Unfortunately, a system of transmuted goods is itself insufficient to explain the most debilitating aspect of the problem of evil: a personal disappointment that God has abandoned us at our most urgent time of need. At a recent conference, the first at which I introduced transmuted goods, this phenomenological worry about the problem of evil presented itself in a powerful way. As I have here, I suggested transmuted goods could explain early modern theodicy in a way that better addresses key difficulties posed by the atrocity paradigm. A number of atheists and philosophers of religion were in attendance, and I called on a prominent atheist for the first question. His response was startling. He capitulated to the idea of transmuted goods and to my suggestion that they offer a better theodical response than what has been given, but he noted that my argument couldn't explain where God was during suffering. When I mentioned in reply that he was communicating a personal, phenomenological narrative in which God had failed him, the scholar tried to retract but, ultimately couldn't. He concluded by stating he was disillusioned with the idea theists posited that God cared generally but really did not or could not care about his individual experience with suffering.

His (what can only be called) anger on display at the conference reminds me a great deal of the existentialist Gabriel Marcel's discussion of the 'death of God' in Frederick Nietzsche and Jean-Paul Sartre.[17]Marcel (1967, 32) argued that those who focused on Nietzsche's apparently-triumphant exclamation, "God is dead!" were both reading the phrase out of context and forgetting Nietzsche's own biography. The full Nietzschean proclamation should be, "God is dead, and we have killed him," which underscores, for Marcel, the personal loss that Nietzsche experienced when he killed his own belief in God. Nietzsche's sentiment communicates that we become murderers of the divine and so, for those who once believed, the moment is fraught with loss and suffering. Marcel contrasts Nietzsche with Sartre, who descended from a plane on D-Day and exclaimed, "God is dead!" Marcel argued that Sartre lost nothing in the exclamation, having never experienced a personal commitment to God's existence, and so did not have the same claim as Nietzsche to make it, and did not experience the same devastation in making the pronouncement. My colleague's response to the problem of evil, and to the inability of transmuted goods to off-set the devastation it displayed, is equally Nietzschean. The transmuted goods account is one of a handful of theodical responses I have offered here on the basis of early modern women's scholarship, but none of them can address the personal disappointment you or I have if we feel that God has done less than what we think God should do.

What transmuted goods do accomplish is a way to get us in the same room. These phenomenal early modern female scholars thought we, as a community, could come together to work towards virtue, to battle evil, to overcome power structures, and to speak out for those who have no voice. My hope is that we can take their cue, so theists and atheists alike can enter into dialogue together, and can agree that acting on our shared secular commitments can lead to a better world. As we work towards that world, our continued dialogue makes progress possible for issues on which we currently disagree.

Notes

1 Perhaps with the exception of Mary Astell, for whom an interesting and potentially successful argument might be made that she is *primarily and essentially* a philosopher of religion.
2 Recently, for example, see Sarah Coakley (2013), *God, Sexuality, and the Self: Essays on the Trinity.*
3 In 1996, Card wrote, "I believe that women who identify as lesbian or gay should be reluctant to put our activist energy into attaining legal equity with heterosexuals in marriage and motherhood—not because the existing discrimination against us is in any way justifiable but because these institutions are so deeply flawed that they seem to me unworthy of emulation and reproduction" (Card 1996, p. 1). Others have argued that, since abuse is neither an essential nor predictable consequence of marriage and mother/child relationships, spousal and familial systems are not institutions of evil. See Todd Calder (2009), pp. 27–29.
4 Ann Cudd, 2009, 108. Cudd draws upon Adam Morton's (2004) "Inequality/Iniquity: Card on Balancing Injustice and Evil.".
5 Cavendish, of course, would reject Lara's conclusion that collective reflection in relation to democracy is necessary to combat suffering.
6 See, for example, Elizabeth Potter 2006, 98; and Sandra Harding 2008, 109.
7 Rosemary Hennessy 1993, p. 30, is helpful here.
8 Many aspects of subjective experiences are universal, including love of family, need for friends, creative impulses, etc.
9 Lynn H. Nelson observes that, "These survive to the extent that, like any common-sense theories, they are empirically successful—allowing the explanation and prediction of experience" (Nelson 1990, 267).
10 See U.N. News Centre 2014..
11 Mercedes (2011), 62, is especially helpful here.
12 My (2015) article expands on the kenotic philosophical theology of Macaulay and Hays, "It is a bit anachronistic to call early modern philosophical theology 'kenotic', but its emphasis on the suffering Christ who empties himself to stand in solidarity with those who are exploited is consistent with kenotic theology, and so aligning the scholarship of early modern women who suffered exploitation and yet defended divine existence and perfection against the problem of evil yields interesting results for contemporary scholarship. Their kenotic-like characterization of the Atonement provides a theory of how a divine Christ could partake in human suffering—he takes up suffering sacrificially for us to relate to those who suffer most, to be an exemplar for us of how to redeem suffering in the world that does not require the lowliest to be made lower. On Macaulay's and Hays's view, divine justice is enacted because all wrongdoers partake in redemption as a natural part of God's creative order, whose completion is in our perfection" (Hernandez 2015, 109).
13 An excellent synopsis of these can be found in Janet M. Soskice 2008.
14 See, for example, Boyle (2013), 526–30.
15 Kantians, however, will be dissatisfied that the arguments of early modern women are not related in a thoroughgoing way to Kant's work on theodicy, apart from a small

mention in Chapter 1. My intent was to put contemporary atheistic arguments in communication with traditional theodical arguments, of which Leibniz's are the best representation. (There are several reasons for this, not the least of which is that Leibniz did not share Kant's belief that theodicy could not answer the problem of evil, nor his conclusion that the problem of evil is primarily an endeavor for faith.) So, there is room for more discussion about Kant and this scholarship. From my perspective, the most interesting point of contact between Kant and the early modern female philosophers of religion is actually how Kant's interpretation of moral improvement might inform a system of transmuted goods.

16 Eschatological justice connotes an all-things-considered, at the end of life justice, in which believers can be comforted about the ills of human existence, by promises of final vindication and reward—results in an even better good into eternity. (See David Aune, 2010, 573).

17 It is not an insignificant point to remember that Sartre and Marcel were contemporaries who became adversaries in close proximity to Marcel's conversion at the age of 40.

BIBLIOGRAPHY

Adams, Marilyn McCord, *Christ and Horrors* (New York: Cambridge University Press), 2006.

Adams, Marilyn McCord, *Horrendous Evils and the Goodness of God* (Ithaca: Cornell), 1999.

Adams, Robert, *Leibniz: Determinist, Theist, and Idealist* (Oxford: Oxford University Press), 1994.

Adorno, Theodor, *Prisms* (Boston: MIT Press), 1983.

Aldrich, Robert and Voltherspoon, Garry, *Who's Who in Gay and Lesbian History: From Antiquity to the Mid-Twentieth Century* (New York: Routledge), 2005.

Almeida, Michael, *Freedom, God, & Worlds* (Oxford: Oxford University Press), 2012.

Althaus-Reid, Marcella, *The Queer God* (New York: Routledge), 2006.

Anderson, Pamela Sue (ed.), *New Topics in Feminist Philosophy of Religion: Contestations and Transcendence Incarnate* (Dordrecht: Springer), 2010.

Antognazza, Maria Rosa, *Leibniz on the Trinity and Incarnation* (New Haven, CT: Yale University Press), 2008.

Antognazza, Maria Rosa, "Metaphysical Evil Revisited," in L. Jorgensen and S. Newlands (eds), *New Essays on Leibniz's Theodicy* (Oxford: Oxford University Press), 2014, 112–134.

Ariew, Roger, "Leibniz on the Unicorn and Various Other Curiosities," *Early Science and Medicine*, 3:4, (1998), 267–288.

Arnault, Lynne, "Cruelty, Horror, and the Will to Redemption," *Hypatia*, 18:2, (Spring 2003), 155–188.

Astell, Mary, *Bart'lemy Fair: Or, an Enquiry After Wit* (London: Wilkin), 1709.

Astell, Mary, *The Christian Religion, as Profess'd by a Daughter of the Church of England* (London: Wilkin), 1705a.

Astell, Mary, "An essay in defence of the female sex, in a letter to a lady," 1721, Rice University Woodson Research Center Special Collection.

Astell, Mary, *Essay on Female Sex*, University of North Carolina at Greensboro Women's Collection, 1696.

Astell, Mary, *Letters Concerning the Love of God* (London: J. Norris), 1705b.

Astell, Mary, *A Serious Proposal to the Ladies: for the advancement of their true and greatest interest*, Vol 1 and Vol 2, (London: Wilkins), 1697.

Astell, Mary, *Some Reflections on Marriage*, (London: R. Wilkin), 1706.

Bar On, Bat-Ami, "Terrorism, Evil, and Everyday Depravity," in R.M. Schott (ed.), *Feminist Philosophy and the Problem of Evil* (Bloomington, IN: University of Indiana and Hypatia, Inc), 2007, 195–205.

Barber, Daniel Colucciello, "Review: Wandering in Darkness: Narrative and the Problem of Suffering," *Religious Studies*, 47:4, December 2011, 537–541.

Barnes, Diana, "Familiar Epistolary Philosophy: Margaret Cavendish's Philosophical Letters", *Parergon*, 26:2, (2009), 39–64.

Boyle, Deborah, "Fame, Virtue, and Government: Margaret Cavendish on Ethics and Politics," *Journal of the History of Ideas*, 67:2, (April 2006), 251–289.

Boyle, Deborah, "Margaret Cavendish on Gender, Nature, and Freedom," *Hypatia*, 28:3 (Summer 2013), 516–532.

Broad, Jacqueline, "Women on Liberty in Early Modern England," *Philosophy Compass*, 9:2, (2014), 112–122.

Broad, Jacqueline and Green, Karen, *A History of Women's Political Thought in Europe, 1400–1700* (Cambridge: Cambridge University Press), 2009.

Brock, Rita Nakishima, *Proverbs of Ashes: Violence, Redemptive Suffering, and the Search for What Saves Us*, revised edition (Boston, MA: Beacon Press), 2002.

Browne, Joanne Carlson and Parker, Rebecca, "For God So Loved the World?", in J.C. Browne and C.R. Bohn (eds), *Christianity, Patriarchy, and Abuse: A Feminist Critique* (Cleveland, OH: Pilgrim Press), 1989.

Buber, Martin, *I and Thou*, Walter Kaufman (trans.), (New York: Touchstone Books), 1970.

Burgelin, Pierre, *Commentaire du Discours de métaphysique de Leibniz* (Paris: Presses Universitaires de France), 1959.

Calder, Todd, "The Prevalence of Evil," in A.Veltman and K. Norlock (eds), *Evil, Political Violence, and Forgiveness* (New York: Lexington), 2009, 13–34.

Card, Claudia, "Afterword," in A.Veltman and K. Norlock (eds), *Evil, Political Violence, and Forgiveness* (New York: Lexington), 2009, 213–217.

Card, Claudia, *The Atrocity Paradigm* (New York: Oxford University Press), 2002/2005.

Card, Claudia, *Confronting Evils: Terrorism, Torture, Genocide* (Cambridge: Cambridge University Press), 2010.

Card, Claudia, *The Unnatural Lottery* (Philadelphia, PA: Temple University Press), 1996.

Cavendish, Margaret, *The Blazing World*, in *Margaret Cavendish Political Writings*, Susan James (ed.), (Cambridge: Cambridge University Press), 2003 (1666b).

Cavendish, Margaret, *Observations upon Experimental Philosophy, to which is Added, The Description of a New Blazing World*. London, 1666a.

Cavendish, Margaret, *Philosophical Letters: Or, modest reflections upon some opinions in natural philosophy, maintained by several famous and learned authors of this age, expressed by way of letters: By the thrice noble, illustrious, and excellent princess, the Lady Marchioness of Newcastle* (London: Privately published), 1664.

Cavendish, Margaret, *Sociable Letters*, JamesFitzmaurice (ed.), (New York: Garland), 1997 (1664).

Cavendish, Margaret, *The Worlds Olio* (London: J. Martin and J. Allestrye), 1655.

Chignell, Andrew, "Infant Suffering Revisited," *Religious Studies*, 37:4 (2001), 475–484.

Clatterbaugh, Kenneth, "Benatar's Alleged Second Sexism," *Social Theory and Practice*, 29 (2003), 211–218.

Coakley, Sarah, *God, Sexuality, and the Self: Essays on the Trinity* (Cambridge: Cambridge University Press), 2013.

Conway, Daniel W., "Circulus Vitiosus Deus? The Dialectical Logic of Feminist Standpoint Theory," *Journal of Social Philosophy*, 28:1, Spring 1997, 62–76.

Cudd, Ann, "When to Intervene: Atrocity, Inequality, and Oppression," in A. Veltman and K. Norlock (eds), *Evil, Political Violence, and Forgiveness* (New York: Lexington), 2009, 97–114.

Curran, Andrew and Graille, Patrick, "The Faces of 18th-Century Monstrosity," *Eighteenth-Century Life*, 21:2 (May 1997), 1–10.

Daly, Mary, *Beyond God the Father: Toward a Philosophy of Women's Liberation*, revised edition (Boston, MA: Beacon Press), 1993.

Daly, Mary, *Gyn/Ecology: The Metaethics of Radical Feminism* (Boston, MA: Beacon Press), 1978.

Darwall, Stephen, "Authority and Second-Personal Reasons for Acting", in D. Sobel and S. Wall (eds), *Reasons for Action* (Cambridge: Cambridge University Press), 2009.

Darwall, Stephen, *Honor, History, and Relationship: Essays in Second-Personal Relationships II* (Oxford: Oxford University Press), 2013.

Darwall, Stephen, *The Second-Person Standpoint* (Cambridge, MA: Harvard University Press), 2006.

Darwall, Stephen, "Two Kinds of Respect," *Ethics*, 88:1, October 1977, 36–49.

Davidson, Donald, "Rational Animals," *Dialectica*, 36 (1982), 318–327.

Davidson, Donald, "The Second Person", in P. French, T. E. Uehling, and H. Wettstein (eds.), *Midwest Studies in Philosophy*, 17 (1992), 255–267.

Detlefsen, Karen, "Margaret Cavendish on the Relation between God and World," *Philosophy Compass* 4:3, (2009), 421–438.

Enoch, David, "Not Just a Truthometer: Taking Oneself Seriously (but not Too Seriously) in Cases of Peer Disagreement," *Mind*, 119:476, (December 2010), 953–997.

Fichte, J.G., *The Science of Knowledge*, P. Heath and J. Lachs (trans.), (Cambridge: Cambridge University Press), 1982.

Flemming, Arthur, "Omnibenevolence and Evil," *Ethics*, 96:2, (January 1986), 261–281.

Fortune, Marie M., "Faith is Fundamental to Ending Domestic Terror," *Women's Rights Law Reporter*, 33:463, (Summer 2012).

Fortune, Marie M., *Sexual Violence: The Sin Revisited* (Cleveland: The Pilgrim Press), 2005.

Fortune, Marie M., Alkhateeb, Sharifa, and Ellis, Sharon, "Domestic Violence: The Responses of Christian and Muslim Communities," *Journal of Religion and Abuse*, 2:1 (2001), 3–24.

Frances, Bryan, *Gratuitous Suffering and the Problem of Evil* (New York: Routledge), 2013.

Franklin, J., "Two Caricatures, II: Leibniz's Best World," *International Journal for Philosophy of Religion*, 52:1 (August 2002), 45–56.

Frazer, Elizabeth, "Mary Wollstonecraft on Politics and Friendship," *Political Studies*, 56 (2008), 237–256.

Geddes, Jennifer L., "Banal Evil and Useless Knowledge: Hannah Arendt and Charlotte Delbo on Evil after the Holocaust," in R.M. Schott (ed.), *Feminist Philosophy and the Problem of Evil* (Bloomington, IN: University of Indiana and Hypatia, Inc), 2007, 110–120.

Gilbert, Margaret, "Shared Intention and Personal Intentions," *Philosophical Studies*, 144 (2009), 167–187.

Gockel, Mattias, "Be Not Overcome by Evil, but Overcome Evil with Good – an orientational approach to suffering and evil," *Modern Theology*, 25:1 (2009), 97–105.

Goldie, Mark, "Mary Astell and John Locke", in W. Kolbrener and M. Michelson (eds), *Mary Astell: Reason, Gender, Faith* (Aldershot/Burlington, VT: Ashgate), 2007, 65–86.

Green, Karen and Weekes, Shannon, "Catharine Macaulay on the Will," *History of European Ideas*, 39:3, (2013), 409–425.

Groarke, Louis, "Reconsidering Absolute Omnipotence," *Heythrop Journal*, 42 (2001), 13–25.

Gunther-Canada, Wendy, "Catharine Macaulay on the Paradox of Paternal Authority in Hobbesian Politics," *Hypatia*, 21:2, Spring 2006, 150–173.

Hampson, Daphne, *Theology and Feminism* (Oxford: Basil Blackwell), 1990.

Hanley, Kirstin, *Mary Wollstonecraft, Pedagogy, and the Practice of Feminism* (New York: Routledge), 2013.

Harding, Sandra, *Sciences from Below: Feminisms, Postcolonialities, and Modernities* (Durham, NC: Duke), 2008.

Harding, Sandra, *Whose Science? Whose Knowledge? Thinking from Women's Lives* (Ithaca: Cornell University Press), 1991.

Harol, Corrinne, "Mary Astell's Law of the Heart", in W. Kolbrener and M. Michelson (eds), *Mary Astell: Reason, Gender, Faith* (Aldershot/Burlington, VT: Ashgate Press), 2007, 87–99.

Hasker, William, "Light in the Darkness? Reflections on Eleanor Stump's Theodicy," *Faith and Philosophy*, 28:4, (October 2011), 432–450.

Hays, Mary, *Appeal to the Men of Great Britain on Behalf of Women* (London: Johnson & Bell), 1798.

Hays, Mary, *Letters and Essays: Moral and Miscellaneous* (London: Knott), 1793.

Hays, Mary, *Memoirs of Emma Courtney* (London: Robinson), 1796.

Hays, Mary, *The Victim of Prejudice, 1799* (Toronto: Broadview), 1994.

Hennessy, Rosemary, "Feminist Knowledge: Feminist Standpoint as Ideology Critique," *Hypatia*, 8:1, (Winter 1993), 14–34.

Hernandez, Jill, "Acquainted with Grief: the Atonement and Early Feminist Conceptions of Theodicy," *Philosophia*, 43:1, (March 2015), 97–111.

—— "Atrocious Evil, Divinely Perfected: An Early Modern Feminist's Contribution to Theodicy," *The Journal of Religion*, 94:1, (January 2014), 26–48.

—— "The Anxious Believer: Macaulay's Prescient Theodicy," *International Journal for Philosophy of Religion*, 73, (June 2013), 175–187.

—— "Moral Evil and Leibniz's Form/Matter Defense of Divine Omnipotence," *Sophia*, 49, (2010), 1–13.

Hodson, Jane, "Women Write the Rights of Woman: the Sexual Politics of the Personal Pronoun in the 1790s," *Language and Literature*, 16:3, (2007), 281–304.

Holmes, Emily and Farley, Wendy, *Women, Writing, Theology* (Waco, TX: Baylor University Press), 2011.

Honneth, Axel and Margalit, Avishai, "Recognition," *Proceedings of the Aristotelian Society*, 75 (2001), 111–139.

Ihde, Don, "'Cartesianism' Redux or Situated Knowledges," *Foundations of Science*, 17:4, (Nov 2012), 369–372.

Intemann, Kristen, "25 Years of Feminist Empiricism and Standpoint Theory: Where Are We Now?" *Hypatia*, 25:4 (Fall 2010), 778–796.

Jaarsma, Ada, "Irigaray's To Be Two: the Problem of Evil and the Plasticity of Incarnation," *Hypatia*, 18:1, 2003, 44–63.

Jaggar, Alison, "Naming Terrorism as Evil," in R.M. Schott (ed.), *Feminist Philosophy and the Problem of Evil* (Bloomington, IN: University of Indiana and Hypatia, Inc), 2007, 219–227.

Jorgensen, Larry and Newlands, Samuel (eds), *New Essays on Leibniz's Theodicy* (Oxford: Oxford University Press), 2014.

Joy, Morny, "Rethinking the 'Problem of Evil' with Hannah Arendt and Grace Jantzen," in P. Anderson (ed.), *New Topics in Feminist Philosophy of Religion: Contestations and Transcendence Incarnate* (Dordrecht: Springer), 2010, 17–32.

Kelly, Gary, *Women, Writing, and Revolution, 1790–1827* (Oxford: Clarendon), 1993.

Kolbrener, William, "Astell's 'Design of Friendship' in Letters and A Serious Proposal, Part I," in W. Kolbrener and M. Michelson (eds), *Mary Astell: Reason, Gender, Faith* (Aldershot/ Burlington, VT: Ashgate Press), 2007, 49–65.

Kondoleon, Theodore, "Moral Evil and the Existence of God," *The New Scholasticism*, 47, 1973, 366–374.

Kraemer, Eric Russert, "Evil, Atrocity, and Harm," in A. Veltman and K. Norlock (eds), *Evil, Political Violence, and Forgiveness* (New York: Lexington), 2009, 175–194.

Laird, Susan, *Mary Wollstonecraft: Philosophical Mother of Coeducation* (London: Continuum), 2008.

Laird, Susan and Bailey, Richard, *Mary Wollstonecraft*, Continuum Library of Educational Thought Series (London: Continuum), 2014.

Lance, Mark and Kukla, Rebecca, "Leave the Gun; Take the Cannoli! The Pragmatic Topography of Second-Person Calls," *Ethics*, 123:3 (April 2013), 456–478.

Lance, Mark and Kukla, Rebecca, *'Yo!' and 'Lo!': The Pragmatic Topography of the Space of Reasons* (Cambridge: Harvard University Press), 2009.

Lara, Maria Pia, "Claudia Card's Atrocity Paradigm," *Hypatia*, 19:4, (Autumn 2004), 184–191.

Lara, Maria Pia, *Narrating Evil: a Postmetaphysical Theory of Reflective Judgment* (New York: Columbia University Press), 2007.

Lara, Maria Pia, "Reframing Perspectives on Evil: Accountability, Moral Responsibility, and Collective Judgment" in A. Veltman and K. Norlock (eds), *Evil, Political Violence, and Forgiveness* (New York: Lexington), 2009, 195–211.

Lara, Maria Pia, *Rethinking Evil: Contemporary Perspectives* (Berkeley: University of California Press), 2001.

Leibniz, G.W., *Confessions, Confessio Philosophi: Papers Concerning the Problem of Evil, 1671–1678*, R.C. Sleigh (trans.) (New Haven, CT: Yale University Press), 2006.

Leibniz, G.W., *Discourse on Metaphysics and Other Essays*, D. Garber and R. Ariew (eds) (Indianapolis, IN: Hackett Publishing), 1989.

Leibniz, G.W., *Theodicy*, A. Farrer (ed.) and E. M. Huggard (trans.) (Chicago: Open Court), 1998.

Look, Brandon, "Perfection, Power and the Passions in Spinoza and Leibniz," *Revue Roumaine de Philosophie*, 51:1–2, 2007, 21–38.

Low, Jennifer, "Surface and Interiority: Self-Creation in Margaret Cavendish's The Claspe", *Philological Quarterly*, 77:2, Spring 1998, 149–169.

Luck, Morgan, "Incommensurability, Slight Pains, and God," *International Journal of Philosophy of Religion*, 75, (2014), 79–85.

Luria, Gina, "Introduction," in M. Hays, *Letters and Essays, Moral and Miscellaneous*, University of North Carolina at Greensboro Special Collection (New York: Garland), 1974.

Luria, Gina, "Mary Hays's Letters and Manuscripts," *Signs: Journal of Women in Culture and Society*, 3:2 (1977), 524–530.

Macaulay, Catharine, *An Address to the People of England, Scotland, and Ireland, On the Present Important Crisis of Affairs* (Bath: Cruttell, for E. and C. Dilly, London), 1775.

Macaulay, Catharine, *Letters on Education: With Observations on Religious and Metaphysical Subjects* (London: C. Dilly), 1790.

Macaulay, Catharine, *Loose remarks on certain positions found in Mr. Hobbes's philosophical rudiments of government and society with a short sketch of a democratical form of government in a letter to Signior Paoli* (London: W. Johnson), 1769.

Macaulay, Catharine, *A Treatise on the Immutability of Moral Truth* (London: E. and C. Dilly), 1783.

Marcel, Gabriel, *Problematic Man*. Trans. Brian Herder (New York: Herder and Herder), 1967.

Mascetti, Yaakov, "A 'World of Nothing, but Pure Wit': Margaret Cavendish and the Gendering of the Imaginary," *Partial Answers: Journal of Literature and the History of Ideas*, 6:1, (January 2008), 1–31.

Mercedes, Ana, *Power For: Feminism and Christ's Self-Giving* (London: T&T Clark), 2011.

Miller, Sarah Clark, "Atrocity, Harm, and Resistance: A Situated Understanding of Genocidal Rape", in A. Veltman and K. Norlock (eds), *Evil, Political Violence, and Forgiveness* (New York: Lexington), 2009, 53–76.

Morgan, Anne, "Simone de Beauvoir's Ethics of Freedom and Absolute Evil," *Hypatia*, 23:4, (2008), 75–89.

Morny, Joy, "Rethinking the 'Problem of Evil' with Hannah Arendt and Grace Jantzen," in P. Anderson (ed.), *New Topics in Feminist Philosophy of Religion: Contestations and Transcendence Incarnate* (Dordrecht: Springer), 2010.

Morris, Thomas, "Duty and Divine Goodness," *American Philosophical Quarterly*, 21:3, 1984, 261–268.

Morton, Adam, "Inequality/Iniquity: Card on Balancing Injustice and Evil," *Hypatia*, 19:4 (Fall 2004), 197–201.

Nelson, Lynn H., *Who Knows: From Quine to a Feminist Empiricism* (Philadelphia, PA: Temple University Press), 1990.

Nussbaum, Martha, *The Therapy of Desire: Theory and Practice in Hellenistic Ethics* (Princeton: Princeton University Press), 2013.

O'Brien, Karen, *Women and Enlightenment in Eighteenth-Century Britain* (Cambridge: Cambridge University Press), 2009.

O'Neill, Eileen and Lascano, Marcy, *Feminist History of Philosophy: The Recovery and Evaluation of Women's Philosophical Thought* (Dordrecht: Springer), forthcoming.

Pickard, Claire, "Great in Humilitie: A Consideration of Mary Astell's Poetry" in W. Kolbrener and M. Michelson (eds), *Mary Astell: Reason, Gender, Faith* (Aldershot/ Burlington, VT: Ashgate Press), 2007, 115–126.

Plantinga, Alvin, "Superlapsarianism or 'O Felix Culpa'," in Peter van Inwagen (ed.), *Christian Faith and the Problem of Evil* (Grand Rapids, MI: Eerdmans), 2004, 1–25.

Pinnock, Sarah Katherine, *Beyond Theodicy: Jewish and Christian Continental Thinkers Respond to the Holocaust* (New York, NY: State University of New York Press), 2002.

Poma, Andrea, *The Impossibility and Necessity of Theodicy: The "Essais" of Leibniz* (Dordrecht: Springer), 2012.

Porter, Roy, "Rape – Does It Have Historical Meaning?" in Sylvana Tomaselli and Roy Porter (eds), *Rape* (Oxford: Blackwell), 1986.

Potter, Elizabeth, *Feminism and Philosophy of Science* (London: Taylor & Francis), 2006.

Pufendorf, S.F.v., *On the Law of Nature and of Nations*, C.H. Oldfather and W.A. Oldfather (trans.) (Buffalo, NY: William S. Hein; reprint of Oxford: Clarendon Press), 1995.

Radcliffe, Mary Ann, *"The Female Advocate, or, an attempt to recover the rights of women from male usurpation"* (1799), University of North Carolina-Greensboro Women's Collection.

Radzik, Linda, "On Minding Your Own Business: Differentiating Accountability Relations within the Moral Community," *Social Theory and Practice*, 37:4, (October 2011), 574–598.

Rankka, Kristine M., *Women and the Value of Suffering* (Collegeville, MN: The Liturgical Press), 1998.

Rateau, Paul, "The Theoretical Foundations of the Leibnizian Theodicy," in L. Jorgensen and S. Newlands (eds), *New Essays on Leibniz's Theodicy* (Oxford: Oxford University Press), 2014, 92–111.

Richardson, Alan, "Mary Wollstonecraft on Education," in C.L. Johnson (ed.), *The Cambridge Companion to Mary Wollstonecraft* (New York: Cambridge University Press), 2002, 24–41.

Richey, William, "'A More Godlike Portion': Mary Wollstonecraft's Feminist Rereadings of the Fall," *English Language Notes*, 32:2, (December 1994), 28–38.

Rolin, Kristina, "The Bias Paradox in Feminist Standpoint Epistemology," *Episteme*, 3:1–2, (June 2006), 125–136.

Roney, Patrick, "Evil and the Experience of Freedom: Nancy on Shelling and Heidegger," *Research in Phenomenology*, 39:3, (2009), 374–400.

Ruether, Rosemary Radford, *Sexism and God-Talk: Toward a Feminist Theology*, revised edition (Boston, MA: Beacon Press), 1993.

Ruether, Rosemary Radford, *Women and Redemption* (New York: Fortress Press), 1998.

Schott, Robin May (ed.), *Feminist Philosophy and the Problem of Evil* (Bloomington, IN: University of Indiana and Hypatia, Inc), 2007.

Schott, Robin May, "War Rape and the Political Concept of Evil" in A. Veltman and K. Norlock (eds), *Evil, Political Violence, and Forgiveness* (New York: Lexington), 2009, 77–96.

Scott, Mark Stephen Murray, "Theodicy at the Margins: New Trajectories for the Problem of Evil," *Theology Today*, 68:2, (2011), 149–152.

Seachris, Joshua and Zagzebski, Linda, "Weighing Evils: The C. S. Lewis Approach," *International Journal for Philosophy of Religion*, 62:2½ (2007), 81–88.

Sen, Amartya, "Mary, Mary, Quite Contrary?" *Feminist Economics*, 11:1, (March 2005), 1–9.

Siegfried, Brandie and Sanderson, Lisa, *God and Nature in the Thought of Margaret Cavendish* (Aldershot/Burlington, VT: Ashgate), 2014.

Sleigh, Jr., Robert C., "Leibniz on Freedom and Necessity," *The Philosophical Review*, 108:2, 1999, 245–277.

Smith, Jane Monckton, *Relating Rape and Murder: Narratives of Sex, Death and Gender* (Basingstoke: Palgrave Macmillan), 2010.

Soelle, Dorothee, *Suffering* (New York: Fortress Press), 1984.

Soskice, Janet M., *The Kindness of God* (Oxford: Oxford University Press), 2008.

Springborg, Patricia, *Mary Astell: Theorist of Freedom from Domination* (Cambridge: Cambridge University Press), 2005.

Steinberg, Justin, "An Epistemic Case for Empathy," *Pacific Philosophical Quarterly*, 95:1, (March 2014), 47–71.

Strawson, Peter, Skepticism and Naturalism (New York: Columbia University Press), 1985.

Stump, Eleanore, "Second-person Accounts and the Problem of Evil," *Revista Portuguesa de Filosofia*, 57 (2001), 745–771.

Stump, Eleanore, *Wandering in Darkness* (Oxford: Oxford University Press), 2010.

Surin, Kenneth, *Theology and the Problem of Evil* (Eugene, OR: Wipf & Stock), 1986.

Swinton, John, *Raging with Compassion: Pastoral Responses to the Problem of Evil* (Grand Rapids, MI: Eerdmans), 2007.

Taylor, Barbara, *Mary Wollstonecraft and the Feminist Imagination* (Cambridge: Cambridge University Press), 2003.

Taylor, Barbara and Knott, Sarah, *Women, Gender and Enlightenment* (London: Palgrave MacMillan), 2005.

Tilley, Terrence W., *The Evils of Theodicy* (Eugene, OR: Wipf & Stock), 2000.

Tirrell, Lynne, "Epistemic Aspects of Evil: The Three Monkeys Meet The Atrocity Paradigm," in A. Veltman and K. Norlock (eds), *Evil, Political Violence, and Forgiveness* (New York: Lexington), 2009, 35–52.

U.N. News Centre, 6.10.2014, "At global summit, UN envoy Angelina Jolie calls for end to sexual violence in conflict," http://www.un.org/apps/news/story.asp?NewsID= 48008#.VZyQi7V2Fnl, accessed 7. 7. 2015.

Vabalaite, Ruta, "Evil, Good, and Freedom in the Best of Possible Worlds," *Logos*, 64:9 (2010), 114–122.

Veltman, Andrea and Norlock, Kathryn, "Introduction," in A. Veltman and K. Norlock (eds), *Evil, Political Violence, and Forgiveness* (New York: Lexington), 2009, 1–12.

Vitale, Vince, "Review, Wandering in Darkness," *Mind*, 122:488 (2013), 1193–1201.

Walker, Michael, "The Atonement and Justice," *Theology*, 91:180 (1988), 180–186.

Walters, Lisa, *Margaret Cavendish: Gender, Science and Politics* (Cambridge: Cambridge University Press), 2014.

Ward, Peter, "The Prejudices of Mary Hays," *International Journal of Law in Context*, 5:2, (2009), 131–146.

Westmoreland, Robert, "The Truth about Public Reason," *Law and Philosophy*, 18:3, (1999), 271–296.

Williams, Garrath, "Sharing Responsibility and Holding Responsible," *Journal of Applied Philosophy*, 30:4, (2013), 351–364.

Wiseman, Susan, *Conspiracy and Virtue: Women, Writing, and Politics in Seventeenth-Century England* (Oxford: Oxford University Press), 2006.

Wolfthal, Diane, "'A Hue and a Cry': Medieval Rape Imagery and Its Transformation," *The Art Bulletin*, 75:1, (March 1993), 39–64.

Wolfthal, Diane, *Images of Rape: The Heroic Tradition and Its Alternatives* (New York: Cambridge University Press), 1999.

Wollstonecraft, Mary, *Letters and Miscellaneous* (posthumous), volume 4, William Godwin (ed.), in the University of North Carolina at Greensboro's Woman's Collection, 1798a.

Wollstonecraft, Mary, *Letters Written during a Short Residence in Sweden, Norway, and Denmark*, University of North Carolina at Greensboro's Women's Collection (London: J Johnson, and J Wilson), 1796.

Wollstonecraft, Mary, *Maria, or the Wrongs of Woman*, University of North Carolina at Greensboro's Women's Collection (London: J Johnson, and GG & J Robinson), 1798b.

Wollstonecraft, Mary, *Mary, a Fiction* (London: J. Johnson), 1788.

Wollstonecraft, Mary, *Thoughts on the Education of Daughters, with Reflections on Female Conduct, in the More Important Duties of Life* (London: J Johnson), 1787.

Wollstonecraft, Mary, *A Vindication of the Rights of Women* (Philadelphia: Mathew Carey), 1792.

Wolterstorff, Nicholas, "Living within a Text," in Keith Yandell (ed), *Faith and Narrative* (Oxford: Oxford University Press), 2001, 202–213.

Yandell, Keith, "Narrative Ethics and Normative Objectivity," in Keith Yandell (ed), *Faith and Narrative* (Oxford: Oxford University Press), 2001, 237–260.

INDEX